THE
NATURAL BEAUTY
OF
CORNWALL

THE
NATURAL BEAUTY
OF
CORNWALL

PETER MAXTED

ROBERT HALE • LONDON

Contents

Acknowledgements

There are far too many books, reports, websites and other forms of source material that I have seen and read over the years to list here, but I would like to express especial thanks to Cornwall Council's Historic Environment Service, the Cornwall Records Office and Cornish Studies Library and to four books in particular that I found invaluable reading before embarking on this journey: *Cornwall's Geology and Scenery* by Colin M. Bristow, *A History of Cornwall* by F.E. Halliday, *Cornwall's People* by Carolyn Martin and Paul White and *Historic Gardens of Cornwall* by Timothy Moat. Where I have quoted these authors directly I have referenced this within the text. A couple of guides that were part-funded by the AONB have also been useful source material: *An Introduction to Bodmin Moor* by Mark Camp and *Five Walks Around Mount Edgcumbe* by Bill Scolding.

Of the people who helped with advice, information and support, I'd like to thank Colette Holden, Peter Mansfield, Nigel Sumpter, June Crossland and Karen Johns, as well as Emma of the AONB team and Paul Walton, the former AONB Manager.

Special thanks go to my mother, Eleanor, who helped with some of the research and proofreading and contributed an original poem. Special thanks also go to Dave Matthews of 'Captured in Cornwall' (*www.captured-in-cornwall.co.uk*) who supplied half the superb photos in this book.

This book is dedicated to Katie and Nick Maxted, my daughter and son who, unlike me, were lucky enough to be born in this most beautiful of counties and, most of all, to my lovely wife Anne whose support and encouragement have been unstinting.

Peter Maxted

Dave Matthews

▲ Tolverne on The Roseland

The big picture

'It's all beautiful, boy!' The gruff, Cornish tones belonged to a local farmer and held a slightly admonitory note. I had asked, shortly after I joined the AONB team, if he knew which parts of Cornwall made up our Area of Outstanding Natural Beauty.

Anyway, there he was, dressed in tweed jacket, shirt and tie, muddy boots and twine-tied trousers, just as my uncle used to look when he farmed up-country. He was, somewhat absently, pulling me down a couple of bales of hay. His weather-beaten face was kind but a little distant; he may have been thinking of the milking to come; he may have been, though polite, impatient with this sassy incomer asking silly questions. So which bits of Cornwall are beautiful? Why, many Cornish people, with their deep affinity for the land, would naturally say that all of it is.

The gruff farmer wasn't that far wrong about Cornwall. There aren't many truly ugly bits, not like parts of our oil-stained cities or the long, dull stretches of agribusiness land, flanked by litter-strewn ditches, skirting the M1. Nearly all of Cornwall is rural, coastal or comprises small and, for the most part, unspoilt and attractive towns. The blue-black, storm-lashed cliffs of the north coast, the brooding solitary mass of Bodmin Moor, the wild, stone-strewn heaths of West Penwith, the mining ruins gradually crumbling back to nature, the patchwork of fields and the tranquil wooded river valleys in the south; all of it *is* beautiful, some of it outstandingly so.

And thus it is that nearly a third of the county has been designated as an Area of Outstanding Natural Beauty and given national status and protection.

Areas of Outstanding Natural Beauty are particularly special landscapes whose distinctive character and scenic value is considered to be so important that it is

Dave Matthews

in the nation's interest to safeguard them. Many were designated at the same time, or shortly after, our great National Parks. Most of the Cornwall AONB was designated back in 1959. But whilst the two protected landscapes have a similar status they are very different types.

We assume that our countryside will always stay the same, but often this is not true. Perhaps the most vulnerable areas are not the wild, open, high places but the gentle, smaller-scale landscapes of England and Wales. These include hedgerows, spinneys and bluebell woods; heath, marsh and meadow. Under pressure for change, much of this traditional countryside has already vanished. AONB status protects the finest examples which remain. AONBs work – with due care for the rural way of life – to conserve the landscape's outstanding natural beauty and ensure its survival for future generations.

Natural England

A brief account of the designation

His Majesty's National Park Committee presented its report (popularly known as the Addison Report) to government in 1931. However, the government was preoccupied with dealing with depression, strikes and the rise of Hitler and Mussolini in Europe and therefore had what it considered higher priorities. Nevertheless, the Standing Committee on National Parks (SCNP) was set up after the Council for the Preservation of Rural England (CPRE) put forward well-argued proposals for National Parks to government in 1938. Significantly, for the future, John Dower, an architect and planner, helped write several SCNP publications.

Things got a little busy in the six years following 1939 but Dower's Report, published in 1945, suggested ten National Parks and a list of 'Other Amenity Areas'. These 'Other Amenity Areas' were put forward as areas of landscape beauty which merited some form of national protection and many of these provided the basis for the fifty-two conservation areas of high landscape quality, scientific interest and recreational value (as apart from the final twelve National Parks) listed in the July 1947 report of the National Park Committee, chaired by Sir Arthur Hobhouse, that followed on from the Dower Report.

The National Parks and Access to the Countryside Act 1949 brought the National Parks into being. The Cornish coastline (pretty well today's AONB) was suggested as one such National Park, though this did not come to pass as we shall see.

In 1955 the National Park programme was so well advanced that the Commission announced its intention to start the designation of Areas of Outstanding Natural Beauty (AONBs).

Dave Matthews

▲ Gentle small-scale landscape

Dave Matthews

There are currently thirty-six AONBs in England and Wales and a further nine in Northern Ireland – forty-five in all. Together they make up around 18% of the country. Natural England (formerly The Countryside Agency) is the organization currently responsible for designating AONBs.

There are also fourteen National Parks and one separate designation – the Broads (Norfolk and Suffolk). Together protected landscapes make up 24% of the land area of England.

INTERNATIONAL CATEGORIZATION

Not many people, even in the environmental field, have heard of the IUCN. The International Union for Conservation of Nature (IUCN) is the world's oldest and largest global environmental organization. Founded in 1948, it has more than 1,200 government and NGO members and almost 11,000 volunteer experts in some 160 countries. Its remit is to help the world find pragmatic solutions to our most pressing environmental and developmental challenges.

IUCN works on biodiversity, climate change, energy, human livelihoods and greening the world economy by supporting scientific research and managing field projects all over the world. But arguably its most important area of expertise is in defining protected area management categories.

IUCN CATEGORIZATION

The definition of a protected area, as adopted by IUCN, is: 'An area of land and/or sea especially dedicated to the protection and maintenance of biological diversity, and of natural and associated cultural resources, and managed through legal or other effective means'. It has defined a series of six protected area management categories, based on primary management objectives. In summary, these are:

CATEGORY 1a

Strict Nature Reserve: protected area managed mainly for science.

Area of land and/or sea possessing some outstanding or representative ecosystems, geological or physiological features and/or species, available primarily for scientific research and/or environmental monitoring.

CATEGORY 1b

Wilderness Area: protected area managed mainly for wilderness protection.

Large area of unmodified or slightly modified land, and/or sea, retaining its natural character and influence, without permanent or significant habitation, which is protected and managed so as to preserve its natural condition.

CATEGORY 2

National Park: protected area managed mainly for ecosystem protection and recreation.

Natural area of land and/or sea, designated to (a) protect the ecological integrity of one or more ecosystems for present and future generations, (b) exclude exploitation or occupation inimical to the purposes of designation of the area and (c) provide a foundation for spiritual, scientific, educational, recreational and visitor opportunities, all of which must be environmentally and culturally compatible.

CATEGORY 3

Natural Monument: protected area managed mainly for conservation of specific natural features.

Area containing one, or more, specific natural or natural/cultural feature which is of outstanding or unique value because of its inherent rarity, representative or aesthetic qualities or cultural significance.

CATEGORY 4

Habitat/Species Management Area: protected area managed mainly for conservation through management intervention.

Area of land and/or sea subject to active intervention for management purposes so as to ensure the maintenance of habitats and/or to meet the requirements of specific species.

CATEGORY 5

Protected Landscape/Seascape: protected area managed mainly for landscape/seascape conservation and recreation.

Dave Matthews

Area of land, with coast and sea as appropriate, where the interaction of people and nature over time has produced an area of distinct character with significant aesthetic, ecological and/or cultural value, and often with high biological diversity. Safeguarding the integrity of this traditional interaction is vital to the protection, maintenance and evolution of such an area.

Dave Matthews

CATEGORY 6

Managed Resource Protected Area: protected area managed mainly for the sustainable use of natural ecosystems.

Area containing predominantly unmodified natural systems, managed to ensure long term protection and maintenance of biological diversity, while providing at the same time a sustainable flow of natural products and services to meet community needs.

It will be seen that Cornwall AONB, like others in the UK, falls into Category 5.

PURPOSE OF AONB DESIGNATION

The primary purpose of AONB designation is to conserve and enhance natural beauty. The 1949 act, reinforced by the Countryside and Rights of Way Act in 2000, stresses the national importance of AONBs.

However, in pursuing the primary objective, 'account should be taken of the needs of agriculture, forestry, other rural industries and of the economic and social needs of local communities'. Particular regard should be paid to promoting sustainable forms of social and economic development that in themselves conserve and enhance the environment.

Unlike in National Parks, recreation is not a requirement under the designation, but the demand for recreation should be met 'so far as this is consistent with the conservation of natural beauty and the needs of agriculture, forestry and other uses'.

Also in 2000, under the Countryside and Rights of Way (CROW) Act, the government confirmed that AONBs had the same status and protection as National Parks.

Cornwall AONB

Cornwall is eighty miles long from the Devon border to Land's End. At its widest it is about forty-five miles across, with the narrowest point between St Ives and Mount's Bay being a mere seven miles wide. About 30% of Cornwall is AONB designated, including the Cornish side of the River Tamar.

Cornwall was originally suggested by Dower as a National Park but Cornwall County Council rejected the proposal in July 1953. Why they did so is not completely clear but pressure from a number of landowners and mining and quarrying interests played a part. It may also be that the somewhat nationalistic council at the time (so different now) resented the imposition of any designation from 'England'.

The consequent need for our amazing coastline to be given an alternative form of national landscape protection was still paramount and this was a key driver of the move, countrywide, to designate AONBs. So although Cornwall was not the first AONB (that distinction belongs to the Gower in Wales) it was a prime mover for the growth of AONBs as a whole.

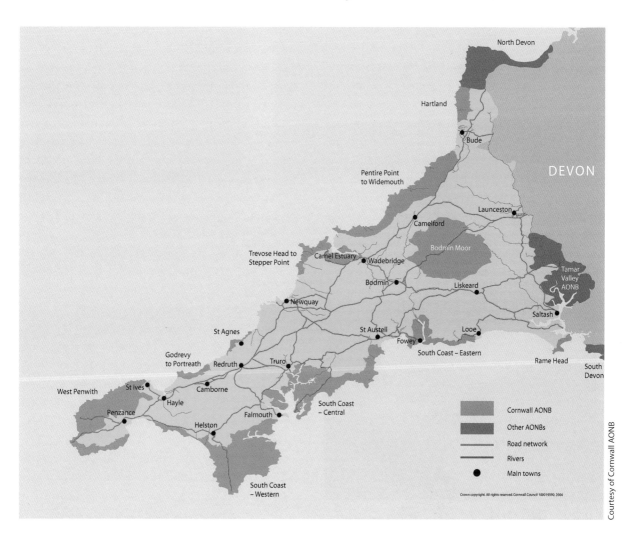

Courtesy of Cornwall AONB

11

Dave Matthews

▲ Why the tourists come

The aforementioned landowners and mining and quarrying interests are probably one of the reasons why the Cornwall Area of Outstanding Natural Beauty is made up of twelve separate geographical areas with somewhat erratic boundaries. Why should one side of a country lane covered in primroses be in the AONB but not the other? Why was it decided that the section north of Newquay should start at Bedruthan Steps rather than Mawgan Porth? Why are the stunning inland hills not part of the South Coast Western section of the AONB? To go back to my introductory farmer, it does seem strange that there are so many beautiful parts of the county that are outside the AONB. Beauty, like art or philosophy, does not recognize frontiers.

Dave Matthews

▲ The Gannel near Newquay – not in the AONB

A few of my own favourite locations include the timeless area around Godolphin and Tregonning, the Allen Valley, the upper Camel and Lanhydrock – all could easily be described as having the potential for protected status. The reasons why some parts of Cornwall missed becoming protected in the fifties are many and various and sometimes still a bit of a mystery. It is interesting to note that many of the great houses of Cornwall: Godolphin, Pencarrow, Trerice (the loveliest of Elizabethan houses) and Lanhydrock, for example, fall outside the AONB areas. Back in the fifties the great estates still had a lot of clout.

Still, as many a Cornishman would say, 'We are where we are'. Cornwall AONB has twelve sections; none of them are physically connected, but it is still one single AONB. It covers approximately 27% of the County – an area of 958 square kilometres (370 square miles). It was designated in 1959 with the Camel Estuary section being added in 1981. A part of the Tamar Valley AONB is also in Cornwall and there is a close relationship with the Isles of Scilly and North and South Devon AONBs. We can be grateful at least that so much *is* protected.

The AONB is a major environmental asset for Cornwall and contributes substantially to the economy, as well as to the enjoyment, health and lifestyle benefits to half a million local people and up to 5 million visitors.

The Cornwall AONB is managed by a partnership of fourteen organizations which meet three times a year. They are supported by a small team of professionals with a wide range of expertise – ecology, landscape architecture, landscape planning, communications, project management and administration.

THE AONB'S ECONOMIC SIGNIFICANCE

Exploitation of natural resources has been the source of Cornwall's wealth since time immemorial. Agriculture, fishing and mineral extraction have been the primary industries since the early Bronze Age and have helped shape the Cornish landscape and the communities within the county. Agriculture is still a significant 'industry' but fishing is on the decline and the resurgence of tin mining is still an aspiration – although recent increases in the price of tin have meant that it is one that is increasingly likely to be fulfilled.

Dave Matthews

▲ Agriculture is still important

As these traditional industries reduced or disappeared, a new dominant industry crept up on Cornwall from around the late nineteenth century, turning into a headlong rush after World War II. Tourism in the county now draws in nearly half a million visitors annually (4.4 million staying visitors were recorded in 2008). And, unsurprisingly, surveys suggest that most holiday trips to Cornwall are motivated wholly or partly by the landscape. Scenery/landscape/views were cited by the largest proportion of visitors in the Cornwall Visitor Survey of 2008/9 as their favourite aspect of the county. In a survey commissioned by one of the country's leading holiday companies, almost one in four (22%) holidaymakers chose the cliffs, beaches, sand and surf of Cornwall, voting it their favourite UK destination. Scotland came second with 16%, the Lake District captured 13% of the votes and, with 10%, Devon (ahem) came fourth. Visit-Cornwall has been marketing the area's 'unique blend of old and new' recently, with 'traditional holidays offered alongside more contemporary and unusual activities'.

But other sectors of the economy besides tourism also benefit from the quality of the Cornish landscape, particularly the AONB, notably the creative industries, new technology developments, horticulture, local produce, marine businesses and new energy sources. Cornwall is becoming an increasingly attractive place for entrepreneurs to establish or expand a business and the roll-out of new super-fast broadband in 2012/13 has only increased this.

Courtesy of Cornwall AONB

The economic value of the environment is not only relevant in terms of jobs and businesses in the tourism, recreation or agricultural sectors. In recent years Cornwall has been actively promoted to businesses, with marketing focusing on the environment and quality of life. The area's attractiveness as a place to live and as a leisure destination is likely to remain as [a key feature] of future economic progress.

Cornwall Council – local economic assessment 2010

If the increasing value of our landscape in economic terms helps its protection and enhancement, then that's fine by me. Just as climate change only started to be properly discussed with the publication of the Stern Report in 2006 when effects on the world's economy and GDP were highlighted, so the putting of monetary value on formerly intangible things such as views, tranquillity and space may give a little pause to those who have formerly seen our land as something simply to be plundered for its resources. The idea that 'just because you can't count something, that doesn't mean it doesn't count' doesn't resonate with everyone.

A sense of place

The qualities of the AONB landscape are represented by its different features – most notably its character, natural heritage, historic environment and cultural associations. These features, I would argue, are all underpinned by its geology. But a further feature of the Cornwall AONB is the protected landscape's importance to the people of Cornwall (and many visitors) and to the economic well-being of the county.

There is a sense of real richness and bewildering variety to the landscape of the AONB. In places it is wild and remote, with treeless moors, spectacular cliffs and sculpted headlands. Yet there is a softer side with sheltered, hidden creeks, south facing slopes, wooded valleys and sub-tropical gardens. The mood of the landscape is

Dave Matthews

Dave Matthews

Jessica Hirons

often dictated by the weather and the influence of the sea, both of which create seasonal changes that, on the north coast in particular, can vary in the extreme.

The coast is for many people the essence of Cornwall. Yet it is far from a homogeneous coastline. Sheltered fishing villages and storm-lashed headlands, exposed cliffs on the north coast and more tranquil tree-lined river valleys in the south, their colour altering with the seasons and the ever-changing light…you could spend a lifetime on the Cornish coast and not appreciate it all.

Inland, Bodmin Moor and West Penwith possess a sense of open, untamed countryside with many visible remains of early periods of settlement and more recent industrial heritage. Much of the Lizard is flat heath-land, while the Roseland comprises rolling fertile farmland and ancient estates.

The Cornwall and Isles of Scilly Landscape Character Study was undertaken over two years from 2005–7. It is a detailed description of the different landscape areas of Cornwall and the Isles of Scilly. The idea of the study was to offer landscape descriptions, vision and planning and land management guidelines and to demonstrate what is unique and distinct about the different areas of Cornwall and the Isles of Scilly. It is now being used by planners to guide development and help ensure that Cornwall's local distinctiveness is maintained, enhanced

and restored. The Landscape Character Study also gives land managers the information they need to manage Cornwall's landscapes well into the future whilst having respect for the way land has been worked in the past.

According to Cornwall Council, the guidance 'has been written to explain the importance of retaining the diverse character of the Cornish landscape, whilst positively planning for future development. It allows an interpretation of the local environment and the wider landscape, to successfully manage development, and provides a framework for future planning and management policies.' These encouraging words suggest that the Council is fully signed up to the value of landscape and aware of its myriad faces.

Based on the 2007 study, an AONB 'atlas' was also produced, which presents the results of monitoring work that is being undertaken by the AONB to build a picture of the current condition of the landscape. This is based on a set of 'indicators' chosen to reflect local landscape character. These indicators will continually be measured over time to build up a picture of landscape change – with the results being updated in the atlas.

So our fabulous landscape is enormously varied and, at last, quite well-documented. It has been shaped partly by nature and partly by man. And because we know that beauty is not just skin deep, let us now take a look beneath the surface.

Geology

AGE (millions of years)	SUB DIVISION	MAIN EVENTS	EARTH MOVEMENTS	LIFE
Tertiary (0–1.8)	Quaternary	**Ice ages** – Cornwall cold but not glaciated	Minor	Man, various mammals and plants
Tertiary (1.8–23)	Neogene	**Pliocene** –St Erth beds – sea level slightly higher than now **Miocene** – St Agnes sands and clays – sea level higher than now	Minor	Gastropods, conifer forests on islands
Tertiary (23–65)	Paleogene	**Oligocene** – St Agnes candle clays **Eocene** – Dutson basin (Launceston) sands and clays. Ball clays in Devon. Crousa and Polcrebo gravels **Paleocene** – No sediments preserved; land with deep weathering, possible silcretes	Major	Seqoula forest, some palms. Forest
Mesozoic (65–146)	Cretaceous	**Upper** – Rising sea levels gradually submerge most of Cornwall; marine sands and chalk deposited **Lower** – Cornwall probably dry land, subjected to deep tropical weathering. Main opening of the Atlantic west of Cornwall	Minor	Ammonities and belemneties in the sea. The remains of algae. Forests with dinosaurs
Mesozoic (146–208)	Jurassic	Cornwall probably above sea level throughout, with tropical forest and deep weathering. Atlantic ocean begins to open up as America drifts west and the continent of Pangaea breaks up	Minor/ moderate	Forests, primitive conifers and cycads. Dinosaurs
Mesozoic (208–245)	Triassic	Land surface hot and dry – Cornwall probably a fairly well eroded mountain range in the centre of a supercontinent – Pangaea	Minor/ moderate	Sparse or no vegetation. Some dinosaurs and primitive mammals
Upper Paleozoic (245–290)	Permian	Land surface hot and arid, sea distant. Metalliferous mineralization at depth. Volcanicity at Kingsand, contemporary with the intrusion of the granites. Volcanoes on top of where we see granites today	Major	Sparse vegetation, some burrowing animals at Kingsand
		INTRUSION OF GRANITES		
Upper Paleozoic (290–363)	Carboniferous	**Upper** – Sands and muds eroded from mountains rising in the south fill trough across North Cornwall. **Lower** – Deep marine conditions in North Cornwall with radiolarian ooze and muds, some volcanicity, mountains begin to rise in South Cornwall	Major (Variscan Orogeny)	Coal measures, vegetation, king crabs. Goniatites, trilobites, conodonts
Upper Paleozoic (363–408)	Devonian	**Upper** – Deep water throughout Cornwall, mountains begin to rise in the south. Crustal extension forms an ocean to the south, floored by oceanic crust **Middle** – Deep water throughout Cornwall, shallower in mid-Cornwall, coral reefs around Plymouth **Lower** – Most of Cornwall part of fairly deep sea, submarine volcanoes around St Austell. Cornwall forms part of a vast plain lying on the south of the O.R.S continent, with freshwater lakes	Major (Variscan Orogeny)	As above, plus crinoids, a few corals and shellfish. Primitive freshwater fish in Lower Devonion
Lower Paleozoic (408–570)	Silurian Ordovican Cambrian	Represented only as fragments contained in younger rocks. The oldest rocks ever discovered were dated at 4,000 million years – found at Western Slave, Canada	Major	n/a

Behind (and below) the landscape of Cornwall lies its geology. Some 400 million years of shifting, grinding, exploding, settling and sometimes even turning upside down have gone into making the shape of the Cornwall we know and love today. Some of the names of the geological features inadvertently suggest that there has been a deep battle going on for millennia. The 'Start-Perranporth Line', the 'Padstow Confrontation', the 'Carrick Thrust', the 'Pentire Succession' and the 'Portscatho Formation' – no wonder science and myth sometimes seem so tightly intertwined in Cornwall.

The geological variety is like few other places in the UK and while a lot of very clever scientists have unpicked the various processes and time scales, notably Joseph Henry Collins, the mining engineer and leading mineralogist (1841–1916), it was not until Colin M. Bristow wrote his *Introduction to Cornwall's Geology and Scenery* in 1996 that it became properly comprehensible to the layman. He writes:

▲ Granite on Bodmin Moor

Most of the sedimentary rocks on which Cornwall is formed were laid down in the Devonian and Carboniferous eras… Even older rocks are found in the Channel Islands and Brittany – a thousand million years ago and more. Two rocky reefs off the coast of Cornwall may be composed of ancient Precambrian rocks – the Eddystone Rocks south of Rame Head and the Man of War Rocks just off the southern coast of the Lizard. Both are composed of metamorphic rock called gneiss which resemble similar ancient rocks found in the Channel Islands and Brittany.

During the Devonian period Cornwall was covered by sea and was way to the south of where it is now – in fact, not far from the equator. The oldest Cornish rocks from this era, known as the Dartmouth group, can be found around Fowey and Polperro, further east at Rame and on the north coast at Watergate Bay.

During the Carboniferous period the wonderfully named Variscan Orogeny (mountain-building) occurred, and roughly between the Carboniferous and Permian eras came the intrusion of graniteshese formations form the basis for the distinctive moorland landscapes on Bodmin Moor with our 'mountains', Brown Willy and Rough Tor, the highest points in the county.

The strange southerly plateau of the Lizard originated to the south of the equator and slowly moved northward. On the Lizard, the most intense metamorphosis of

▲ The western side of the Lizard

any south-west area gave rise (after further complex chemical activity) to the spectacular red-green serpentine rock much used in building (as stone facing) and in the carving of artefacts. Serpentine is similar to marble and may be worked in much the same way.

The spectacular heights at Crackington Haven originated on or near the equator and are so important geologically that they are known worldwide as the Crackington Formation.

The geological forces that shaped the landscape also laid down the ore-bearing that provided the basis for the mining industry, the remains of which contribute hugely to the character of Bodmin Moor, Pendeen, St Just and St Agnes in particular. Many of these post-industrial landscapes now have World Heritage site status.

In spite of all this activity hundreds of millions of years ago, most of the Cornish landscape that we know today was formed much more recently, indeed, almost within a time scale that we can actually comprehend.

▲ The tranquil Helford

Recent (i.e. post-Ice Age) developments have seen first the incising and widening of the river valleys – ice melt and tumbling boulders scoured out the drowned rias of the south coast – and then the creation of the now tranquil soft scenery of the Helford, Fal and Fowey rivers. The sea level rise drowned some coastal areas and helped shape the cliffs and coves. As the ice disappeared so the frozen tundra that would have been Cornwall began to gain tree cover and lower lying areas formed wetlands. Grassland areas came into being too (although this had much to do with the hand of man, as we shall see). Later still, human influence became even more apparent, as we both dug into the surface and built on it.

Today's landscape

So, if we look out on this astonishing landscape moulded by millions of years of geological transformation, thousands of years of history and hundreds of industry, what do we see today?

I think it is fair to say that everyone sees something different. There are the cliffs, of course, and the beaches – still what nearly all tourists think of first. Most of the protected landscape of Cornwall has a coastal aspect and naturally this is where the up-country visitor nearly always heads for. The almost unimaginable depth of time that created Cornwall's geology gives us the high cliffs, the rocky foreshores and the sandy (and sometimes pebbly) beaches. Inland the bare granite tors are bunched like great grey fists about to punch the sky.

But the locals and long-established foreigners (like me) tend to see other aspects. We love the river valleys, the small fields, the winding lanes. We love the mine remains standing like sentinels as we round a bend or come over the brow of a hill. We love the bleak (until you look closer) heaths and moors. We love the trees, the hedges, even the built environment – for much of it is still unspoiled and much of today's development (though sadly not all) is in keeping with the land.

CLIMATE

'All you need in Cornwall,' said my mother in the 1970s, 'is wellingtons and sandals.' The climate is notoriously mild (is that a non-sequitur?) often not dipping below

Helen Rushworth

Paul Hughes

▲ There is little light pollution in Cornwall

freezing at all in the winter. Sometimes we hear of snow elsewhere in the UK and look wistfully out of the window at the puddles, sodden grass and damp, dripping trees. As I write this paragraph, in late December, the temperature outside is around twelve degrees.

The summer is occasionally hot but again more often mild and damp (sorry, Cornwall Tourist Board). Yet the advertisers have got one thing right: spring comes early, with primroses in February and daffodils in March, and autumn lingers on, with trees still leaf-clad in protected hollows well into December.

This mildness is good for crops. The aforementioned daffodils are grown commercially and are always ready for Easter, whenever it falls. Early potatoes, often grown under plastic, rival those of the Channel Islands and even the Mediterranean. The prevailing warm, damp wester-lies mean we are rarely short of water; the droughts that the south-east and East Anglia now regularly face are not likely here in the near future.

Yet there are some signs of a shift, even in Cornwall. When we have a heatwave, it is often a significant one with temperatures flying into the thirties. When the storms come in they do seem to be more ferocious of late. And we have had more flooding, not all of it directly linked to our uncanny ability to concrete or tarmac over flood prevention land.

SPECIAL SKIES

Natural beauty in Cornwall is not confined to the land-scape. Look up and you may see spectacular storm clouds over the sea or scudding mares' tails in the blue summer sky. At night there is little light pollution (compared with much of the rest of the UK anyway) and in the AONB sections especially the skies are notably more dark, tran-quil and, often, star-speckled. That said there has been an overall reduction in dark night skies across the AONB since 1990, largely as a result of continued housing and infrastructure development.

The Campaign for the Protection of Rural England (CPRE) in partnership with the Campaign for Dark Skies (CfDS) carried out a lighting nuisance survey a couple of years ago. The survey found that, across the country, eight out of ten people have their view of the night sky affected by light pollution and half have their sleep disrupted by light spilling into their bedrooms.

UK astronomer Steve Owens commented last year: 'People have been looking at the night sky, telling stories, for the entirety of recorded human history. But when we moved into cities, we lost that deep connection with the universe.' In Cornwall that connection is still alive and kicking. There are a number of observatories, the one on the Roseland being, perhaps, the best known. But you don't really need an observatory or even a telescope to appreciate the beauty of the night sky. On the plateau of the Lizard, on the hills of West Penwith, on the tors of Bodmin Moor, all you need to do is look up.

SEASCAPES

Always, there is the sea. You are never far from it in Cornwall and its influence can be felt everywhere.

Dave Matthews

While you would logically expect the varied landscape to be more interesting, in Cornwall it is so often the sea that takes our eye. Ostensibly featureless apart from the odd wave or small boat, it can nevertheless hold our gaze for hours. It is no coincidence that you always see visitors (and locals) looking out. On beaches, on benches, in cafes and on cliffs, our eye is inexorably drawn towards the sea.

Partly it's the sea and sky combination, of course, for even on the bright clear blue days (which abound in summer) there is always the interaction of water and light. And when the storm clouds roll in over a slate grey winter sea, the vista can astonish.

The Cornish have a natural affinity for the sea; many would say it is in their blood. It is not altogether surprising – centuries of fishing, trading, piracy (and its more respectable twin, privateering), exploration and, more recently, surfing and other sea-based recreation have informed most of our coastal communities. But the distinction between land and sea is often blurred (as anyone who has stood on a rock as the tide comes in will testify) and seascapes often do not get the attention they deserve.

Phil Dyke, the National Trust's Coast and Marine Adviser, told me last year: 'As an island nation it does seem strange that it's taken us more than six decades to start thinking about how we protect our seascapes, these wonderful but fragile places that mean so much to most people, and especially those in Cornwall.'

The Trust has been asking for the identification of marine areas that are of national importance and a means by which they can be conserved by the planning process – in the same way that the 1949 National Parks Act created the system that led to the formation of the National Parks in England and Wales and the setting up of Areas of Outstanding Natural Beauty.

Dave Matthews

If seascapes have been given little attention when compared with the land, what lies under the sea has been given even less. There are a few Special Areas of Conservation (SACs) around the coast which afford some protection. SACs are strictly protected sites designated under the EC Habitats Directive of twenty years ago; they are intended to maintain or restore natural habitats and species of European interest. There are 189 habitat types and 788 species listed – those considered to be most in need of conservation at a European level (excluding birds). Nearly half the habitat types, seventy-eight, are believed to occur in the UK. There are sixteen SACs in Cornwall including pretty much all of the Lizard, the upper Camel and De Lank rivers, several stretches of coastline and the Fal and Helford Estuary.

Marine Conservation Zones have now been proposed (after years of pressure). The Marine and Coastal Access Act of 2009 promised a coherent network of protection around the coasts by 2012. The 127 marine sites around England's coast, including 12 small inshore ones in Cornwall, have been recommended by 4 regional stakeholder groups to become Marine Conservation Zones this year. However, it appeared at the time of writing that many of these might not be implemented even though they are the result of two years of consultation with more than 1 million stakeholders and are desperately needed.

According to the Cornwall Wildlife Trust: 'The exclusion of any of the sites agreed in the process would be striking a blow at the future of Cornwall's marine ecosystem as a whole. The twelve carefully chosen sites around Cornwall represent a tiny fraction of the total coastal waters.'

The incredible diversity of Cornwall's natural and semi-natural habitat, offshore and on land, is the result of thousands of years of interaction between humans and nature. And though it is the blink of an eye in geological terms, it is probably reasonable to assert that our recent history has changed the landscape just as much as the great upheavals of the distant past. So let us take a tour of these more 'recent' times.

History and the land

For at least 5,000 years, people have helped shape the landscapes that we have inherited. The fields, roads, settlements, villages and the monuments to past industry are the result of several millennia of constant quarrying, building, adaptation and abandonment. Much of our landscape is valued for the depth of time that it

Dave Matthews

Dave Matthews

21

demonstrates – some of our field systems and village remains are prehistoric. Some areas have changed very little whilst others seem to be in a state of constant flux. If we look at any of the rich (in terms of time depth) landscapes around us we can see and almost feel the texture of the past. This 'past in the present' is at the heart of Cornwall's very strong sense of cultural identity.

So how far back can we go? The best places to look for our earliest activity are West Penwith and Bodmin Moor. Here, on the safe high ground, the signs of the Neolithic period are everywhere. But even during the earlier hunter-gatherer period, Cornwall saw some significant changes. From the last effects of the Ice Age the history of Cornwall can be roughly broken down into the following periods:

moorland being not unlike today. And, of course, the first settlers arrived as the climate became more hospitable.

Between 5000 and 6000 BC the land bridge between Britain and the rest of Europe was flooded – the beginning of our island history. The nomadic hunter-gatherers who had regularly crossed to southern England, including Cornwall, continued to move around with the seasons and food sources, gathering nuts and berries and hunting in the woodland in autumn and winter, following the upland grazing herds and gleaning the seashore for shellfish in the summer. Coastal tribes no doubt fished from the shore or in small crude boats. These Mesolithic people have left few traces on the landscape bar the archaeological finds around Gwithian, Trevose Head and Padstow on the north coast that have

Courtesy of Cornwall Council Historic Environment Service

Mesolithic Period	8000–4000 BC: Hunters and gatherers
Neolithic Period	4000–2500 BC: Monuments of the first farmers
Bronze Age	2500–800 BC: Settlement and ceremony, organized landscapes
Iron Age	800 BC–43 AD: Farmers and fighters
Romano-British Period	43–410: Under new management
Early Mediaeval Period	410–1066: Cornish kings and Celtic saints
Mediaeval Period	1066–1540: Tin, fish and farming
The industrial centuries	1540–1900: Mining and engineering
The modern age	1900–2012: Communications, energy and the motor car

Once the ice had retreated and the water and rocks had done their valley-incising work, climate and vegetation changed rapidly from about 8000 BC. In the later stages of the Ice Age, Cornwall would have been very similar to today's frozen tundra in Russia; then the cold grassland gave way to birch woodland and, as the climate warmed, to oak and hazel with some elm and lime. The high ground, even when the forest was at its densest, still had only sparse tree cover, the exposed granite and grass

revealed flint tools, arrow heads and fishing harpoons. They built little and if they did it was temporary, tents of hides, temporary shelters of woodland material, all remains now gone.

However from around 4000 BC some tribes began to settle down. Over maybe a thousand years domestication of animals had begun and now woodland clearances, often by burning, began to produce pasture. No doubt brought in by another northwards migration, farming practices, already well developed in Egypt and the Middle East began to be introduced to Britain. The deliberate cultivation and harvesting of plants for food meant that communities were increasingly tied to the land in specific places. Here we can begin to date with some certainty the effects that early man had on the landscape of Cornwall for, according to Cornwall's Historic Environment Service, it is from this period that our first monuments have survived.

[Although] it is known from flint scatters and other artefacts that settlements developed throughout the county, often on the sites of earlier Mesolithic camps, there are no visible remains of these first farms to be seen today. As the heavily wooded landscape was increasingly cleared and farmed, the growing population developed a social organisation and sense of territory that is reflected in their monuments. The massive 'megalithic' Chamber Tombs (Lanyon Quoit, Trethevy Quoit, Mulfra Quoit, Chûn Quoit) would have required the co-ordinated labour of a sizeable community. Generally known in Britain as 'Portal Dolmens' these monuments of the fourth millennium BC would have served as ritual foci and marked the community's ancestral territory. Long Cairns are rare in Cornwall and appear to be contemporary with the Chamber Tombs (e.g. Lanyon Quoit, Woolley Barrow as well as several on Bodmin Moor). It is clear that landmarks such as tors and hills with distinctive profiles were important and there is increasing evidence that structures were being built both to mimic and to view these. In the fourth millennium, tribal centres developed, perhaps controlling relatively large territories. There may be as many as seven Tor Enclosures in Cornwall, including Helman Tor and Carn Brea. That at Carn Brea is an astonishing achievement for such an early date. A series of massive defensive ramparts enclose 46 acres. These ramparts take the form of a 2m wide and 2-3m high stone wall faced with upright stones back and front and stretch over at least 3,750m; no less than fifteen stone-lined entrances have been found. Other enclosures at Roughtor and Stowe's Pound may be of similar date.

THE BRONZE AGE

During the Bronze Age (from about 2500 BC to about 800 BC) the landscape changed again, in some cases quite dramatically. Of course the ages in the table on p.22 are nothing like as precise as they seem. The Iron Age in the Middle East and parts of the Mediterranean began long before it did in Britain. There are tribes in far-flung parts of the world who have only relatively recently emerged from the Stone Age. When would you say our 'modern' age really began? With the French Revolution? The first railways? With the discovery of electricity? The combustion engine? The computer? Not so easy, is it? Ages, such as they are, segue into each other and older cultures often continue for a long time alongside newer ones.

However, the introduction of bronze, the beginning of the working of tin and further waves of migrants from Europe and Ireland did take place between 2000 and 1000 BC. It was during this time that the north to south routes across Cornwall, firstly from Hayle to The Mount, later from Padstow to Fowey, began to be well travelled. Ireland was a relatively advanced culture by northern European standards and her trade routes with Europe and the south cut across Cornwall rather than having the traders brave the dangers of the seas around Land's End.

It seems there were Bronze Age settlements at St Michael's Mount (where a bronze and copper hoard was found in the sixteenth century) and on Rough Tor on Bodmin Moor, and there may well have been others where later Iron Age fortifications or mediaeval castles are now prominent; after all a defensible place doesn't lose its usefulness as tools and ages change (or at least not until recent times).

The two most famous stone circles in Cornwall, the Merry Maidens between Penzance and Land's End and The Hurlers on the eastern edge of Bodmin Moor also date from Bronze Age times.

The later Bronze Age saw a rise in farming – bronze sickles and ploughshares have been found – so some of our prehistoric field systems, which can still be seen today, may be from this period. If you look down from Rough Tor or Brown Willy you can make out quite a number of field systems and round houses. These would

Peter Maxted

▲ Rough Tor summit

probably have extended into the lowland area but, of course, the remains would now be lost beneath 3,000 years of agricultural development, not to mention concrete and tarmac.

Interestingly, in spite of the number of settlements found on Bodmin Moor and other upland areas to the east, nearly all the important Bronze Age finds have come from west Cornwall, suggesting that around 1000 BC it was the most prosperous part of the county. This would have been due to it having the shortest north/south trade route from the Hayle Estuary to St Michael's Mount and, of course, a certain metal. It's been plausibly suggested that the Mount was the 'Ictis' mentioned in 400 BC accounts as a port for the tin trade. It was perhaps at this time, due to the trade with the Mediterranean area, that Cornwall was by far the most prosperous and advanced part of Britain – far more so than the little villages of London or Manchester.

THE IRON AGE

Around the time that Homer was devising *The Iliad* in far-away Greece, iron began to replace bronze for use in weapons and tools. There is some evidence that the small number of iron deposits found in Cornwall began to be worked around then. No doubt tin was also traded for the iron with areas such as Gloucestershire and Kent.

Three features from this period can be seen in Cornwall today (as well as the aforementioned fields). Farmsteads often had sheltered central areas such as Arthur's Hall on Bodmin Moor, which may also have had a protective and perhaps a ritual significance. Then there are the strange stone tunnels known as *fougous* – Cornish for cave (although not exlcusive to Cornwall. The best preserved one I have seen was in the west of Ireland). These again may have been defensive – perhaps temporary refuges during brief onslaughts by raiding parties – and may also have been used as cold stores (for dairy products or meat) or for religious purposes. There are several in West Cornwall, one between Newquay and Padstow, and one outside Constantine near Falmouth.

The most significant structure to have an effect on the landscape during the Iron Age and into the post-Roman era was probably the hill fort. Some, as previously mentioned, were developments of Bronze Age fortifications such as on Rough Tor or even of the earliest Neolithic ones such as Carn Brae. But many more date from the first millennium BC. The names of Castel an Dinas in Penwith and Castel Dore near Fowey remain evocative even today. But it seems there is barely a scrap of coast where an Iron Age fort *didn't* stand. Almost every coastal section of the AONB can boast a couple, some like West Penwith have ruined hill forts as numerous as the caravan sites in the unprotected areas. Hill forts, cliff forts, forts everywhere.

But boy, did they need them in the Iron Age. To begin with it seems that the fortifications were erected as a protection against waves of Celtic and perhaps Teutonic invaders in successive centuries during the first millennium BC. As each was assimilated there was nearly always a new invasion or threat to follow. Pirates were a further threat as were raiding parties from Brittany and Normandy. So the 'Cornish', actually a continuing surge of invasion, settlement and assimilation by different peoples, kept building and strengthening. Some hill forts survive sufficiently so that the layman can make out ramparts or entrances such as that on Trencrom Hill near St Ives. Others, such as Rosemullion near Falmouth or on the point above Trelissick, are simply grassed or wooded mounds indistinguishable, to the untutored eye, from natural landscape features.

THE ROMANS

In his *A History of Cornwall*, F.E. Halliday sums up the story so far with his usual precision:

> By the beginning of the Christian era a hundred generations of men had modified the natural landscape of Cornwall. To the memorials of the dead, the great stone tombs and monuments of Neolithic man, to the stone circles and grass grown barrows of the Age of Bronze, the men of the Iron Age had added their trophies of the living – their citadels, forts, cliff castles and villages. Most of these had been built on high ground, those of the first two ages for religious reasons, those of the last for more practical motives of defence.

To this description we can add the early field systems, some farmsteads and small settlements, as well as some of the tracks that are still the course of today's roads. The landscape of 2,000 years ago is all around us today.

The first Roman invasion under Julius Caesar was probably no more than a distant rumour in far Cornwall. The second, in the first century AD, saw the Emperor Augustus's legions march west and found a fortified camp at Exeter. This was known as Isca Dumnoniorum, the first recorded time that the Cornish and Devonian Celts were known by their ancient name, the Dumnonii. Their subjugation was not as harsh as that of some eastern tribes and it seems that the Romans did not press on across the Tamar in any great strength. The Cornish were a division of the Dumnonii tribe, known as the Cornovii.

Cornwall was incorporated into the administrative area but while some of the hill forts were abandoned during the military occupation the most important rounds were not and were probably left in the hands of local chiefs who paid allegiance to Rome.

During the 400 years of Roman occupation, Cornwall was changed subtly. The local tribe became more 'Romanized' and while there may have been the occasional visit from a genuine Roman administrator the Dumnonii simply adapted to a different and, for their leaders, a richer and more civilized, way of life. There were no Roman towns or major roads west of the Tamar but there have been many finds of pottery, jewellery and coins.

There is evidence of one Roman villa near Camborne and a fortified farm near Bodmin. Most other settlements from this period are still Iron Age Celtic such as the courtyard houses at Chysauster near Penzance.

In the early days of the Roman Empire the tin trade declined but, once the easier-to-access Spanish tin was used up, Cornwall again became a trading centre. Thus Roman influence probably increased with visits from traders to St Michaels Mount, Fowey and other south coast ports as well as down the Camel Estuary in the north.

In 410 AD the last of the legions withdrew, leaving a much-changed Britain. Cornwall had adapted too in terms of expanded trade, better farming, new administration and, towards the end of Roman rule, the introduction of Christianity. However there is no doubt that Cornwall was still, despite 350 years of Roman influence, essentially Celtic.

THE DARK AGES

Although some historians and archaeologists call the period between the departure of Rome and the arrival of the Normans the early mediaeval period, most of us know this as the Dark Ages. The implication of chaos and disaster is not without foundation but the term really refers to the lack of certain knowledge passed on through the written word. After the (fairly) well-documented Roman era the next 600 years are a bit more obscure.

The main reason for this is the fact that much of Britain was invaded and ruled by the Saxons and the Vikings – both of whom had an oral rather than a written tradition. The last of the Celtic Britons, both originals and those pushed west by subsequent invasions, were left in their strongholds of Wales and the West Country.

Dave Matthews

A number of immigrants arrived in Cornwall in the early part of this period as well. Significantly, they were Christian and among them were the saints who gave their names to so many Cornish towns and villages. From Ireland came the Cornish patron saint St Piran who landed at Perranporth near Newquay, St Ia who gave her name to St Ives, and St Just as well as a host of others. From Brittany came St Melor (Mylor) and St Germans, from Wales came St Kew and St Petroc. I haven't counted them all but there must be the best part of a hundred towns and villages named after a missionary saint, probably the most of any similar sized area in Europe. Although the early settlements from the great age of the saints have almost completely disappeared, the names live on in the town and in the stone churches built in mediaeval times.

Of the kings of Dumnonia known by name, Constantine in the sixth century and Gereint in the eighth century are definitely recorded, but three far more famous names from the sixth century are also still with us – though so embroidered by legend that all truth has long been hidden. They are King Mark along with his son (or nephew) Prince Tristan and, of course, King Arthur.

Battles against the Saxons continued throughout the period with mixed results. Two notable defensive features from the time, both in the AONB, are linear earthworks, the Bolster Bank at St Agnes (still visible between Trevaunance Cove and Chapel Coombe) and the Giant's Hedge (originally stretching between Lerryn near Fowey and Looe), large sections of which are visible north of Lanreath). Both may have been defences built during this period, though some historians place them much earlier. What is fairly certain is that the battle near Camelford which gave its name to Slaughter Bridge was the site of the Saxon King Egbert's victory against the rebellious Cornish (and not the site of King Arthur's last battle as legend, and Tennyson, would have it). It is also the case that Tintagel was a stronghold from the sixth century onwards and it is certainly possible that it was occupied at some point by the Royal Prince Arthurus. More of him, fact and fiction, later.

The Saxon influence on Cornwall was slight although

there is some remnant of it in the east of the county; Morwenstow and Kilkhampton are both fusions of Cornish words with Saxon endings. There was, however, continual conflict with the expanding Saxon kingdom of Wessex before King Athelstan, in 936 AD, set the boundary between England and Cornwall at the Tamar.

MEDIAEVAL TIMES

The Normans defeated Harold and his exhausted Saxons at Pevensey near Hastings and within twenty years there was no part of Saxon England that had not felt their heavy hand. Even distant Cornwall was no exception.

Very few Cornish Celts would have accepted their Saxon overlords but the Normans were a different case. Robert of Mortain, William the Conqueror's half-brother, was given Cornwall as his domain and he set up his 'capital' at Launceston where he built his castle. By the time of the Domesday Book in 1086 Robert had taken over almost all of the 300 Cornish manors, regardless of whether they had Celtic or Saxon owners, and most of the religious establishments. Other early castles, Motte and Bailey types, later replaced with the stone

Dave Matthews

keep and two bailey (wall) style that we can still see today, were constructed at Tintagel, Restormel, Kilkhampton and elsewhere. Gradually the castles fell into decay and ruin in part because Cornwall was remote from the main wars against the Scots, Welsh and French and then the great civil Wars of the Roses.

By the twelfth century there was a significant amount of agriculture, particularly in the more fertile east of Cornwall. There was also still extensive woodland, certainly by today's standards. But one of the most significant landscape features that developed during the Middle Ages was, of course, the church.

As elsewhere new stone buildings leapt up across the land, from the great monastic centres at St Germans in the south-east and St Gluvias in Penryn to the small granite churches in almost every village of any size. There are well over a hundred mediaeval churches in Cornwall — repositories of history unmatched by any other type of building. Around the churches the villages grew slowly, and the towns, especially if they received a market charter, rather faster. Tolls from markets and fairs were as important to mediaeval lords as tithes from the agricultural workers — Truro, Penryn, Helston and Fowey were just a few of these early urban centres. Bodmin, dating from an earlier period, was the largest.

From the twelfth century onwards an increasing number of markets and towns are recorded in documents. All of the new towns that had developed by the end of the twelfth century were coastal or inland ports, and trade was the obvious factor in their location. During the thirteenth and fourteenth centuries many new towns were established, developing from fishing ports. Cornish trade at the time included the export of tin, fish, slate and cloth, and the import from Brittany, Ireland, France and Spain of salt, linen, canvas, wine and fruit.

At the end of the thirteenth century Helston, Truro, Liskeard and Lostwithiel were Stannary towns. Each Stannary town contained a Coinage Hall for the biannual assaying of tin (testing it for purity and taxation purposes). At Lostwithiel the Coinage Hall formed part of the 'Duchy Palace', a large administration complex which was the centre from which the Cornish estates were managed and which contained the county court.

In late mediaeval times Henry VIII resurrected the castle building of the earlier period, this time not to repress his own subjects but to repel the French. The dominating castles of Pendennis at Falmouth and St Mawes and Fowey bear witness to his efforts.

Richard Carew, born in 1555, bestrides the period linking the mediaeval and industrial eras, the late Elizabethan and early Jacobean period. He is the author of *The Survey of Cornwall* published in 1602/3 just as Elizabeth was being succeeded by James I. The survey is an astonishingly detailed snapshot of the landscape at the time and the first really detailed description of Cornwall including the Godolphins, Arundells, Killigrews, Grenvilles and St Aubyns.

Carew trained as a lawyer, held most county offices and was an MP twice. He spent his lifetime collecting noteworthy facts about Cornwall, travelling its length and breadth. He lived at Antony in the south-east, and was related to most of the great families of Cornwall

The first part of his survey describes the Cornish landscape, its mining, farming, fishing, communications and recreations, including hurling. The survey began some time before 1586 and was completed and published in 1602. 'It [the survey] bespeaks a sense of Cornish identity rooted in a profound attachment to the geographical space,' wrote Exeter historian Alexander Walsham in an introduction to a modern reprint. The survey is dedicated to Sir Walter Raleigh, Lord Warden of the Stannaries and Lieutenant General of Cornwall.

THE INDUSTRIAL ERA

While it was in the period between the Elizabethans and the twentieth century that saw the great upsurge of industry and the greatest change to the face of Cornwall in human times, the story of our industrial past goes a lot further back.

I suppose you could argue that the first 'industry' was hunting, perhaps as early as 7000 BC, before we even became an island (Britain, not Cornwall, that's still to come). This would also include the earliest types of fishing, for the shore-dwellers of Stone Age times would have been dependent on fish and shellfish for survival especially in winter. There is thus a justifiable claim that our declining fishing industry can make to being Cornwall's oldest.

For centuries, perhaps millennia, fishing remained largely unchanged. Not too far from shore, small boats caught fish with line and net much as they do today. Yet even before the arrival of the deadly pair trawling system and the ghastly factory ships that we've seen recently, there was a period of fishing on an industrial scale.

From about 1700 to the early 1900s the trade in salted pilchards was as big a contributor to the Cornish economy as tin mining. The great shoals would be spotted from special lookout points called huers' huts around the coast, up would go the cry, '*Hevva! Hevva!* and the boats would be launched from Mousehole, St Ives, Boscastle, Mevagissey – a dozen or more places around the coast. A number would circle the huge mass of fish then draw their conjoined nets into the middle, a process known as seine netting. On shore the fish would be salted, packed in barrels and sent to London or farther afield to the Mediterranean countries that considered them a great delicacy. Many of the fishing ports, large and small, that decorate our coast today grew up during this era thanks to the humble pilchard.

Today the fishing industry is in decline, not just in Cornwall but worldwide. The reason isn't the dreaded EU with its quotas or even Russian factory ships and Spanish pair trawlers (sorry Newlyn). Or at least it's not just for these obvious reasons. The main reason for declining fish stocks is over-fishing caused by over-consumption. And *that* is largely caused by an increasing and increasingly wealthy world population. (Oh dear, he's on his environmental soap box again!)

There are some things we can do to limit this damage; we can conserve stocks through robust fisheries policies. We can cut waste. We can introduce protected breeding and spawning zones (Marine Conservation Zones are a good start). And we can move towards eating sustainably. Sustainable fish is a massively complex issue with no easy solutions as stocks vary from area to area and even from season to season. But to choose hand-line caught mackerel or bass over the trawled stuff or to eat pollack or whiting rather than cod or, especially, imported fish, would be a good start. And please, only eat scallops rarely and those that are dived-for rather than dredged; scallop-dredging is probably the most destructive fishing method – it ploughs up and virtually destroys the entire seabed.

Agriculture

For a county with relatively poor soil, certainly when compared with the rich earth of Devon or Somerset, Cornwall has a history of farming that goes back further than almost anywhere else in the UK. We have evidence of much prehistoric agricultural activity and some of the earliest field systems in the country are still visible today with their stone boundaries intact. The best examples are in the far west near Zennor but traces remain on the edge of Bodmin Moor too (there is more on farming the upland areas of Cornwall in Chapter 8).

Farming seems to have stabilized under the Romans and declined during the Dark Ages (though people still had to eat, so there must have been some). During the Middle Ages more land came under cultivation, though methods were still primitive and, whether the Celtic small field system or the Anglo/Norman strip-farming system was used, the method of oxen ploughing and hand harvesting would have seemed very familiar to farmers 1,000 or even 2,000 years earlier. The main reason for the increase in land farmed, if not the yield from any particular patch, was the repeal of the Forest Laws (Cornwall paid King John the huge sum of 2,200 marks, allowing it to cut down former royal forest and cultivate the land).

The late Middle Ages saw an increase in farming again, this time as a result of changing working practices as peasant farmers began to work for themselves rather than for feudal lords. By late Tudor times there was plenty of reasonably prosperous agriculture although there was a dip after the end of the Civil War.

The great leap forward in agriculture (with apologies to any Maoists reading this) came with the Industrial Revolution proper and the beginning of mechanized farming in the nineteenth century. This was, however, preceded by a devastating drop in farm produce prices following the end of the Napoleonic Wars.

Dave Matthews

Interestingly, the twentieth century agricultural practices that have seen parts of the east of England turned into 'green desert' have largely passed the hillier regions of the south-west by. Some hedgerows were ripped up in the middle of the twentieth century (I remember watching in impotent fury as an ancient stone hedge was destroyed near my mother's cottage) but on the whole farms have remained small, fields are still enclosed and the landscape stays beautiful at least in the lowland areas.

Peter Maxted

trating on cattle less suitable for the moors. Sheep farmers too may be 'turning away' from the uplands. Without the hardy breeds and the skills of the hill farmers, the uplands will change – gorse and bracken will cover important archaeological sites, ancient field systems will disappear and access for the public will become much more difficult. The chapter on West Penwith (Chapter 8) has more on farming the uplands.

It may be that the tradition of common grazing that has effectively 'looked after' the uplands for over 6,000 years will be broken.

Mining

Some might argue that Cornwall missed the beginning of the Industrial Revolution, others that we started it. Certainly Cornish industry, in the shape of granite quarrying, tin and copper mining, smelting and charcoal

While fields themselves may not have changed that much, farming practice has, and that has influenced the look of the landscape. Many older people remark on how few animals there seem to be in our landscape today compared with fifty or even thirty years ago.

In a ten year period from 1984, common market agricultural policy to restrict milk production drastically reduced dairy herds and prompted shifts to beef and lamb production. Pig farming declined too. The subsequent damaging effects of the BSE and foot-and-mouth crises saw another notable change – the growth of horticultural activity. The daffodil fields in early spring seem to increase year on year. And much larger crops of sugar beet, oilseed rape and flax have seen a changing colour scheme come to our farmed landscape too.

One of the greatest threats is to the Cornish uplands with the loss of grazing animals and the decline in the number of hill farmers with the necessary skills to manage the land. The naturally hard conditions that made it more difficult for farmers to compete meant that in the past hill farmers often also worked in other local industries such as quarrying and mining. A survey of south-western hill farmers in 2007 found that 43% had recently reduced their breeding beef herd. As improving the value of their livestock was the only solution, that meant moving away from hardy hill stock and concen-

Rachel Martin

burning predates the beginnings of the Industrial Revolution in South Wales. And Cornwall is the UK's first post-industrial county too, the last tin mine closed in the 1980s and the land is dominated, in many areas, by the ruins of mine buildings. Mining affected much more than just the immediate landscape around the mines. Towns and villages were transformed by a growing industrial population with newly built rows of distinctive terraced cottages, shops, chapels and substantial public buildings.

The great days of tin mining took place during the eighteenth and nineteenth centuries, but the history of tin, bound up with the very essence of Cornwall, goes back somewhat further. It is fascinating to consider who first merged the soft copper, probably from Ireland, with the new metal found in Cornish streams to form bronze. Some 4,000 years ago, in the early Bronze Age tin production began in Cornwall, almost certainly in the far west near the land trade route from Ireland (and later Wales) to the continent. The method of accessing the tin, known as streaming, continued in a similar fashion at least until late mediaeval times, just as agricultural practice remained more or less the same. Tin streaming is still practiced today, at Blue Hills near St Agnes, the last, for the time being, tin produced in Cornwall. The tin is found where streams have eroded the surface rock and cut across tin seams. These are known as alluvial deposits.

The Elizabethans (well, some of them) believed that tin was washed down from the remnants of Noah's flood and was thus a God-given asset. But it was in the late Tudor period that mining as we know it began. Tin had been dug out since the late mediaeval period – the first lodes, those exposed or close to the surface, were strip-mined. When these surface lodes and alluvial deposits became exhausted or ever harder to find, mining went underground.

Some of the earliest mines were on the Godolphin Estate near Helston. Extraction was not easy – for the deeper a mine went the more expensive it was to shore up, to pump and to extract the tin. Nevertheless, the mines and estate prospered through the next century. The Godolphins flourished under the Stuarts, supported the Royalist cause, helped the young Charles II to escape and, in the reign of Queen Anne, financed the Duke of Marlborough's campaign and victories – all thanks to the wealth generated by tin.

Yet, up until the early nineteenth century copper was mined more extensively than tin, although both are found together in many areas. In the early 1800s Dolcoath mine in Camborne produced over £1m worth of copper – equivalent to perhaps £200 million today.

As the copper was gradually exhausted, or became too uneconomical to extract, tin took over. Its heyday was during the early years of the nineteenth century. In 1837 over 28,000 people were employed in Cornish mines including 7,000 children, and a survey of 78 mines that year noted an annual consumption of 50,000 tons of coal and timber equivalent to 140 square miles of Scandinavian forest. From 1819 to1840 nearly 300,000 tons of ore were raised and over 63 miles of development levels and shafts were cut.

Victorian engineers helped this industry to grow – Richard Trevithick (whose steam engine was earlier than Stephenson's famous Rocket) invented the mining beam engine and Humphrey Davy, protégée of Faraday, developed his miners' safety lamp. The railways began in Cornwall to transport tin (and quarried stone) to the ports for export. Before long, of course, they began to carry passengers and other goods and it could be argued therefore that tin had a direct effect on the early tourist trade. Today tourists and locals can walk or cycle on the nearly forty-mile long network of multi-activity trails around some of the main mining areas, notably on the Great Flat Lode trail near Camborne. Many of the new trails follow the tramway and railway routes once used to transport ore.

The long, slow decline of tin mining began in the mid-nineteenth century and was accompanied by an exodus of Cornish mining families to all parts of the world where new mines were being opened up. Australia, South Africa, Mexico and many others saw the Cornish arrive, bringingtheir traditional skills with them. Today it is estimated that around 6 million people worldwide have Cornish roots. This Cornish diaspora is around fourteen times the size of the current population of Cornwall.

Dave Matthews

As the tin industry declined, other natural products offered extraction possibilities. China clay was discovered in the mid-1700s and was used principally in the production of porcelain and paper. The 'Cornish Alps' above the St Austell area are supposedly one of the few man-made structures visible from space (unlike the Great Wall, contrary to popular belief) and the great spoil heaps and pits give the landscape an eerie feel. Above Penryn lie a number of ancient granite quarries (and a few that are still working) from where the stone was exported around the world. And on the north coast there are the slate quarries. Today the massive operation at Delabole Slate Quarry, 'the largest man-made hole in Europe', is the only survivor, but remains of the old quarries can be found throughout the northern part of the county, not least along the Camel Estuary where I counted over forty in one small AONB section. Many of the tin miners moved over to work in these slate, granite and especially china clay industries, during the nineteenth century.

The last tin mine closed in the 1980s but it is impossible to travel far in Cornwall without being aware of how prevalent the industry was. The skeletal engine houses and desolate chimneys are a constant reminder.

THE WESLEYS

Since John Wesley, and to a lesser extent his brother Charles, were intimately bound up with miners and the mining communities of the eighteenth century, this seems an appropriate place to introduce them. John, whose journeys took him the equivalent of ten times round the earth, is an important figure for the Cornish Mining World Heritage organization who summarized his influence thus: 'John Wesley was known for his stirring oratory – he was said to captivate the spirit of the Cornish audiences he spoke to. During his lifetime he is thought to have preached more than 30,000 sermons, travelled 250,000 miles and edited over 200 books.'

The message that John Wesley preached was comforting to the mining communities. The words spoken by him and the other Methodist preachers brought hope and security to those who faced the nonstop hazards of the mining work they undertook. The Methodists became the most relevant institution for these working-class communities. In part, the expansion of the newer Anglican churches in parts of Cornwall can also be attributed to the work of John Wesley. His influence and that of those who preached the same doctrine were seen by the Church of England as a threat and they built new churches to slow the spread of Methodism.

Methodism, like the humble pasty, travelled with the miners that left Cornwall and went to work overseas. This migration of men, women and belief resulted in the setting up of Methodist chapels throughout the Cornish communities that appeared in the mining areas of the world.

John Wesley, the Methodists and the chapels that were constructed in the years that followed his preaching, remain just as important as the engine houses and other significant reminders of Cornwall's world-changing industrial past.

Charles Wesley has, according to Carolyn Martin:

largely been overshadowed by [the] achievements of his older brother. It was as a hymn writer that Charles excelled composing the words for over 6,000 hymns…whilst at Oxford he and his brother became involved with a group of religiously-minded students, whose members visited the sick and prisoners as well as keeping sensible hours, praying, fasting and generally behaving unlike proper Oxford undergraduates!

Charles did have bragging rights over his brother in one respect; he was apparently the first Methodist preacher to arrive in Cornwall, in 1743, though John followed very soon after. Both seem to have preached at the astonishing Gwennap Pit near Redruth, outside the AONB but one of the sights that any visitor to Cornwall should see. The pit is still used for religious services and outdoor performances today.

WORLD HERITAGE

The Cornwall and West Devon Mining Landscape World Heritage site, popularly known as 'Cornish Mining' was designated quite recently in 2006. It gave formal recognition to the importance that Cornish mining played in shaping the world.

It is the largest World Heritage site in mainland UK, covering nearly 20,000 hectares stretching from the St Just mining district in the far south west to Tavistock in Devon, and it coincides with five of Cornwall and Devon's Areas of Outstanding Natural Beauty. As a World Heritage site, it can claim to be as important as the Pyramids, the Great Wall of China or the Taj Mahal.

In 2011 the 'Discover the Extraordinary' Project was launched. This tells the story behind the Cornwall & West Devon Mining Landscape and has been funded by a European Union and DEFRA grant through the Rural Development Programme for England (RDPE). Money has been invested in eleven Cornish Mining WHS partner attractions, implementing substantial improvements to their visitor facilities and public presentation. The next phase of the Project is being aimed at target visitor audiences, public events at mining heritage attractions and a series of tourism familiarization days (I went on one, to Geevor) to introduce journalists, Cornish

Dave Matthews

accommodation providers and other tourism businesses to the World Heritage landscape and attractions.

Delve deeper into the Cornish mining story and we find that Cornish miners introduced pasties and football to Mexico and rugby to South Africa. And many of the great gardens and houses of Cornwall, including the massive Lanhydrock, were developed from the proceeds of Cornish mining

THE MODERN ERA

If the mining industry had the greatest effect on the Cornish landscape since the forest clearances and river valley creation of the last Ice Age, the last seventy years must come a close second. After the war (many World War II buildings are still to be found in the landscape) there was an explosion of house and road building. The National Trust protected much of the coast and the AONB designation ensured sensible, sustainable building in some areas but many industrial estates, housing complexes, small factories and, of course, dramatically increased road networks still transformed much of the county – and not always for the better. Even today, much land is still post-industrial and contaminated with arsenic, heavy metals etc. Cornwall now has more derelict land than any other county in England, with 12% of the total national resource at 4,888 hectares. All 'wild' land needs management. This is an extract from a Cornwall Council information leaflet:

What we see on rough ground today…is not a 'natural' landscape but rather the results of a century or more of neglect. The wildlife and scenic value of these landscapes has been reduced and archaeological features are hidden and can be damaged by the growth of bracken and scrub. To maintain and enhance its unique historic, wildlife and scenic value, heath-land needs to be actively managed: in particular, scrub and bracken need to be controlled. These can be cut by hand or machinery over small areas and small controlled fires can also be used. The best solution for long-term care, however, is to restore the low-intensity livestock grazing which for so long was the major use of these areas.

Recent large developments have, on the whole, been of a higher calibre. The new university at Penryn, the Heartlands project between Redruth and Camborne, the Eden Project – all have enhanced the county as well as providing employment and bringing prosperity. But over-development is an ever-present threat – the price of beauty is continued vigilance.

One of the largest landowners in Cornwall, and one whose activities nearly always have a beneficial effect on the landscape (even if this sometimes isn't recognized at first) is the National Trust.

The National Trust is a charity independent of the government. Its income comes from membership fees, donations, legacies and revenue raised from commercial operations. The Trust has over 4 million members and 55,000 volunteers. More than 14 million people visit their properties and they estimated 50 million per annum visit our open air sites. The Trust is one of Britain's richest charities.

With over 350 historic houses, gardens and ancient monuments in its portfolio the Trust is also a huge landlord, owning forests, fens, beaches, farmland, downs, moorland, islands, archaeological remains, castles and nature reserves – even whole villages. It was founded in 1895 by three Victorian philanthropists – Octavia Hill, Robert Hunter and Hardwicke Rawnsley. Concerned about the impact of uncontrolled development and industrialization, they set up the Trust to act as a guardian for the nation in the acquisition and protection of threatened coastline, countryside and buildings.

Social reformer Octavia Hill said at its founding: 'The need of quiet, the need of air, the need of exercise, and the sight of sky and of things growing seem human needs, common to all men.' Interestingly, coastal preservation was not high on the three founders' list of priorities. The coast was viewed, rather as the countryside was before the romantic poets, as a dangerous wild place and not somewhere anyone would want to visit or live unless they had to. This was especially true of the north Cornish coast whose reputation seems as bleak as it was in Parson Hawker's time, eighty years earlier. In 1901 *The Times* published an article entitled: 'The Danger of the North Cornish Coast,' highlighting its unpopularity as a vacation destination and writing of its 'dangerous nature'. The roads were difficult also (although more towns were served by the railways than today).

However, one of the National Trust's very earliest acquisitions was the twin headlands of Barras Nose and Tintagel Castle in 1896. It seems coastal land *was* worth saving if it had a historic connection or was culturally important to the local community or, perhaps more importantly, if it was connected to one of Britain's great myths or legends.

A number of prominent coastal sites were purchased in the early part of the twentieth century, including the Dodman in 1919. In 1936 there were moves to build an estate of bungalows on Pentire Head and The Rumps. After a local outcry, the National Trust moved to buy the two headlands. In the 1960s 'Operation Neptune' was launched to raise funds to save the coastline, leading to the purchase of Lizard Point and Cape Cornwall, though, sadly, not Land's End.

Ian French

▲ The Rumps – saved from being a housing estate

By this stage the Trust had a policy of buying 'one farm deep', meaning that much of the hinterland was also protected. The whole coastal landscape, up to the first skyline, was the target, rather than just the cliff or promontory.

The Trust's conservation decisions have not always been popular – locals object when a footpath is moved or a car park closed and the subject of coastal grazing is a contentious one in certain areas but it is nevertheless true that without 116 years of the National Trust Cornwall would be a much poorer place.

Nature and wildlife

Cornwall's remoteness, together with some good and some fortunate management, has meant that, in wildlife conservation terms, it remains one of the richest and most diverse counties in Britain. Its 400km coastline provides a haven for an enormous range of notable species including the globally rare grey seal and gannet.

The bluebell woodlands are of international importance and the extent of our ancient woodland comes, surprisingly, to nearly 7,000 hectares (over 27 square miles). Woodland wildlife includes foxes and badgers, roe deer and many smaller mammals while wild ponies still roam the moors. The sand dunes (or *towans*) contrast with the towering cliffs on the north coast and

Andy Hay

▲ Gannets on the cliffs

35

▲ Yellow gorse flowers in spring

are important for their scenic qualities as well as their suitability as wildlife habitats.

Cornwall also has approximately 12% of Britain's lowland heath, home to many rare plant and insect species. Heath and moorland often tend to be lumped together as 'rough ground' whether upland, lowland or coastal. They are characterized by a vegetation cover of heather, ling (another sort of heather, not the fish), gorse, bilberry, bracken and a range of grass species. It is interesting to note that gorse, often now seen as a nuisance, was once a primary source of fuel (it was known as furze). Gorse is a legume (like beans and peas) and thus has a useful ability to fix nitrogen in the soil. Colonies of bacteria, which occupy nodules in the root system, can take up nitrogen from the surrounding soil and make it available to the gorse plant. By shocking the plant (coppicing or pollarding) some of the nitrogen is released and becomes available to other plants using the same root space.

Some of the west Cornish heath-lands are also home to three rare plants, two types of squill and the confusingly named Cornish Heath. Interestingly our heathland can give us clues to the time depth of the landscape better than many other areas. On Treen Common in West Penwith deposits of fine herbaceous material including sedge, rush leaves, seeds and roots and ling leaves (some of them charred) have been found. Could the charring have been the work of early man? If so, we may have to re-write the history books as radiocarbon dating suggests the vegetation comes from just before 10,000 BC – the late glacial period. Were Mesolithic hunters already in Cornwall then?

Pools on the heath and moorland support frogs, toads and newts while the rivers that rise on Bodmin Moor have salmon and brown trout. Bats lurk in old mine buildings, shafts and adits. Once busy workings that echoed to the shouts of miners and the rumble of machinery now lie silent all across our landscape – home

to many kinds of wildlife who now have the crumbling industrial buildings to themselves. Many of the mining areas particularly in the west are home to grass snakes and adders too, although spotting either is rare except on calm sunny days when you may find them basking on trails and footpaths.

In summer the bird-life is prolific all across the protected landscape but particularly on the coast, with the once extinct (in Cornwall) chough now back and breeding well in at least three locations (one of them still secret at the time of writing). The gentle climate of the county means that almost as many birds arrive in the autumn as depart. The southern coastal estuaries are a vital resource for overwintering birds; waders and wild-fowl gather in vast numbers over the winter months.

More exotic wildlife to be seen nowadays includes ostriches, alpacas and llamas, farmed for meat and wool. And then, of course, there is the 'Beast of Bodmin'. This has often been sighted (nearly always at dusk or during the night) but rarely photographed. It has been identified as anything from a feral native cat to a black panther. The skull of a large cat (identified by the Natural History Museum) found in the River Fowey suggests the story is not without foundation. The existence of the Beast is a lot more likely than the legend of Morgawr, Cornwall's very own sea monster and rival to the one in Loch Ness, which has been 'seen' off and on for over a hundred years in and around Falmouth Bay.

There are also plans to re-populate parts of West Penwith and the Lizard with the red squirrel, last seen in Cornwall in 1984. The Cornwall Red Squirrel Project was launched by the Duke of Cornwall, Prince Charles, at the 2010 Royal Cornwall Show: 'The importance of preserving Britain's reds cannot be overstated. They are one of the most charming and irresistible of British native mammals and are under ceaseless, pernicious attack by the relentless march of the imported greys.' As can be seen by the language used by the Prince, this is an emotive subject. The project has been received with rapture by many visitors and indeed much of the Cornish public, but several conservation organizations have been more cautious, notably over the proposed cull of the grey and the ability to provide an exclusion zone for the reds. If the red is successfully re-introduced, however, there will be tourism benefits. In other strongholds in Scotland, in parts of the north-east and particularly at Formby Point, Merseyside, around which a 'buffer zone' free of grey squirrels has been created, visitors flock to see the reds.

Finally, a word about some of the smaller creatures and plants around us. I must admit to finding it hard to get excited about insects and certainly about slugs and snails. However, naturalists I have been out with never fail to find not only an abundance of micro-life but an amazing variety. And where I gasp at sweeping carpets of heather-clad heath or wild seascapes, my wife will often delight in a tiny violet or delicate spider. After years of looking into the distance at the great canvas of our astonishing landscape, I am slowly learning to appreciate some of the more intimate world close to my boots.

Dave Matthews

THE WILDLIFE TRUST

Cornwall Wildlife Trust is the leading local conservation charity that works to protect Cornwall's wildlife and wild places. Like many others around the UK, Cornwall Wildlife Trust conserves habitats by managing 55 nature reserves, covering over 500 acres, giving refuge to rare and endangered species and advising landowners on how best to manage their land for wildlife.

The Trust also campaigns and runs projects on land and at sea to protect wildlife and its environment. It records and monitors wildlife, allowing us to share in its information, knowledge and expertise. It also aims to inspire people by encouraging locals and visitors to explore and enjoy Cornwall's natural heritage, and to help children to have fun with nature through the (primary school age) Fox Club.

The Trust was founded in 1962 by a group of local naturalists who were concerned about the severe decline in wildlife at that time. Now it employs over 40 staff, is helped by thousands of volunteers and supported by nearly 14,000 members.

NATURE RESERVES

There are three National Nature Reserves in Cornwall – Golitha Falls on Bodmin Moor, Goss Moor which is not in the AONB and now has a new dual carriageway running through it, and the Lizard. In total there are also fifty-five smaller reserves, mostly private donations that are managed by the Cornwall Wildlife Trust. There are eight Local Nature Reserves managed by Cornwall Council of which four abut the Area of Outstanding Natural Beauty, two on the Godrevy–Portreath section and two at either end of the South Coast Eastern section. All of the NNR sites are, of course, also Sites of Specific Scientific Interest, giving them considerable protection.

According to Cornwall Wildlife Trust in 2011, there were 498 County Wildlife Sites in Cornwall covering nearly 33,000 hectares. This is nearly 10% of the county's land area and is under both public and private ownership. County Wildlife Sites range from small copses and linear features like river valleys to ancient woodlands, large moors and wetlands. Many of these are Biodiversity Action Plan (BAP) habitats; these are habitats that are

Mullion and Predannack Cliffs

The Lizard National Nature Reserve is made up of many varied sites. Mullion and Predannack offers a mix of cliff, heathland and coastal grassland unique in Britain. The combination of mild climate, an exposed southerly location and rare serpentinite and schist rocks has resulted in this internationally important habitat.

The heathland includes the common early summer flowering bell heather (1), the rare western gorse (2) and the pale beautiful Cornish heath (3), a heathland plant found almost solely on The Lizard. The shallow soil has led to a maritime turf which supports a wide variety of plants. Among the rocky outcrops you can find thrift (4), kidney vetch (5), and a low-growing form of ox-eye daisy (6). Scattered throughout are many much rarer plants such as the green-winged orchid (7) and the autumn and spring squills (8).

The cliffs and offshore islands provide nesting sites for a variety of seabirds, peregrine falcons (9) and ravens. Inland the heathland supports

many birds, with skylarks and stonechats (10) especially common. The conservation of this special landscape relies on sensitive management. Firebreaks protect the Reserve from accidental fires, whilst carefully sited fencing helps confine livestock. When traditional grazing fell into decline during the 1950s, coarse grasses and scrub rapidly spread, shading out many smaller rare plants. Since the early 1980s grazing has been re-introduced to much of the Reserve using Shetland ponies and Soay sheep. Winter scrub clearance and controlled heath buring have also contribute to the restoration of the site, with long-dormant seeds flowering and carpeting the clifftops once more.

www.naturalengland.org.uk

Dave Matthews

considered to be of conservation significance either locally or nationally.

County Wildlife Sites were identified and selected during the 1980s and 1990s using a combination of aerial photograph data, past and local knowledge and, where possible, ground based surveys. They were selected because of their high nature conservation value. Selection was based on distinctive, important or threatened species and habitats, in either a national, regional or local context and aimed to link and buffer other important areas for nature conservation, such as SSSIs.

Anette Anderson

Unlike SSSIs or Special Areas of Conservation (SACs), County Wildlife Sites are non-statutory designations. This means they have no legal protection although there are some minor planning constraints.

HEDGES

Cornish hedges are a particular feature in their own right, combining natural heritage and historic environment. As the most common means of enclosing land for centuries they have become important habitats supporting a wealth of plant species and providing shelter for a wide range of fauna. It could even be argued that they are the defining feature of the inland Cornish landscape, varying in construction and appearance according to the geology and history of the area.

The Cornish hedge is a unique form of hedging peculiar to Cornwall (and some parts of Devon). Similar hedges are found in Wales and Ireland but differ slightly in design. A Cornish hedge is built with layer upon layer of stone, often in a herringbone pattern. It is then packed very tightly with soil. The top is a dome of compressed soil with a turf border often with hawthorn or black-thorn planted to improve stock control. The Guild of

Cornish Hedgers helps keep the ancient craft of hedging alive and provides practical advice and historical information. Fifteen or twenty years ago many hedges were grubbed up (though nothing like as many as in other parts of the UK). It is notable that both Cornwall Council and many private landscape architects and gardeners specify and build Cornish hedges when boundaries are required. This seems to be one unique feature of the Cornish landscape that is back in rude health.

CORNWALL'S TREES

Trees? Cornwall is always thought of, and described as, a 'treeless' county. True, we don't have the dense woodlands of the Kentish Weald or the remains of the great forests of the Midlands. But there are far more trees in our Cornish landscape than you might think – from the stunted, seemingly bent (but actually 'wind-pruned') hawthorns near the coast to the wild, ancient oaks along the river valleys and the strange exotic great trees in our parks and gardens.

According to Nigel Sumpter, landscape architect and AONB Officer, 'native' trees are those that were here after we separated from Ireland but before the land bridge to Europe was submerged and Britain became an island, sometime after 5500 BC. He told me:

Careful analysis of ancient tree pollen preserved in successive layers in the wet Cornish marshes proves that our native woodlands, following the last ice age, were composed almost entirely of sessile oak and hazel which were found on dry land and throughout the upland forested areas and alder, which was found in damp valley bottoms. These then are the true native woodland trees of Cornwall. To this we can add the Cornish elms which genetically can be traced to Brittany and were mostly brought over in the Bronze Age for shelter belts around fields; they are very resistant to salt winds and spread by suckering not by seed. The shorter and much narrower Cornish elm is distinct from the English elm which is only found east of the Tamar and today mostly only in Sussex. The widespread sycamore is a relatively late

arrival having been brought over from Europe (probably northern France) in the 1600s. Its wind-dispersed seeds freely colonise all the places from which we have removed our native trees. However it is possible sycamore could become the replacement for elm in our hedgerows as it spreads vigorously and is also resistant to salt winds.

The Cornish, like most Celts, have a special affinity for trees. This may go back to the days of the Druids, or further; oaks and oak groves in particular formed part of religious activities and philosophy for centuries and traces remain. Even today, throughout Britain, people still touch wood to ward off misfortune – a relic of the days where guardian spirits were supposed to live in trees. Touching the tree was both a mark of respect and a request for a wish to be granted.

The Cornish place name *Kelli* or grove, is still to be found throughout the county, even though most of the tree-cover has now disappeared. Other place names, such

Dave Matthews

as *coos* (wood) as in Barncoose, and other tree names like *elaw* (elm) as in Treloan, can show where important trees were to be found.

Trees became sacred as their useful properties – wood for building and fire, fruit and nuts for food – began to be venerated. This is not so uncommon – I recently went to a Diwali Festival in Cornwall (proof of the county's increasingly cosmopolitan culture) where 'cow-honouring' took place. It was rather interesting and it got me thinking; the cow, once prized for its milk, then meat, then hide, is now sacred and often untouchable. Perhaps the same happened with trees – that they were first prized for their utility and then gradually (because they were so useful) venerated as holy. During the next 2,000 years this veneration died out and exploitation became the norm. If we are to save our forests, not just in the UK but worldwide, then a balance, between loving trees for their usefulness and appreciating their beauty, needs to be struck – and soon.

In the same way that trees were venerated, so was water nearby. This may go back to an introduction to the Ancient Greek spirits of Naiads and Dryads. Trees that grew near springs were gradually given magical or mystical properties as was the water source. The trees around 'Holy' wells were often decorated with offerings, a tradition that goes way back in time but is still to be seen today (I recently found evidence of this at Madron in the west) even where Christian saints have taken over the guardianship of healing wells.

Our great Cornish trees have been well-documented recently. Loveday Jenkin, Project Officer with the Cornwall Ancient Tree Forum, told me: 'Over three years volunteers, experts and community groups have undertaken a Cornwall-wide survey of ancient, veteran and notable trees and attended training, community events and activities across the county.'

Few very large, ancient trees still exist today in Cornwall unlike in other more arboreal regions. The Trebursey Oak is a shadow of its former self and the Great Elm of Rosuic (originally with a circumference of twenty-six feet) succumbed to Dutch Elm Disease (although it is, apparently and encouragingly, putting out new shoots). The incredible Twisted Beech at Tehidy still

astonishes though, and the Darley Oak at Linkinhorne, close to Bodmin Moor, still flourishes and is thought to be over 1,000 years old; it loses a branch from time to time and the tea-house inside is gone, but it is still a delight to its owners and tourists alike and its acorns are locally thought to have charms that will ensure a successful pregnancy. From the early 1800s until the 1980s, tea parties were actually held inside the trunk; eventually the collapsing canopy made continuation too dangerous.

Perhaps the least tree-inhabited part of Cornwall is the Lizard Peninsula. Yet several significant trees are situated there including the Cury Great Tree, a large ash that was on the site of a factional fight between the men of neighbouring parishes, quarrelling over their share of smuggling booty. Another is the Mulberry Tree at Bochym Manor, mentioned in the Domesday Book.

Most large trees that we see today date from the eighteenth and nineteenth centuries and were planted by newly rich landowners (nearly all had made their fortune from mining) keen to landscape their gardens and the surrounding park land. And more recent plantations of conifers are significant features of the moorlands and elsewhere.

Many of the 'garden trees' are exotic species that have reached exceptional size in the mild, Cornish climate. Those in the great gardens, such as Trebah and Trelissick, are good examples.

The coast path

There are a number of ways to appreciate the beauty of Cornwall. Even if you flash down the A30 (though not on a summer Saturday) you'll catch glimpses of tors and beacons, ancient fields and woods, even tantalizing hints of cliffs, beaches and open sea. You could see the landscape by bike, taking in leisurely views over estuaries or ruined mining country (and, of course, gazing at the view of your own front wheel as you slog up one of our endless hills!). But the nicest way to see and come to love Cornwall is on foot. There are footpaths almost everywhere, and where there are not there are quiet country lanes. Ewart Jones wrote: 'Cornwall is a paradise for the walker if he will only enter into it, the holiday crowds, rushing from cove to cove in their motors, will not touch the basic lovely loneliness of the countryside.' You may infer from the language that this was written a while ago – in fact, it was in 1948. However, Jones also wrote: 'Here in Cornwall footpaths and rights of way are disappearing; many are already overgrown or barred.' It is to the credit of various councils, voluntary groups such as the Ramblers and changing attitudes among rural folk that this trend has been reversed. There are now an enormous number of footpaths – most well-signed and in good repair. And there is one crowning glory to our marvellous walking network.

The Cornish coast path is part of the much larger South West Coast Path that runs 650 miles from Poole in Dorset to Minehead in north Devon. The Cornish stretch covers 260+ miles, near enough ten marathons if you are thinking of doing the whole thing in one go. Walking the path, whether on a short stroll from a gateway town or a day-long hike, is the best way to see the stunning Cornish coast. But do be warned, this really

isn't a stroll in the park; even seasoned locals can get a bit fed up with the endless ups and downs. One of my very first Cornish walks was from Porthcurno to Lamorna (see Chapter 8). We checked the map carefully (including the contours), calculated the distance at around six miles and estimated a two-hour walk. Four hours later we were still going!

It is difficult to calculate the precise amount of revenue the Coast Path generates for Cornwall each year, but estimates range from £100 million upwards. This seems like a huge amount, but how much less appealing would it be if we could only look at the coast from towns, lay-bys and beaches. Just over ten years ago, this scenario was played out for real during the dark days of the foot-and-mouth crisis when the countryside was closed to many visitors, especially walkers. Although farming suffered badly, the greatest financial impact in the south-west was in the tourism sector, as visitors were forced to go elsewhere.

Each year around £300,000 is spent on routine maintenance of the Coast Path in Cornwall; some comes from donations and earned income but the majority of it is provided by Natural England. The money pays for the path to be kept clear of overgrowing vegetation, for sections to be made safe, less muddy or even re-routed and for signs, stiles and gates to be repaired.

Appreciating the landscape from the Coast Path is no longer simply the preserve of the fit and able-bodied. Countryside Mobility is a relatively new project that

▲ Tramper above Loe Bar

aims to make access to the countryside easier for people with limited mobility, whether alone or with friends, and so make for a truly accessible visitor destination. Based on the principle of urban Shopmobility schemes, 'Tramper' all-terrain mobility scooters and wheelchair accessible 'Wheelyboats' are now available at a number of countryside and lakeside locations in Cornwall.

The Natural England budget is already being cut significantly and will be much reduced over the next few years. This is likely to impact on the amount they are able to spend on the Coast Path. More will need to be raised from other sources to keep this much-loved and vital visitor resource open and functioning.

Architecture and Art

Ah, buildings. Nine thousand years of history have meant they are omnipresent, ruined, preserved, old, new, beautiful, ugly and every stage in between. Ancient hut circles, mediaeval churches, great houses, small farms, Victorian public buildings, modern bungalows – not many counties have such a rich diversity of buildings and architecture.

There are around 12,500 listed buildings in Cornwall with the greatest concentration in the north-eastern part. This may be because that part of Cornwall has been relatively free from 'development' with the A30 and the railway passing a long way south. Listing means a building or structure is of national historical or architectural interest. The 'list' is administered by English Heritage and includes all buildings built before 1700 that have survived in anything like their original condition, most buildings from 1700 to 1840 if they are relatively untouched and buildings up to 1914 of high quality and historic interest. Few twentieth-century buildings are included and none from the twenty-first. Buildings are listed to give them protection from unsympathetic alteration and demolition and the main criteria is that they are of 'special interest' in a *national* context.

There are also 145 Conservation Areas in Cornwall, mostly in towns, covering 407 square kilometres of land.

The built environment is an integral part of our landscape and it is almost everywhere you look. But almost nothing upsets people (including me) more than an inappropriate or badly sited building sticking out of the countryside or sitting on the cliffs like the proverbial sore thumb. Planning, development and construction are controversial topics in Cornwall, as in many a beautiful part of the UK, with debate rampaging across the spectrum from the 'just say no' brigade at one end to the 'growth at any cost' crowd at the other.

It would be wrong to assume that all development is bad in the eyes of the AONB. If it is truly sustainable, rights past wrongs or adds real value it should be, and will be, applauded.

The Cornish Buildings Group was founded in 1969. This not-for-profit organization aims 'to stimulate interest, appreciation and knowledge of good building in Cornwall, and to encourage the erection, protection, repair and recording of such buildings.' There are many fine buildings in Cornwall and much recent careful, appropriate building. There are also some right eyesores – out-of-town shopping centres, 'anytown' suburban estates, military establishments, 1970s industrial areas and get-rich-quick holiday developments. Fortunately most of the rubbish isn't in or near the AONB but there's still too much of it.

One of the big concerns of those who administer, and live in, Cornwall is the preponderance of second or 'holiday' homes. Many current and former fishing villages such as Port Isaac and Gorran Haven are now facing a situation where more houses are owned by people from up-country who only live in them for part of the year than by locals (born and bred or immigrants). In 2008 the number of second homes registered in Cornwall rose by 3% to 13,600. Cornwall's housing stock has more than doubled in the last forty years, making it one of the fastest growing places in the UK. But over that time, the housing problems of local people have got markedly worse. Therefore, simply building more unaffordable homes, especially second homes, is not the answer. Balancing the need for local people to have somewhere to live, and the equally pressing need to preserve the environment and landscape that makes people want to live here, is a far from easy conundrum to solve. I shall revisit this thorny issue in the conclusion (Chapter 15).

Dave Matthews

Peter Maxted

▲ A Hepworth bronze sculpture

For now, suffice to say that there is an easy test as to see whether 'development' should be permitted both within and outside the AONB (for, surely, the same level of quality is desirable everywhere?). My question to a developer would always be this: 'How does the proposed development *enhance* our landscape?' Cue, usually, much muttering and shuffling of feet.

Cultural Associations

History and the landscape intertwine to create a very strong sense of place in our county. Artists and writers have been visiting Cornwall for over a century but the earliest indigenous one was probably John Opie, born in 1761. Today there are many artists and craftsmen who were born here but Cornwall was a magnet for artists and writers from the late nineteenth century onwards, many of whom settled here and called it home – maybe even becoming accepted by the natives (hope for me yet!).

The roll call of famous writers who have lived and worked in Cornwall is extensive. Just in the last hundred years we have been blessed with the talents of Hardy, Lawrence, du Maurier, Golding and Le Carré. Artists, both native and incomers, also offer up a roll call of some significance in recent times. We have been home to Sickert and Whistler, Nicholson, Leach, Hepworth, Frost, Lanyon and Heron – and there are many others. Today the Art College at Falmouth, recently merged with Dartington, produces a huge wealth of talent every year, much of which stays in the county.

Peter Maxted

▲ Filming on the iconic coast

Musically, there are choirs and brass bands, classical virtuosos and talented composers everywhere you look. And in every town, and even some small villages, you'll find live music any night of the week. I bet there are more 'music pubs' in Cornwall than there are in London with fifteen times the population.

Equally, the relative isolation of Cornwall – in terms of distance from London and other major cities – means that specific expressions of local culture such as food, festivals, the Cornish language and local sports survive and reinforce the identity of Cornwall as a special place, distinct from anywhere else. We might, with some justification, be accused of over-egging it recently, but it is still true.

The landscape has a pervading influence on paintings, sculpture, poetry, music, literature, film, photography and many crafts. This has led to a parallel cultural landscape now recognized far and wide – and even occasionally appreciated locally for its economic benefits.

SPORT

Look out from any beach these days and you'll see distant black dots. As they come closer some will be rising from the white foam in a graceful, swaying, snaking dance. Or as comedian Jeremy Hardy put it on a visit last year: 'In Cornwall there's so little to do, people

Dave Matthews

▲ Surfers on the north coast

45

have to stand up on the sea.' All year round the surfers ride the waves. In the sailing waters around the Fal and Fowey, racing yachts large and small decorate the ocean with the AONB as a backdrop. All round the coast the pilot gigs race throughout the summer.

Gig racing is one of the fastest growing sports anywhere but it has an ancient history. Strictly speaking they are 'pilot' gigs; traditionally, as a boat approached a harbour such as Falmouth or St Ives, a number of gigs would race out to meet it. Each carried a local pilot who knew the waters well and the first there would get the job. This was particularly important on the Scillies with its maze of rocks and reefs so it is appropriate that the gig 'World Championship' is held there in May each year. Gigs were used as early lifeboats, to obtain goods from wrecks and almost certainly for smuggling. The design has changed little.

Diving is very popular too and the wrecks around the coast make it the best place for scuba diving in the British Isles (at least so diving friends tell me – you'll not find me in that water, let alone under it. On top in a sailboat or, better still, a kayak, yes; in it, no.)

Inland, Cornwall is lucky that it still retains many of its sports fields, council owned in some cases, which in other parts of the country have been sold off for development. Rugby is popular, as is football, of course, and cricket in the summer. There are more than a few racing

cyclists on the hilly roads and leisure-riders on the trails. Mountain biking in the Tamar Valley is booming. Participation in youth sport is healthy and I'd warrant that the children of Cornwall are healthier, as a whole, than anywhere else in the UK.

One ancient sport that has seen a comeback in recent years is Cornish wrestling. The equally ancient sport of hurling (very different to the Irish version) is also kept alive at summer festivals. Although some commentators have described it as an early form of football, it actually sounds remarkably like rugby. Here's what Richard Carew had to say about hurling in the late sixteenth century: 'the hurler must deal no foreball, or throw it to any partner standing nearer the goal than himself. In dealing the ball, if any of the adverse party can catch it flying ... the property of it is thereby transferred to the catching party; and so assailants become defendants, and defendant assailants.'

The parishes around Newquay (it is believed by some to have first been played in St Columb) and Penzance were particular hotspots historically for the game, which was often violent and sometimes ended in deaths.

The game survives in two communities. In St Ives, a children's game is held in February and in St Columb Major a full hurling game is held on Shrove Tuesday. The St Columb game is far more similar to the original played widely across Cornwall and is played between two sides: town and country. Hurling balls are in several local museums including Penlee House in Penzance where they used to form part of the civic regalia of the town.

FOOD AND DRINK

Since we are on the subject of all that is beautiful, and there is little more beautiful to a Cornishman or woman than a proper homemade pasty, a brief word on food and drink.

Europe has recognized the particular significance of Cornish cream and pasties, and saffron cake is still popular, but in recent years Cornwall has developed a significant reputation for a much wider variety of good food and drink. The quality of local produce is remarked on by many tourists and means that local diets are

Dave Matthews

arguably better than in most of the UK.

Fresh fish is still landed in quantity at Newlyn and Padstow and good shellfish abounds, particularly the world-famous Helford oyster. Artisan cheese, such as Cornish Blue or the nettle-wrapped Yarg, and local bread have both been national award-winners recently. Meat from animals that graze outdoors on pasture or heath and moor, and local fruit and vegetables that benefit from the longest daylight hours and mildest climate in the UK also contribute to a minor but significant cottage industry. Farmers' markets abound, pretty well every town has one at least once a week

It is arguably this quality of fresh produce that is attracting some of the best chefs to the county and has meant that new restaurants open weekly – even during the recent recession.

Small and micro-breweries abound. A new one seems to open almost every week, and the larger long-established ones such as St Austell have had to up their game. Wines, particularly those from the Camel Valley, are now of a quality that is achieving international recognition.

Something that is gaining popularity at the moment, especially with transition groups (these are sustainable, local organizations acting where coherent government environmental policy should apply but often doesn't) is the planting of fruit trees and community orchards (there's even one at County Hall). Many of the Cornish apple varieties being planted are particularly suited to our warm, damp climate.

THE PEOPLE AND LANGUAGE

Cornwall has a distinct sense of its own identity. In 1994, the Local Government Commission reported on Cornwall:

> Cornwall's Celtic roots create a strong sense of identity within the county. The 13th century Mappa Mundi shows the four parts of the island of Britain as England, Scotland, Wales and CORN-WALL. Some suggest that Cornwall has never legally been incorporated into shire England. Cornwall is rich with artistic, literary and religious expressions of its history, it has its own flag, and

patron saint and has the highest number of recorded ancient monuments in Britain.

Unlike Yorkshire, another proud independent county, where you are a Yorkshireman or woman if you were born in the county, to be 'proper' Cornish you need to be able to trace your family back at least eight generations. I certainly can't claim the privilege and nor will my great grandchildren. But most of the indigenous Cornish are enormously welcoming to 'forriners' that settle and make their home here. There are still a few curmudgeons who write bitter diatribes to the local papers about incomers (as if Cornwall hadn't seen waves of these for around 8,000 years!). There is a significant nationalist movement and Mebyon Kernow is still a force (mostly for good) in the land. However, for the most part, the Cornish today are not unlike those of the Bronze Age who traded with people from all over the known world and made visitors welcome.

Many Cornish surnames begin with a prefix that mirrors that of the towns and villages: 'By Tre, Pol, Car, Lan and Pen, Shall you ever know Cornishmen.'

The Cornish language is closely related to Breton and Welsh. It was the main language to the west of a line between Padstow and Fowey (roughly the Saints' Way) until the time of Queen Mary. In 1547 Andrew Borde published the first multi-language phrasebook with 'useful' questions and answers. One of the languages included is Cornish.

The main reason for the decline of the language was because it was very much a rural, peasant tongue. This meant few, if any books – very little Cornish was written down. In the west of Cornwall, Cornish was widely spoken in 1620 but was confined to the very far west. Carew wrote in 1602: 'The English speech doth still encroach upon it [Cornish] and hath driven the same to the uttermost skirts of the shire'. It had ceased to be a community language by 1800 and the last semi-speakers died around 1890. Dolly Pentreath of Mousehole is supposed to have been the last purely native speaker although there were probably several others. Cornish is undergoing a vigorous revival today with quite a number of people being able to converse fluently. Most town signs have a Cornish translation as do some of the more important designations. Our Cornwall Area of Outstanding Natural Beauty is *Ranndir a Dekter Naturek a vry Kernow.*

Much the best place to find the Cornish language spoken is at the Cornish Gorsedd (Gorsedh Kernow), an annual celebration similar to the Welsh Eisteddfod. And it is very much in the same bardic tradition. This is how the organization describes itself:

> The Gorsedd of Cornwall, or to give its Cornish language title, Gorsedh Kernow, is an organisation dedicated to the preservation of Cornwall's unique Celtic spirit, through literature, language, music and the arts, and the recognition of all forms of important service to Cornwall and its people. It is neither political nor religious, although some of its members are active in Cornish politics and church services in Cornish are held on special occasions throughout the year. It is allied to the Gorsedds of Wales and Brittany and has strong links with both these Celtic countries. It cannot be stressed too strongly that it has no connection whatsoever with Druidism nor with any pagan practice.

> In ancient Celtic times, Bards – story-tellers, poets and singers had great importance as keepers of the heritage. They had places of high honour at important assemblies regularly held at venerated sites throughout Britain, one of which was the stone circle at Boscawen-un, in the parish of St Buryan on the high moors of West Cornwall.

This tradition, following that of Wales, was revived in Cornwall in 1928 at a Gorsedd, or meeting of Bards, at Boscawen-un, when Cornwall's first Grand Bard, Henry Jenner and 12 Bards were initiated by the Arch-druid of Wales, Jenner taking the Bardic name Gwas Myghal, Servant of Michael. (The Welsh title 'Arch-druid' also has no connection with Druidism and is merely a title for the Senior Bard).

Since then a Gorsedd has been held every year on the first Saturday in September, except for the war years 1939–45. Over 1,000 men and women have been invited to become Bards and the current roll is 496, 56 of whom live abroad, particularly in Australia where Cornish traditions are very strong.

Myth and legend

Traditional folklore in Cornwall is made up of tales of giants, mermaids, piskies (please note, *not* pixies) or the *pobel vean* (little people). Spriggins lived in the stones, Knockers in the mines. The cultural landscape is strewn with myths and legends and these in turn influence many a festival and event.

Cornwall is intimately associated with one of the great figures of British legend – King Arthur. I studied Arthurian literature and legend at university, so it was a delight when I arrived in Cornwall to find even more references to him than I had known existed. From Tintagel and Slaughter Bridge in the north, past Dozmary Pool on the Moor to Castle Dore and the Tristan Stone in the south and even out to the Isles of Scilly, the land is awash in Arthurian stories. The Welsh claim Arthur too, of course, and the people of Somerset seem to think he was theirs with his Camelot at Cadbury near Yeovil and his supposed burial under Glastonbury Tor.

The earliest mention of Arthur as a Celtic leader is

Peter Maxted

found in the *Historia Britonum,* written around the end of the seventh century and edited in the ninth. This places him as a late fifth- or early sixth-century warrior who defeated the Saxons on a number of occasions but it is unclear whether he was Cornish or Welsh. This is probably the factual basis upon which the legend was overlaid. The beginning of the embellishment was in the twelfth century when Geoffrey of Monmouth placed Arthur's birth at Tintagel and his death by the River Camel. Geoffrey interwove his narrative with stories from Northern France – hence the introduction of Lancelot and the tale of Holy Grail.

Three centuries later Thomas Malory wrote his *Morte D'Arthur* while in prison, bringing together most of the scattered tales into one book. This saw the beginning of the round table legend with Arthur's knights now firmly mediaeval. Four centuries further on Tennyson romanticized Arthur still further in his *Idylls of a King,* intertwining him and his knights with his Victorian idea of chivalry. By this time little remains of the Romano-British leader from the far dark ages – except for here in Cornwall where he still whispers to us among the ancient stones.

There are many other Cornish myths and legends, of course; giants in particular seem to have inhabited most of our AONB areas. There are tales of mermaids from far Penwith, of sea monsters in Falmouth Bay, of piskies almost everywhere, of spriggins and of knockers, of ghosts and demons too. Some of these myths will unfold as we travel through the different parts of Cornwall.

For now that we have a flavour of the landscape and have touched on its geology, history, industry, architecture, flora and fauna, rich culture and its myths and legends, let us look at each of the twelve sections that make up the Cornwall AONB and the western side of the Tamar Valley, in more detail.

You will find many references to other writers who have traversed the county before me but two deserve a special mention in terms of my 'standing on the shoulders of giants': Between 1534 and 1542 the king's librarian, Robert Leland, toured the whole country and left a mass of writings including detailed information on Cornwall, which he visited in 1538. Some seventy years later, in the last years of Elizabeth I's reign, Richard Carew completed his *Survey of Cornwall* - a vivid description of the land and its people 400 years ago.

Dave Matthews

Hartland

North of Bude there is, it seems to me, a strange feel to the land. There are still high cliffs of black rock lowering over wave-cut platforms below. Walking the coast on a winter's day, the wild Atlantic is no more or less white-capped and ferocious than it is at Boscastle, Hell's Mouth or Land's End further south and west. There is still farmland, grassy expanses of springy turf grazed close by sheep and hardy cattle. Inland there are woods and tiny hamlets, served by twisting country lanes. So what is unusual? What makes it feel so *un-Cornish*? Perhaps it is the thatched cottages one comes to suddenly round the bend of a narrow lane. Maybe it is the valleys, narrow, stream-filled and deeply incised – coombes perhaps, ending in sharply tumbling waterfalls that feed the ocean. It feels a long way from anywhere. It feels like (whisper it) *Devon*.

This is the 'Hartland' section of the Cornwall AONB – even the name refers to a headland in Devon rather than Cornwall (as was, pointedly, remarked on by several locals at the Royal Cornwall Show last year). It is one of the smallest stretches and covers an area from just above Bude to the Cornwall/Devon border. Here the small river known as Marsland Water meanders through a wooded coombe before reaching the sea at Marsland Mouth. And this is where it joins the North Devon AONB in a seamless transition. Beauty is indivisible.

Yet it is less than a mile as the chough flies from the source of Marsland Water to the source of the river Tamar. It would not take much effort to join the two (and don't think Mebyon Kernow haven't thought of it) which would effectively make Cornwall an island!

The area is haunted by the memories and stories of two extraordinary men who lived two centuries apart. In the early 1600s Sir Bevil (sometimes called Beville or Bevelle) Grenville, immortalized by Daphne du Maurier as the king's general in her novel of the same name ruled the land around from his manor in Stowe. He was born in 1596 further west near Bodmin, and was a grandson of Sir Richard Grenville, captain of the *Revenge* and contemporary of Francis Drake. Educated at Oxford, he became MP for Launceston and commanded troops against the Scots in the 1630s. The Grenvilles, who probably came over with the Conqueror and certainly date back to William Rufus, also include a fourteenth-century Archbishop of York and a captain who went down with the ill-fated *Mary Rose*. They were landowners and lived, for nearly five centuries, both at nearby Kilkhampton and at the Manor of Stowe in the wooded Coombe Valley. The valley is probably not much changed from Sir Bevil's day but the manor is sadly long gone. However, the National Trust-owned farm, Stowe Barton, was built from materials left over from the demolition of Stowe Manor and some of the interior panelling and furniture has been preserved in Prideaux Place near Padstow (see Chapter 5).

At the outbreak of the Civil War in 1642 Bevil declared for King Charles and raised a Cornish army to fight for him. He was much loved by his men; well before the war he had been described as the 'most influential and best-beloved man in all of Cornwall'. When the Parliamentarian forces crossed the Tamar Sir Bevil fought at Braddock Down near Lostwithiel, in which he led an uphill charge that won the day for the Royalists, and in May 1643 he defeated superior forces at the Battle of Stratton, just south of Bude. He launched a dawn attack on the Earl of Stamford's forces that were encamped in an Iron Age earthwork, killed over 300 and took 1,700 prisoners. He then led his men on a victorious march through Devon into Somerset. 'The Cornish exploded out of their county and swept all before them.'

In July 1643, when fortune seemed to be favouring the King's side, the Royalists won the battle of Lansdown Hill outside Bath. Grenville's Cornish infantry stood firm even when the Royalist cavalry was routed early on (Prince Rupert must have been elsewhere) then Grenville led a counterattack against the Parliamentary position at the top of the hill. The Cornishmen succeeded in gaining the hilltop but Grenville was wounded and later died. His Cornish soldiers refused to fight under any other officer and returned home, carrying his body. He was carried from the field by his servant Antony Payne – an interesting character in his own right.

Payne was one of the few, and some have deemed him 'the last', of the Cornish giants. At the age of twenty-one he measured seven-foot two and weighed well over twenty stone. His farmer father offered him as a servant to Bevil who was his landlord and, we may suppose, would have been happy to have a servant with the strength of nearly three men. Antony was reputedly as witty and intelligent as he was strong, with very quick reflexes.

When war began between the King and Parliament, Payne became Sir Bevil's bodyguard. At the Battle of Stratton he is said to have killed ten of the enemy by himself. Once he had returned to Cornwall he took no further part in the war but, after the Restoration, King Charles II appointed Sir Bevil's son, John, as governor of the garrison at Plymouth and Payne became his halberdier. The King took a liking to the friendly Cornish giant, received him at court and commissioned Sir Godfrey Kneller to paint his portrait. This painting, titled the *Loyal Giant,* can be seen today in the Royal Cornwall Museum in Truro. There is also one of Payne at the ancient Tree Inn at Stratton.

It is worth noting that, as with many legendary and quasi-legendary figures, Antony Payne's story may have been somewhat embellished. In *Cornwall's People*, Paul White writes:

He is a vital part of the tourist publicity of Stratton, virtually no real evidence about him survives except a portrait in the Royal Cornwall Museum…also the

burial record, probably of him, in 1691. Almost everything else you may read about him is based on the fabrications of RS Hawker who effectively created Payne as a symbol of Cornish conservative and royalist patriotism.

Ah well, another romance exploded – thanks, Parson Hawker.

Bevil Grenville was buried at Kilkhampton Church and a monument to him was erected on the field of Lansdown to commemorate him and his Cornish pike-men.

Sir John Grenville, son of the heroic Sir Bevil, succeeded to the Kilkhampton estates; at a very early age he had a command in his father's regiment, without Cornish troops, one supposes, and was left for dead in the field after the Battle of Tewksbury. He was appointed Governor of the Scilly Islands when they declared for the King rather than Parliament, and was one of the chief instruments in effecting the restoration of King Charles II. For this, he was given the title Earl of Bath. John completely refurbished the mediaeval manor at Stowe; it was described by a contemporary as 'by far the noblest house in the west of England'.

The sons and grandsons of the ferocious Cornish soldiers who fought with Sir Bevil would, no doubt, have been among the 'twenty thousand Cornishmen' who marched to London a generation later to demand the release of Bishop Trelawney from the clutches of James II. They were immortalized in 'The Song of the Western Men', better known as 'Trelawney', the Cornish national anthem. This stirring song was penned in the early nineteenth century by a local priest; and so we come rather neatly to the second of the two great men to bestride this area.

Close to the coast lies the village, actually not much more than a hamlet, of Morwenstow. Here one of Cornwall's most famous eccentrics lived as its priest from 1835-75. He was married twice; the first time when he was still a 20-year-old student at Pembroke College, Oxford, to Charlotte, a 41-year-old woman, the daughter of a local landowner. Against all predictions, given the twenty-one-year age gap, they were wonderfully happy

Dave Matthews

together until Charlotte died in her eighties, when he promptly married again – to Pauline, a woman of twenty-one. His name was Robert Stephen Hawker.

Besides being a priest Hawker was a poet, and a very prolific one. He built himself a hut on the cliff, using wood from the hull of a wrecked ship, and would spend hours there overlooking the sea, which he loved, in all its moods. In the hut, Hawker according to the local church guide, used to 'meditate and compose verse'. The guide is, of course, being coy. Parson Hawker was, like his contemporary Samuel Taylor Coleridge, a well-known opium smoker. Apparently, he also entertained guests in his hut, including Alfred Tennyson and Charles Kingsley – though the hut is so small it would have to have been one guest at a time.

Hawker dressed outrageously and spent his first wife's money – for Charlotte was rich – with great abandon, building a handsome vicarage but also giving very

generously to the poor of his parish, of which there were many. Their income would be supplemented by cargo from the many wrecks that took place on that ferocious coastline. Though there is no hard evidence for the reports that ships were deliberately lured onto rocks for this (that story comes from the fertile brain of a certain Mrs du Maurier) there may be some truth in the stories that seamen, washed ashore and barely alive, were sometimes dispatched by the locals as, if they recovered, the cargo would belong to them by law and not to the scavengers. One of Hawker's most admirable traits was that he set about altering this, teaching and preaching the sanctity of life, and making sure that any drowned sailor was given a Christian burial in his churchyard.

Hawker was about sixty when he presented the parish with his second bride. Pauline Kuczynski was of Polish descent: her family had moved to London but lost all

Peter Maxted

▲ Hawker's Hut

their money there and Pauline was governess to a Yorkshire family. They had a holiday home (surely one of the earliest of these ubiquitous and mostly unpopular dwellings) in Morwenstow and it was there that Hawker met her. There were objections to the match on account of her youth but Hawker travelled to London by train and must have persuaded her parents to agree. Incidentally he thought little of London, finding it 'dirty and crowded and very expensive' – so nothing new there. His new wife was a great success in the parish and he wrote many love poems to her. Though Hawker was noticed and visited by his contemporaries, including Tennyson, he never succeeded in becoming well known for his poetry. On his deathbed, after all those years as an Anglican priest, albeit a 'high one', he converted to Roman Catholicism.

Morwenstow is a part of England once known as 'furthest from the railways' and no doubt this remote-

ness was what attracted Parson Hawker to live there. Certainly he, and possibly Grenville, would recognize much of the area today; this, of course, is one of the great benefits of the Cornwall AONB – that future generations will be able to see and appreciate the beauty of the landscape unchanged in many ways. Hawker would have known the tiny villages of Stibb, Shop and Woodford and the marvellously evocative Bush Inn at Morwenstow, dating from the thirteenth century and serving excellent beer and good, if slightly expensive, pub food.

Hawker would also have recognized the A39, if not the tarmac, running up into Devon and on to Bideford and Minehead, still following much the same route. He would, no doubt, have often visited the market in the nearby ancient wool town of Kilkhampton on the boundary of the AONB and one of its two gateway towns.

Kilkhampton

Kilkhampton, known locally as Kilk, is an old ridgeway from Bude to Bideford (mostly now the route of the A39) that dates back to Roman times, and like all North Cornwall and Devon has a colourful history that goes back so far that much has been lost to the mists of time. The parish of Kilkhampton includes much of the Hartland AONB section and stretches from the edge of the Tamar lakes to the beaches of Sandy Mouth and Duckpool. It sits on a plateau about 580 feet above sea level and there is evidence that the area has been occupied since the Bronze Age. It was certainly a Saxon town and is mentioned in the Domesday Book as having three leagues (nine miles) of woodland of which the surviving remnants can be seen as Stowe woods and a few other copses. Remains of the Norman castle can be seen west of the town.

Kilkhampton church was probably rebuilt in the late fifteenth century, but still retains the magnificent south doorway that was built about 1130.

From the Middle Ages onwards the town was supported by local agriculture, especially the wool trade. Today, as with so many small Cornish towns, tourism is the most important industry.

Cleave Camp

One aspect of the scenery Hawker would definitely not have recognized is the GCHQ station on the cliffs, which was formerly the military base known as Cleave Camp. The white satellite dishes can be seen for miles, certainly from Tintagel in the south and come as something of a surprise to the coast path walker, though they are nothing like as well-known as those on Goonhilly Downs on the Lizard (see Chapter 8). Whilst no doubt something of a blot on the landscape we can be grateful the camp area is not much larger. In 1953 the Ministry of Defence wanted to expand it enormously and add an artillery range. The fledgling National Parks Committee and, perhaps surprisingly, Cornwall County Council, opposed the plans and argued that any development could be accommodated within the existing camp.

For a flavour of how the war affected even this remote rural area, let us consider the words of Ray Shaddick of Kilkhampton (adapted and reprinted with permission from the BBC's People's War).:

I will always remember the day war was declared. I came out of Church Sunday School and saw the village men congregated outside the London Inn, Kilkhampton. I was told instructions were given to them, that on Monday they were to go down to the Thynne Estate to cut sticks to ward off the enemy should an invasion take place....Attendance at the Home Guard duties were strict, and if you missed one or two parades you were in trouble. One day the Home Guard was going to be inspected by a high ranking Officer and one farm labourer went hay harvesting instead of attending parade. For not attending he was dismissed from Home Guard but appointed Fire Warden of some 25 houses for which he was issued with a stirrup pump and a bucket of sand.

Late in the War years the American soldiers were stationed at Cleave Camp Morwenstow, and as children we would go to the head of the village and eagerly await the American Convoy when we were sure to receive chewing gum and candies, and dried rations. Another occasion to look forward to was at school when we received parcels which came from the Red Cross, and I would generally receive a bag of marbles.

There were isolated instances when a bomb was dropped in the area. One such occasion was when one was dropped in the Tamar Lake and another time the local Postman waved to an aeroplane that passed overhead, only a few hours later to learn that the plane dropped a bomb at Cleave Camp.

Exercises involving the Home Guard A.R.P Special Constables and the W.R.V.S Red Cross were periodically held in the village. For us young people it was great excitement and we were eager to take part because when we got to the Medical Centre which was the Grenville Rooms (the village Hall) we were given tea and refreshments. I remember, on one such occasion, I had supposedly been shot in the leg;

I had to lay on the pavement outside the London Inn and wait for a stretcher to carry me to the Grenville Room. At times exercises took place between the local Home Guard and the American Soldiers, who showed no regard for People's Gardens or land. In my case they ran all over my father's garden and even tore down my dad's kidney bean row and trampled over his 'small tilling'. Was the air 'Blue' the next day as these exercises usually took place over night.

Rationing was as we know at a premium, and one of the slogans was, 'Make do and Mend'. As a family we did very well, we had a greengrocer in the small hamlet of Wolley who could supply his friends with almost anything you wanted, with relatives in Canada and America we had a constant supply of clothes, and food such as sultanas, currents etc. Our local Policeman would bring us back fresh eggs which he obtained from the American Cookhouse at Cleave Camp. These eggs were concealed in his Policemans Helmet, in case he met a Superior Officer.

We had two evacuees billeted with us and at night we would go up to the local playing field called the Lamb Park, when looking towards Plymouth we could see the sky lit up as Plymouth was being bombed.

Today, the activities of GCHQ Morwenstow, as Cleave Camp is known, usually remain classified. However, as some European member states have been concerned that Morwenstow is responsible for industrial espionage and

▲ Folded rock near Crackington Haven

Peter Maxted

the interception of civilian communications, a report by the European Parliament was made public in 2001 that provides some details about the station. Apparently GCHQ has the power, 'To monitor or interfere with electromagnetic, acoustic and other emissions and any equipment producing such emissions and to obtain and provide information derived from or related to such emissions or equipment.' This includes e-mail, text and audio messages.

As always, the debate between civil liberties and freedom from surveillance versus the need to combat crime and terrorism rages on. One thing is for certain – it is unlikely that the white satellite dishes will disappear from the landscape any time soon.

Geology

A high plateau of carboniferous sandstone and slate, known as the Culm Measures, meets the sea in this section of the AONB in sheer cliffs up to 475 feet high. The rocks were deposited around 300 million years ago in an east–west marine channel or strait, known to geologists as the Culm Basin. During the Carboniferous period, a type of anthracite known as 'culm', which had been exploited in the past further east in Devon, was laid down. This low-quality culm makes up the most extreme tip of the great coal fields of the North and Midlands. This culm has made the soil unusually acid for Cornwall and north Devon.

The geology of the area makes for many a dramatic sight on the coast, with features such as wave-cut platforms and great tiered nappes (rocks which have been driven over the underlying ones by a thrust fault). Sharply angled cliffs show where gigantic pressures have folded, sliced and compressed layers of sedimentary rock into sections like a vast pack of cards thrown upwards and then suddenly frozen.

Biodiversity

Beauty, as mentioned at the beginning of this book, has no boundaries and most of the Cornish landscape's appealing characteristics continue on northwards to Hartland Point and the North Devon AONB. The northern boundary of Cornwall is Marsland Water,

which runs inland from Marsland Mouth. Marsland Valley is a nature reserve situated in two large valleys which straddle the border. The steep-sided coombes that run inland from the sea have a mix of coastal heath, grassy meadows, bracken-covered slopes, woodland, streams and ponds. Both valleys, covering some 550 acres, make up the Marsland Nature Reserve, which is jointly managed by Cornwall and Devon Wildlife Trusts. As well as being an SSSI, the reserve is also an SAC. Thirty-four of our fifty-eight butterfly species have been recorded here, but the main interest is for pearlbordered and small pearlbordered fritillaries. There are also regular records of high brown fritillaries, grizzled skippers and purple hairstreaks.

Marsland Nature Reserve was donated by the late Christopher Cadbury (former President of the Royal Society for Nature Conservation, 1962-1986) to the Trusts.

Roe deer, badgers and foxes can all be seen here, as well as the extremely rare and endangered Scarce Blackneck Moth. Some of the trees have been coppiced to create clearings, and vegetation has been thinned to keep it low so that flowers and insects can flourish.

Walking the landscape

From Marsland Mouth the coast path south takes you through the nature reserve, along to Vicarage Cliff below which lies Morwenna's Well – a pretty-much inaccessible site (please don't take this as a challenge) where an early Welsh saint, St Morwenna, is supposed to have established a cell or hermitage. It seems that there was a holy well here so this may have been an earlier pagan site. Morwenna was the daughter of a Welsh prince, Brychan, who had many children. Another of his offspring was Nectan (see Chapter 3). The nearby church at Morwenstow is named after her. This was, of course, the one presided over by Parson Hawker who, incidentally, is credited with the re-introduction of the harvest festival at this church.

The church itself has Saxon origins and retains the Saxon font. Constructed in Norman times it was greatly enlarged in the fifteenth century. Just outside the lychgate lie the graves of three thieves who were hanged and could not be buried in the consecrated churchyard itself.

The route back from the church to the coast takes you over the cliff edge and down a steep, sometimes muddy and treacherous path to 'Hawker's Hut', which is timber-framed with a turf roof. It looks down the nearly sheer cliff and out to sea – on a clear day you can see Lundy Island. The coast continues in a similar style, high cliffs and deep valleys up and down to Duckpool, over Stowe Cliffs and all the way to Sandy Mouth. Several of the coombes end abruptly in small but steep waterfalls, tumbling to the beach below.

All down the coast the high hinterland consists of exposed, treeless farmland running right to the cliff edge. Hardy cattle and sheep graze there for most of the year. Further inland the pastures, many mediaeval in origin, are enclosed by grassy banks or stone Cornish hedges.

Dave Matthews

▲ Hardy cattle graze the coastal strip

From north to south, the AONB is cut by deep river valleys with woods of ash, willow, sycamore, ancient oak and beech as well as a few small conifer plantations. Footpaths run inland up several of them and it is possible to take a number of circular walks to appreciate the hinterland as well as the coast.

In these coombes and river valleys can also be found rare acidic wet pastures known as the 'Culm grasslands'. To look at, these have all the attributes of a traditional water meadow – a landscape feature that is fast disappearing from much of the UK.

The Hartland section of the Cornwall AONB is sparsely populated with isolated farmsteads and a few single track roads weaving up the valley sides. It is not driving country as many a tourist will no doubt testify; even if you do brave the seemingly endless country lanes you will almost certainly meet a farm tractor at some point. Much better to leave the car behind and strike out on foot or, if you're feeling fit enough (it is hilly) by bike.

There are very few villages and even these are tiny, barely more than hamlets. Mostly the buildings comprise isolated farms and cottages. They utilize local slates and sandstones or cob, formerly lime-washed or slate-hung and now more often rendered. In some of the hollows, ancient thatched cottages remain – another feature that is unusual in Cornwall today though not in its neighbour, Devon. There are only a couple of real eyesores in the whole of this part of the AONB – one static caravan park and the aforementioned 'radio station' as it is marked on the maps - though that is, of course, two too many.

From the 'Song of the Western Men' (aka 'Trelawney', the Cornish national anthem) by the Reverend Stephen Hawker:

A good sword and a trusty hand!
A faithful heart and true!
King James's men shall understand
What Cornish lads can do!
And have they fixed the where and when?
And shall Trelawney die?
Here's twenty thousand Cornish men
Will know the reason why!

Widemouth Bay to Pentire Point

Enormous cliffs, lashed by Atlantic gales, granite cottages clustered around ancient wharves, seaweed-clad rocky foreshores and quiet sandy coves – this section of the Cornwall AONB is a complete tapestry of our marvellous coastline. Yet, for me, the most special of many special places is to be found a mile inland. A gentle winter's walk through dripping trees – with nothing but the squelch of footsteps and the life-affirming smell of decaying leaves for company. There is the sound of water growing louder. Emerging from the dank semi-darkness of the woodland into a clearing surrounded by ancient trees, the sound becomes a roar. A cataract cascades through the stone ring it has made for itself into a wide pool. It is rare indeed to find a waterfall this magical in Britain. No wonder St Nectan built a hermitage here.

This part of the Cornwall AONB runs from just below Bude some thirty miles to Pentire Point overlooking the Camel Estuary. Now, just as two people seem to dominate the landscape to the north of Bude, so three different villages seem to somehow crystallize this coastal section – although with the caveat that there is much to see and feel in between them.

Eva Kocianova

▲ Widemouth Bay in winter

Debbie Ashton

Bude

The main gateway town is Bude on the north edge of the AONB. I feel that if Bude went to a counsellor it would be diagnosed as suffering from a lack of self-esteem. Many of the attributes it claims on websites and in guide books are actually those of the hinterland (great walking, famous for wreckers). Widemouth Bay, outside the town limits and with its own village community, is described as the town's surfing beach. Sometimes Bude claims or describes attractions that are some miles away such as Crackington Haven.

Such obfuscation is anyway unnecessary. It has its own beach, Summerleaze, which is also where the Neet River meets the sea and is the starting point for Bude Canal. This is now just a few miles long but it once ran as far as Launceston and lays claim to being Cornwall's only link with the famous navigational era of the eighteenth century.

The town hall is housed in a castle, albeit a nineteenth-century one. It was built by Sir Goldsworthy Gurney who was born along the coast in Padstow in 1793. He was a gifted scientist and a friend of Richard Trevithick (see Chapter 6). Among his innovations was the first steam carriage service, which went from London to Bath (at an average speed of fifteen miles per hour). This was eventually kiboshed by an alliance of horse-drawn carriage owners and the landed gentry who successfully lobbied for the journey to be priced at £2. This compared with the two shillings charged for a horse and coach journey.

Gurney turned his attention to chemistry and developed the Bude Light which used oxygen to increase the power of a standard oil lamp. The oxy-hydrogen blow-pipe, which produced a hot flame from a jet of oxygen and hydrogen, is still in use today. However, the term with which he is most associated is 'limelight'. He used the blowpipe on a piece of lime, increasing the light produced massively. His light system is most associated with theatres, of course, but was also used to illuminate the House of Commons and Trafalgar Square. Gurney has been called 'the forgotten Cornish Engineer', which, when he is compared to giants such as Trevithick and Davy, is perhaps unsurprising.

Apart from the Canal and the Castle, Bude has a small harbour dating from the nineteenth century. It was then and in the early twentieth century that the town became a popular and genteel tourist resort dwarfing the nearby (and much older) town of Stratton, which until then had had the bragging rights. The railway came to Bude late, in 1898 and was axed in 1966. There is lots going on in Bude and lots to see. It doesn't need to be so self-effacing.

Just south of Bude, the northernmost feature of this AONB section is the popular surfing beach of Wide-mouth Bay. The beach is unusual for this part of the coast, having low sandstone cliffs, but these soon give way to the spectacular heights at Crackington Haven and beyond, where the grey/brown rocks seem to be piled in folded layers. Originating (on the equator!) some 325 million years ago, and compressed into the folds you can see today after the last Ice Age, these (mostly) carboniferous rocks are so important geologically that they are known worldwide as the Crackington Formation. This according to Colin Bristow is, 'A sequence of dark slaty shales alternating with sandstones. The latter are clearly turbiditic in character (sedimentary particles produced underwater by a turbidity current)…. The erosion of the mountains to the south was feeding vast quantities of muddy sediment via the rivers draining their northern slopes and a series of deltas, into

Peter Maxted

▲ Lichen – a sign of clean air

the marine trough to the north.' These mountains mentioned are from the Upper Carboniferous period some 300 million years ago.

At Crackington is also to be found the thirteenth century church at St Gennys whose churchyard is the last resting place of many shipwrecked mariners and perhaps a few smugglers. (The old name for those from St Gennys was 'wreckers & wrestlers'.)

Between Widemouth and Crackington is Dizzard Woods, a thick blanket of sessile oak trees which are stunted by the force of the Atlantic winds. The woodland is of international biological importance because of the many rare lichens and mosses thriving there thanks to the exceptionally clean air of the North Cornwall coast. Dizzard Woods is one of the few remnants (another is on north Dartmoor) of the prehistoric oak forest that once covered the whole of Britain.

This last tribe of oaks/each dwarfed and blasted back-wards/every branch bare-knuckled and calloused/ snagged and barbarous.

Extract from a poem by Mark Gibbons

Two miles further south, the prosaically named High Cliff is the highest sheer-drop cliff in Cornwall at 735 feet (224 metres). Up and down goes the path as it follows the coast, with features such as listric faults where the cliffs are slumping seaward, hanging valleys that end abruptly at a cliff edge (often featuring a waterfall) and, below the cliffs, stunning wave-cut platforms where the sea has carved the rock in ways a Turner prizewinner could only dream of producing.

There was mining in the area too. Although Cornwall is renowned for its tin and, to a lesser extent, copper mines, it is interesting to note that zinc, silver, lead and even wolfram (the ore of tungsten, the hardest of all metals) were mined around here.

Boscastle

There are few places along the 130 miles or so of the north Cornish coast where boats large or small can find a haven. Boscastle, however, is one such place. The harbour is set back between two high cliff walls and the

sea inlet winds between them, breaking up the Atlantic's fierceness. Finally two staggered stone quays (built by Sir Richard Grenville in the sixteenth century) jut out to create a safe natural harbour – in fact the only sheltered one between Padstow and Bude. For centuries small ships have loaded and unloaded their cargoes here.

Safe from all the sea could hurl at it, Boscastle thrived, first as a fishing port, then as a nineteenth-century staging post for the import of limestone and coal and the export of slate and perhaps some tin. It continues to prosper this century as a popular and pretty tourist desti-nation.

Safe from the sea Boscastle may be but, ironically, not from the land. Two deeply incised, wooded valleys cut down to sea level, the old mediaeval village running down one side and the Valency River rushing down on the other. In 2004 a freak flood, resulting from heavy rain, caused the Valency to overflow, culminating in a ten-foot high wall of water sweeping down the valley into the village. You may remember the TV pictures, for it was shown extensively on the national news. More than fifty cars were thrown into the harbour, the bridge was destroyed and the visitor centre washed away. Ninety-one people were rescued, many by helicopter from roofs where they were sheltering, in the largest peacetime rescue operation ever launched in the UK. Not a single person was badly hurt.

Rebuilding began, although the lower part of the village was virtually evacuated for a while as the sewage system had been destroyed. A flood plain was created, walls were heightened and strengthened, and a new bridge was built – though the modern design didn't please everyone at first. Today you can see marks on some of the buildings showing the level the water reached. One such was on the wall of a hotel we stayed at, several feet above the window to our room. Boscastle was flooded again in 2007 but the repairs and improve-ments meant the scale of damage was nothing like as bad as in 2004.

All is tranquil now in the dripping woods above the village. In the streets tourists sit in pubs and cafes, watching the Valency gurgle peacefully past. The spanking new visitor centre and the refurbished youth

Peter Maxted

▲ Boscastle Harbour

hostel sit by its banks. The old cottages in the northern valley were unaffected by the flood, as were some buildings in the lower part of the village. It is a pretty place, as testified by the number of visitors who throng the narrow streets and riverside, especially in summer. Perhaps it was not always so, though; John Leland in 1538 described it as: 'A very filthy toun and il kept'.

One of Boscastle's attractions that was damaged but survived the floods (leaving some locals to ask darkly, 'why?') was the Museum of Witchcraft. Apparently 90% of the artefacts were saved. The museum was the lifelong work of Cecil Williamson who began the museum on the Isle of Man (after being refused permission in his native Stratford) then moving it to Cornwall in 1960. Cecil, the most un-witchlike character it is possible to imagine, supposedly became fascinated after meeting a witch during a childhood holiday in Devon. His interest was fuelled by a spell in Southern Africa where he met several witchdoctors. Cecil ran the museum for many

years until 1997. He died three years later, aged ninety.

Even quite recent dictionaries define witches in purely negative terms. Mine says: 'A woman who practices black mages and sorcery or is believed to have dealings with the devil. An ugly or vicious old woman, a hag.' Interestingly, this dictionary was first published in 1987, not 1487. No wonder the current owners of the Museum of Witchcraft still receive a fair amount of abusive hate-mail – much of it from America.

I spoke to a (white) Cornish witch recently, named Lorraine. She loves the witchcraft museum for, in spite of all the horrors visited on old women in the past (many of which are documented here), the museum explains much of what witchcraft is truly about today. It seems that apart from a few herbs and spells to give people something they ask for or desire (a bit like Christian prayers perhaps) most of it is about walking lightly on the planet and revering its sacred places. In Cornwall, unsurprisingly, these are mostly antiquities, standing stones, circles, barrows, 'holy' wells and ancient wood-land. Witches look after these things too. A meeting of witches (a moot) will often involve scrub clearance or litter picking – keeping our ancient monuments clear of rubbish. It sounds like a kind of altruistic paganism to me; indeed, I was told they are closely linked. Anyway if it involves protecting and enhancing the environment, it's OK in my book.

Another notable building among many in Boscastle is the Cobweb Inn. This granite-built, slate-flagged hostelry has beamed ceilings and a splendid open fire in winter. Outside there are benches around a brazier for those who wish to smoke, in an area so cosy that it even lures non-smokers.

Walk up the valley away from the village and you will come to St Juliot's church where a young Thomas Hardy met his first wife, Emma Gifford, while he was working as an architect there. She died in 1912 and a year later he wrote an elegy entitled 'Beeny Cliff' (a landmark a mile to the north) which includes the line: 'Though still in chasmal beauty looms that wild weird western shore…'

As you leave Boscastle on the coast path south to Tintagel, you skirt the edge of the very well preserved mediaeval open field system of Forrabury Stiches, the whole area now protected by the National Trust. Then the path runs up and down in true Cornish fashion over cliffs, above sea caves and across small river valleys. At Rocky Valley, an impossibly picturesque stream leaps down to the sea.

This is the very stream fed by the waterfall at St Nectan's Glen. I've already mentioned this precious gem of a place, with its sixty-foot waterfall, St Nectan's Kieve, plunging into the dark pool below. St Nectan is supposed to have arrived in Cornwall around 500 AD and the story goes that he is buried under the waterfall, along with the treasure he collected. The church (or chapel) dedicated to him later became a hermitage – it is now a tea room. Two witches lived there too for a while appar-ently, though presumably not at the same time as the hermit.

If you carry on inland from Nectan's Glen you will begin climbing to Condolden Barrow, a large Iron Age burial site over a thousand feet above sea level. Thomas Hardy suggested it romantically (and fictionally) as the tomb of Queen Isolde. Many scholars believe that the barrow is the burial place of Cador, the sixth-century king of Cornwall. Geoffrey of Monmouth linked Cador to King Arthur and had him as a principle knight and the king's sword-bearer.

This brings us neatly on to Tintagel, Arthur's spiritual, if fictional, home. The name probably comes from the Cornish *din* (fort) and *tagell* (narrow).

Although in the AONB, Tintagel is, sadly, not of exceptional beauty. There are pretty corners of this ancient village and a recent £2.4 million regeneration project has led to a number of improvements but the overall impact on the visitor is that commercialism rather than quality is the order of the day. The spurious claims to an association with a certain king have led to a strong feel of Arthurian overkill. You can't blame the locals for cashing in, nor the tourists for flocking there, but when pub toilets are labelled 'Lancelots' and 'Guineveres' you

▲ Rocky Valley

Peter Maxted

know things have been taken a little too far.

But in spite of the tackiness of much of the village, perhaps nowhere in the whole county is as evocative as Tintagel Castle, especially on a blustery winter's day with the waves crashing on the rocks. Merlin's Cave lies below the very place where he allegedly spirited the baby Arthur away and is now home to a gigantic sea serpent known locally just as 'The Dragon'. There is probably nowhere else that has had so many myths woven around it, stories told about it or, let's face it, downright lies associated with it as Tintagel Castle.

So let's start with some facts. There *is* a castle. It is situated partly on the mainland and partly on a rocky headland, almost an island, with a deep channel between spanned by a narrow bridge erected in 1975. The castle dates from the twelfth and thirteenth centuries and was begun around 1140 – some seventy-five years after the Conquest.

There was probably an earlier Iron Age fortification and there was certainly a monastery on the 'island' as the twenty-seven-acre headland is called. Bronze Age artefacts have been found as well as goods from the Mediterranean. The castle itself was first built by Reginald, Earl of Cornwall, the bastard son of Henry I, and the date we have for its completion is 1145. The date is interesting because Geoffrey of Monmouth, gatherer, creator and chronicler of many early Arthurian legends, mentioned Tintagel in his writings of 1136. This suggests that a fortification was already associated with the place before the mediaeval castle was begun and there might be something in the Arthurian connection.

One further mention of Arthur must be made; in 1998, excavations discovered the 'Arthur stone' with the name Artognou inscribed on it. The stone is a 1,500-year-old piece of slate on which there were two Latin inscriptions. The second one translates: 'Artognou, father of a descendant of Coll, has had [this] made.' There was much excited speculation as to who Artognou was; most historians, however, do not believe the inscription refers to King Arthur himself – even if such an Iron Age chieftain existed.

Richard, Earl of Cornwall, extended the castle in 1233 – and it is mostly the ruins of this that we see today.

Peter Maxted

There was a Norman chapel dedicated to St Julietta inside the castle walls, now in ruins, which was excavated in the 1930s.

As mentioned, there are a few attractive buildings in the village itself, notably the old post office which was a manor house dating from the 1300s. It became a post office during the nineteenth century. The roof has an undulating look to it; locals will tell you that the dragon from the cave below the castle sleeps there sometimes and that has given it its unusual shape.

To the north, at Bossiney, there are the remains of an earlier castle probably predating Tintagel by some seventy years. A Roman milestone was found making up part of the walls of the churchyard in 1889 and can still be seen in the church. King Arthur's Hall was built in the village in the 1930s, with seventy-three stained glass windows

Peter Maxted

illustrating the Arthurian tales.

South of Tintagel the coast and hinterland were quarried extensively for slate (the last Tintagel cliff quarry was closed in 1937) and, of course, the great slate quarry at Delabole is only a short distance inland. The cliffs are now mostly owned by the National Trust for some way south as is the idyllic little cove at Trebarwith, a mecca for surfers.

Trebarwith Nature Reserve lies two miles south of Tintagel in a steeply sloping valley running down to the sea. It has a rich diversity of wildflowers and a thriving aquatic community in the stream and water meadows. Brown trout live in the stream, a sure sign that the water is clean and well oxygenated. Trout can weigh from as little as ten grams to a massive ten kilos, although you are unlikely to find one of that size here. The fish feed on small invertebrates and flies unfortunate enough to land on the water's surface.

The germander speedwell, sometimes known by its Latin name *Veronica,* is a pretty little flower that grows well here among the more common campion and primroses. It is usually sky blue and blooms from April until mid-summer. Sometimes on the reserve large numbers are out all at once, making a stunning display. The name speedwell is a reminder of the medicinal value that the plant was long considered to have.

A footpath through the reserve, possibly a 'churchway' for agricultural workers, is thought to date from the sixteenth century.

As the coast sweeps around westwards, past sixteenth- & seventeenth-century farmhouses, the villages of Port Isaac and its smaller cousin Port Gaverne come into view, both nestling into the cliffs. In contrast to Tintagel, Port Isaac has retained much of its unspoilt charm – and this in spite of its recent leap to fame as the fictional location for TV's *Doc Martin*, Port Wenn.

Port Isaac

The name means 'port of corn', so it is likely that grain from inland farms was once the staple trading commodity. Later, as the harbour developed (the pier is sixteenth-century) coal was landed and slate and other stone shipped out. Fishing has existed since time immemorial and still today small boats land their local catch. Rather surprisingly for such a small seaside port, there was a railway station just above the village for seventy years – one could travel direct all the way to Okehampton in Devon. The village is criss-crossed with very narrow streets with overhanging houses, like parts of Mousehole or Looe this is not motoring terrain. If you

want an idea of the narrowness of the alleyways (or *drangs* as they are known locally) one is named 'Squeeze-Belly Alley'.

Apart from *Doc Martin* a number of other films and TV programmes have been made here. *Oscar and Lucinda* was one, *The Shell Seekers* another. And, of course, the ubiquitous *Poldark* used many locations around and about – though the same could be said for nearly all coastal Cornwall (I remember my parents being extras in the famous series back in the 1970s).

Port Isaac now has another famous cultural association. Cornish choirs have long been as talented as their Welsh counterparts, if not always as well known. Now the 'Fishermen's Friends', sea-shanty singers from the village, have received national acclaim and appeared on TV and on the great stages in the capital. They signed a record deal with Universal in 2010.

A steep valley runs inland through the AONB here

Dave Matthews

towards Trelights and St Endellion church. Local people have been working hard to make St Endellion a 'Climate Friendly Parish' (the first in the county) with a commitment by individuals, the Parish Council and local businesses to reduce carbon emission by 5% per year.

Nearby are Long Cross Gardens, designed in the late nineteenth century and marked on tourist maps as Victorian Gardens. This cultivated three acres was designed either to emulate on a small scale or possibly parody the great gardens of an earlier age. There are follies and mazes, arches and artfulness and, best of all, a prehistoric garden with *menhirs*, *dolmen* and a mock *men an tol* stone. The gardens were carefully restored in the 1980s.

Back on the coast to the west of Port Isaac is the tiny village of Port Quinn. This suffered more than most from the arrival of the railway, its little quay no longer needed for the export of slate or the import of coal. The cottages were abandoned one by one and the village was deserted – a rumour went round that the population had been washed out to sea! Today the little houses are mostly owned by the National Trust and offered as holiday lets.

The sandstone cliffs give way to the vast promontory of The Rumps which have a narrow neck that will no doubt one day disappear to create an island. The prominent mounds on The Rumps are the remains an early Iron Age cliff castle, probably just pre-Roman. In the rock is a significant amount of greenstone (or blue elvan as the locals call it); its proper name is dolerite. It is hard not to gaze out to sea from The Rumps and if you look long enough at the right time of year you will be rewarded with the sight of dolphins or even whales.

From here the path runs to Pentire Point. The rocks here are largely of pillow lava (telling us that these vast cliffs were once underwater) with their distinctive bulbous or spherical shape. Pillow lava is produced when lava flow occurs beneath the sea. Each time there is a squirt of hot magma, it cools incredibly fast in the salt water producing the strange bulbous shapes we can see around here today. Great piles of pillow lava can also be seen on the south coast around Gorran Haven and Nare Head (see Chapter 10). Where the stone was removed for hedge-building there can be seen indents in the landscape known locally as 'borrow pits' – sites of small-scale quarrying. As this stone has also been used to create the many Cornish hedges found in the area, I love the idea of it being 'borrowed' from one part of the landscape to create another, a properly symbiotic relationship. These hedges can be seen if you walk south through Pentire farm, owned by the Trust and managed sustainably – over half the arable land does not use herbicides or pesticides with a resulting increase in biodiversity.

The path through the farm will take you to the car park at Pentireglaze lead mine. Mines once abounded in this area – particularly to extract the seams of galena ore, the source of lead and silver.

On the cliffs between Pentire Point and The Rumps, there is a stone plaque to commemorate the writing, in 1914, of the sombre poem 'For The Fallen' by Laurence Binyon. The lines are quoted rather often these days, not just on Remembrance Sunday:

> *They shall grow not old, as we that are left grow old:*
> *Age shall not weary them, nor the years condemn.*
> *At the going down of the sun and in the morning,*
> *We will remember them.*

The whole headland of Pentire is an SSSI. At Pentire Point this section of the Cornwall AONB ends. This is 'rough Pentire', the headland that Betjeman dreamed about while stuck in the city. 'Is it rounding rough Pentire in a flood of sunset fire/The little fleet of trawlers under sail?'

And from Pentire you can gaze across the Doom Bar to Padstow and the beginning of the Trevose Head AONB section or inland over sand and mud-flats to the Camel Estuary.

The Camel Estuary

'The five and a half miles beside the broadening Camel to Padstow is the most beautiful train journey I know,' wrote John Betjeman, the Poet Laureate from 1906 to 1984. It is hard not to hear Betjeman's sonorous, upper-class English voice as I lean my bike against a gate and gaze across the Camel Estuary from the outskirts of Padstow. There are the dunes hiding the little church in which he is buried. There are the beaches, where as a boy he played and ate picnics ('sand in the sandwiches, wasps in the marmalade'). Further in the distance is Pentire Point which he longed for in his city exile. Cornwall has seen greater writers, but none for whom it became such a special place, who loved it perhaps even more than those who are born here and take its beauty somewhat for granted. I know how he felt.

Betjeman's beloved Atlantic Coast Express puffed its sooty way from London Waterloo to Padstow for nearly a hundred years but the last passenger train to run along-side this stretch of the Camel River was back in 1964 and the line was finally closed in 1967. The rails and timber sleepers were taken up and in 1984 the track, estuary and farmed hinterland became part of the Cornwall AONB, coincidentally the year that the area's greatest literary champion died.

The Camel Estuary section of the Cornwall AONB is one of the smallest and is one of only two 'inland' sections. Yet water features more prominently than in many of the coastal sections. The old railway line is now a multi-use cycleway and footpath, the Camel Trail, so Betjeman's train journey must now be undertaken on foot or by bicycle (you do the puffing rather than the train!) but the view of water, reeds, mud and sand is still the same, if not better. Away from the river the AONB slopes upward both north and south, past narrow tidal creeks and ancient quarries and across fertile farmland.

Gateways to the AONB are gastronomic Padstow and wealthy Rock on the north-west and north-east sides near the mouth of the Estuary, as well as the ancient wool town of Wadebridge to the south. The River Camel itself rises at 715 feet above sea level on the northern edge of Bodmin Moor then winds over through upper and middle Devonian slate rocks through Camelford, around Bodmin, into Wadebridge and on to Padstow and the Estuary mouth at Stepper Point and Pentire Head.

Wadebridge was originally the small market town of Wade, the 'bridge' part being added when the old bridge was built in the fifteenth century. Wade was named because of a ford across the river here. The crossing had two chapels either side of the river, Kings Chapel on the north side and St Michael's on the south. People would pray for a safe crossing at one of the chapels before wading across at low tide; once they had made it to the other side they would give thanks to God in the other chapel. In 1312 a licence was granted for Wade to commence with a market and several taverns opened.

There are two stories as to why the bridge was built. There is no doubt that it was constructed thanks to the efforts of a local priest, Thomas Lovibond (the vicar of nearby Egloshayle), but one tale has it that the Reverend became distressed at the number of humans and animals that had died during the crossing of the river Camel, the other that he planned the bridge to stop drunk parishioners being drowned as they made their way through the tidal ford. The story has it that the bridge was 'built on wool' with woolsacks as the base for the bridge's seventeen arches. It is, however, much more likely that phrase means the money to pay for it came from local wool farmers and merchants. Even after the bridge was completed in 1468, boats could navigate the channel upriver from Padstow as far as Guineaport quay where their skippers had to pay the steep price of a guinea to moor up.

The bridge has one further historical claim to fame. It was considered an important strategic position and towards the end of the English Civil War, in 1646, Oliver Cromwell himself came with 1,500 men to take it and with it the route into Royalist West Cornwall.

The new bridge to take the busy A39 away from the town was completed in 1991.

The Bodmin and Wadebridge Railway Line opened in 1834 – and is now the third oldest in the world. Originally it carried slate from the quarries inland and sand in the other direction to lighten the local heavy soil on the farms. It was also one of the first to carry passengers. During the mid-1900s gruesome excursions took place so the public could see live hangings at Bodmin Gaol.

South of Wadebridge, the Camel is still a small freshwater river but the tide comes in up past the old bridge and just north of the town the river opens to form a broad valley vista. Like other prominent Cornish estuaries such as the Fal and the Helford, the Camel Estuary is a *ria,* a deep valley that has been drowned by post-glacial rising sea levels.

At low tide mud- and sandbanks are exposed and in the sheltered creeks the mud is colonized with reed-beds and salt-marsh flats teeming with wading birds. The hinterland takes in secluded farms and windswept hilltops with long distance views down the Estuary to the sea.

From the old quays at Wadebridge the river passes under the new A39 bypass where the AONB begins. Following the Camel Trail (now used by nearly half a million people a year) the narrow Camel river is on your right, then, opposite Burniere Point, the valley suddenly widens by nearly five times with acres of salt marsh where the River Amble enters the Estuary from the east. There are birdwatching hides on both sides of the river here; the one on the northern side can easily accommodate ten or twelve people at a time.

The Estuary sides and its mud- and sandflats are home

Peter Maxted

▲ Camel Estuary at low tide

to a wide variety of birds. In the winter you'll see wildfowl such as wigeon and long-tailed duck, goldeneye, grebe and any number of waders. Migrant birds visit throughout the year and in the summer the waters and shoreline provide rich feeding-ground for heron, little egrets, cormorants, shags, oystercatchers and gulls. Smaller birds are the prey for peregrines while ospreys swoop down to catch small fish and pairs of mute swans glide gracefully past.

Continuing north on the trail, at the old Camel slate quarry, with its strange piles of broken stone, you can look across to Cant Cove below the 250-foot bulk of Cant Hill.

At this point, the character of the Estuary changes as mudflats give way to sandbanks. The narrow channel that cuts the mud at low tide becomes a wide expanse of water with windsurfers, pilot gigs, dinghies and canoes a common sight. On the left Old Town Cove is a small stream-fed creek with the remains of an ancient house and chapel at its head.

The house was a mediaeval manor named Halwyn (White Hall in Cornish) once a seat of some magnificence. All that is left are some bramble-covered ruins but the ancient dovecote just a hundred metres from the path, dating from 1347, was restored in the 1990s by English Heritage and Cornwall County Council. This 'culverhouse' (*culver* is Old English for wild pigeon) would have been an important source of food for the manor providing up to fifty birds a week for the table.

Still on the trail, another half mile takes you to the old railway bridge across Little Petherick Creek where sudden gusts of wind can catch the unwary cyclist or walker. The Victorian iron bridge has recently been restored and strengthened, with the old floor timbers and their disquieting gaps being replaced by reassuring concrete. Above, on Dennis Hill, a granite needle obelisk, erected to celebrate Queen Victoria's Jubilee of 1887, surveys the countryside for miles around.

There are paths inland here and elsewhere along the trail, winding up past creeks and alongside fields to tiny hamlets and secluded farms. The path that runs alongside Little Petherick Creek (often somewhat overgrown) joins up with the Saints Way at Little Petherick itself.

Here too is the Grade I listed St Petroc's church, built in the fourteenth century and restored in the nineteenth. The area is littered with quarries and the remains of several small copper mines.

Padstow

As you enter Padstow from the trail one of the first buildings you come to in the old station complex is the national lobster hatchery from where some 10,000 baby lobsters a year are grown to be released off the coast of Cornwall and the Isles of Scilly.

Padstow is the gastronomic heart of Cornwall. Rick Stein is ubiquitous with his seafood restaurant, café, deli and cookery school and he is now being given a run for his money by Paul Ainsworth at Number 6. Across the river in Rock, Nathan Outlaw serves Michelin-starred food to the wealthy, the famous and the pretentious.

It's probably best to avoid Padstow in high summer when it can get almost as busy as St Ives. The other time the town is jam-packed is on May Day when the 'Obby 'Oss celebration takes place. 'Obby 'Oss is the traditional May Day celebration with the 'Oss, whose costume looks for all the world like something an African witch doctor might wear, being taunted by red and blue teams of 'teasers', symbolizing the going of winter and the coming of spring.

There has been a ferry at Black Rock Passage since 1337. Known as the Black Tor ferry, at low water it docks just north of the town at St Saviour's Point (note there is no Sunday service in winter). Above the point was once a high outcrop of rock, a type of quartz known as elvan or greenstone. This must have looked black from below thereby giving its name to the ferry and passage. The stone was quarried away many years ago, as it makes splendid building material, but the name remains.

From the town you can look east across the Camel to Rock or north to Treberthick, where Betjeman is buried in St Enodoc's churchyard. Known today as 'The Church in the Dunes', St Enodoc's was built in the twelfth century on the site of a hermit's dwelling. The wind-blown sand gradually mounted alongside and around it until it was virtually buried. For 200 years (until around 1850 when excavation began) it was known to the locals as 'Sinking Neddy'. A little further north near Rock is Brea Hill where outdoor readings of Betjeman's poetry are held each summer.

Padstow is also the starting (or finishing) point for the Saints' Way which was designated in 1986 and follows the route taken by early Christian pilgrims. They would land at Padstow from Wales and travel the twenty-eight miles (forty-five kilometres) to Fowey to take ship for France. For a short while the Saints Way runs adjacent to the Camel Trail through the AONB before splitting off at Little Petherick Creek. The Saints' Way can be walked in a day (start early) or in two sections with a break.

If you fancy a circular walk, or better still cycle, then take the Camel trail to Padstow, grab a pasty from one of more than a dozen pasty shops (and no, I'm not going to step in the quicksand of pasty recommendation) then cross on the ferry. Take a detour to St Enodoc's and then turn south-east on the little road that follows the river to Cant Hill past Gentle Jane cove – named for a local lady

who treated ailments. The road turns inland and past Tregenna farm joins the B road running from Wadebridge to Port Isaac, Tintagel and beyond. Shortly thereafter it crosses Trewornan Bridge over the River Amble and Camel flood plain which was built in1791 by Rev. William Sandys, who seems to have been as enthusiastic for architecture and engineering as he was for things theological. Its dressed stone pointed arches are in the mediaeval style and there is a legend attached that once a year, always on the night of a full moon, a ghostly coach and horses clatter over it.

According to the *Magna Britannia: volume 3: Cornwall* (1814):

Trewornan-bridge, in this parish, was built about the year 1791, in the place of a dangerous ford, impassable at high tides, in the road leading from St. Minver to Egloshayle, by the exertions of Mr. Sandys, and has been made a county-bridge: it is over a rivulet which

▲ Looking across the estuary from Padstow

Peter Maxted

separates the parishes of St. Minver and Egloshayle; and which, by the flux of the tides, is rendered navigable for barges as high as Amble-bridge, in the parish of St. Kew.

Crossing the A39 you leave the Area of Outstanding Natural Beauty and re-enter Wadebridge.

Industrial heritage

Like so much of Cornwall the landscape of the Camel Estuary is littered with remnants of its industrial past. All along the Estuary banks are disused slate quarries, many with piles of broken slate still lying around. I counted fourteen on the last visit. Inland, of course, is the enormous slate quarry at Delabole where high quality slate is still produced. Two centuries ago barges bringing slate from the quarries would ply the Camel, leading to the growth of Padstow as a port.

Other designations

The 'inter-tidal areas' (those exposed at low tide) around Rock and Polzeath are designated as a Voluntary Marine Wildlife Area. This contains ten species of seaweed and five species of animal that are of special conservation importance in south-west England, including the Celtic sea slug and the *Polysiphonia* seaweeds.

The Camel Estuary is also an SAC, making it a strictly protected site under the EC Habitats Directive, which established 'a European network of important high-quality conservation sites that will make a significant contribution to conserving 189 threatened habitat types and 788 species'.

Recreation versus conservation

As with many sections of the Cornwall AONB, there is a tension between the desire to enjoy recreational activities in the Estuary and the need to conserve and enhance the landscape and look after its flora and fauna. The marine environment and the wildlife it supports can be highly sensitive to damage and disturbance from human activities.

One of the UK's rarest and most protected mammals, the otter, frequents the Camel and has been seen on the edges of Padstow. The Camel is one of the otter's main strongholds in south-west England. Surveys have indicated a (relatively) dense population along most of the river and records show that this persisted even when the otter was in serious decline over much of the rest of its range in England. Thus the Camel may have acted as a nucleus for the re-colonization of other parts of England. The river and its tributaries represent both the upland and lowland habitat types loved by otters with an adequate food supply throughout the year. The wooded lower reaches of the river also provide a good habitat for breeding.

The Estuary is also a sea bass conservation area providing protection for the breeding of this most sought-after fish. The Camel is one of the most productive rivers for salmon and sea trout in the south-west, due to its high water quality. Much of this is due to the recent Cornwall Rivers project, which worked with farmers to reduce pollution and run-off and improve nutrient and soil management.

Rare greater and lesser horseshoe bats feed along the watercourses while beneath them scurry water vole. On the banks and inland there are rare plants to be found amongst the more common blackthorn, gorse, thrift and campion. At the mouth, inter-tidal reefs provide protection for seaweeds and a myriad of fish and other sea creatures.

Fortunately, the main shore-based activities like walking, cycling and horse riding do little damage. Some marine recreation activities such as canoeing, sailing and wind-surfing are also relatively harmless. Rock sailing school runs a series of races near the town each year and dinghies, catamarans and shrimpers can be seen competing. You will see the occasional motorboat too but there's an eight miles per hour speed limit (this is when the bow of the boat lifts out of the water) imposed to protect nest and roosting sites on the northern side.

The Camel Estuary section of the Cornwall AONB may be small but it is a very strange and beautiful place unlike anywhere else either on the coast or inland. Its protected landscape designation will, hopefully, safeguard it for future generations. Betjeman would have approved.

Stepper Point to Bedruthan

Early evening. The sands stretch flat, smooth and empty into the distance, lit red-gold by the setting sun. To the north the sea sparkles as if with rubies from the last of the light. Pentire Head opposite is bathed in a golden glow. You have the beach wholly to yourself from north to south and from sea's edge to dune, apart from a single, solitary fisherman way to the south, a black silhouette in the distance.

Welcome to Harbour Cove on an autumn evening; one of my favourite beaches (as if you hadn't guessed!), unspoilt and empty. And yet Padstow is barely a couple of miles to the south. This section of the AONB, which nominally runs from Stepper Point to Bedruthan Steps but actually begins on the very outskirts of Padstow, has probably more fine beaches than any similar-sized stretch of coast in the south-west. Harbour Cove, Hawkers Cove, Harlyn Bay, Mother Ivey's, Booby's Bay, Constantine, Treyarnon, Porthcothan, on to Bedruthan Steps and beyond to Watergate Bay and the surfing Mecca of Newquay. In between the bays, with their rich golden sands, are cliffs and promontories, all served by the undulating, ubiquitous coast path.

But before we head out along the coast, I want to take you briefly back to Padstow for one of the area's (relatively) undiscovered gems.

Padstow is a corruption of *Petroc-stow* (aka Petrocstowe, or Petrock's Place), after the Welsh missionary Saint Petroc, who landed at nearby Trebetherick early in the sixth century. Petroc founded a monastery named Lanwethinoc (*lan* meaning church and Wethinoc being

▲ Harbour Cove

Ashley Thomas

73

an earlier holy man) which lasted until it was laid to waste in a Viking raid in 981, according to the Anglo-Saxon Chronicle. The monks fled to Bodmin, taking with them the relics of St Petroc. There must have been some remnants, for Lanwethinoc is mentioned also in the Domesday Book. During mediaeval times, Padstow was commonly called Aldestowe (as the 'old place' in contrast to Bodmin the 'new place').

Walk through the town towards the church past pretty flower-bedecked cottages following the signs for Prideaux Place. You enter a parking area with the old Elizabethan manor on your left and the deer park on your right. This is reputed to be the oldest in Cornwall and one of the oldest in Britain.

Prideaux Place has been in the same family, the Prideaux-Brunes, for over 400 years. First built four years after the Armada, the house has been enlarged and modified by successive generations. It combines Elizabethan and Georgian architecture in a rather successful way, unlike many other great houses.

Prideaux Place can be visited by arrangement – they are happy to take parties round to look at the architecture, portraits, furniture and the Prideaux Porcelain Collection. When I visited last summer with a group from the National Association of AONBs, we were treated to a fascinating tour.

Peter Prideaux-Brune himself welcomed us at the gates with the easy charm of true aristocracy, and gave us a brief history of the house, gardens and the deer park which is his particular passion. He also apologized for the mess! Everywhere we went, guided by the charming and knowledgeable Carmen Hocking, we were tripping over cables or navigating props and cameras, because, for the umpteenth time, Prideaux Place was host to a film crew. This one was German, filming one of Rosamund Pilcher's novels – apparently she is enormously popular in Germany. The house has been the backdrop for many other films, including an all-star version of *Twelfth Night*.

There were two particular highlights to our visit; one was our first sight of the astonishing ceiling in the Great Chamber. This was only uncovered in the 1980s so is possibly the best-preserved Elizabethan ceiling in the

country. Part of the panelling in the same room was taken from the manor of Sir Bevil Grenville at Stowe when it was demolished (see Chapter 2). The second was the pleasure of watching the deer come to feed. The deer park, probably the oldest in Britain (it may have been enclosed in Roman times), is right opposite the front entrance. The herd ranges from pale cream to dark brown and new deer are constantly being introduced to keep them from these two extremes. Paul Messenger of the British Deer Society told us how they are managed and how the landscape is constantly being adapted to ensure optimum conditions.

The Prideaux family chose the 'wrong' side in the Civil War, for while most of Cornwall was Royalist, they supported Cromwell and the Parliamentarians, although perhaps not entirely. Just before the restoration of the monarchy in 1660, Edmund Prideaux married his sister to Sir William Morice, Secretary of State to Charles II. Prideaux was subsequently pardoned for his unfortunate choice. Perhaps this explains the miniature to be found in the drawing room. This has a portrait of Charles I on one side and Oliver Cromwell on the other. Incidentally, the pardon forgives the family for crimes past, present *and* future!

The gardens, which were one of the earliest known types of *Jardin Anglais*, dating from Edmund Prideaux's work in the 1720s, have been sympathetically restored over the last twenty-odd years with help from experts who cut their teeth at Heligan (see Chapter 10). However, much of the house has been untouched since the 1940s. This is because it was home, for two years, to the US Army's 121st Engineer Combat Battalion; many of the rooms are exactly as they left them at the end of World War II.

Retrace your steps into town and take the coast path north. From Padstow the path runs through a park with a war memorial and great views across the Estuary, then past overgrown disused World War II buildings and a Napoleonic Wars gun emplacement, up to Harbour Cove and on to Hawker's where you pass the old lifeboat launching station, now a holiday home. Hawker's Cove faces the sand bar that almost blocks the estuary at low tide. It is known as the Doom Bar, graveyard of ships (over 300 foundered there up to the 1920s) and a name of terror for centuries. Now, however, 'Doom Bar' has a more pleasant connotation and is most likely recognized as the name of a popular Cornish ale from the Sharp's brewery at Rock across the estuary!

The path runs on to spectacular Stepper Point. Here you can look north-east to Betjeman's 'rough Pentire', west to Trevose and south back to the Camel Estuary across the Doom Bar where the treacherous sand bar is submerged by a mere couple of feet just after low tide. Stepper Point itself is a beautiful headland overlooking the mouth of the Camel along with its twin sister Pentire Point on the far side. The small whitewashed building on the very edge of the point is a lookout hut belonging to the National Coastwatch Institution, the charity that helps to oversee the safety of people and vessels along the whole UK coastline.

Dave Matthews

▲ Trevone Bay, evening

The road and the coast path skirt either side of Trevone and head on to Harlyn Bay. Above Trevone Bay there are the striking Marble Cliffs at Porthmissen Bridge which are not actually marble but, according to English Nature, 'an extensive exposure through a sequence of alternating shales and turbiditic limestones, which have yielded conodonts indicating an early Frasnian age...a detailed section through an Upper Devonian basinal facies which is unrivalled in Europe'. You'll just have to take their word for it! Perhaps they should have contented themselves with the words of Colin Bristow: 'They consist of an alternating sequence of limestones and slates. The marble is not true marble because it has not been fully re-crystallised by heat and pressure.' They do look like marble though and, most interestingly, for the lines of alternating rock are almost completely horizontal, fossil records have proved that the whole cliff is completely inverted through 180 degrees.

A little further on is the amazing collapsed inland sea cave known as Round Hole. At Harlyn Bay, early Bronze Age artefacts have been found – suggesting it was once on a trading route, probably with Ireland. A third century BC cemetery has also been found here with over a hundred bodies lying in slate kists. It was thought from the grave goods that these were Bronze Age Cornish inhabitants conquered by Iron Age Celtic invaders, possibly the La Tene Celts from the area we now know as Switzerland. However, the bodies showed no sign of violent death so this may have been a graveyard much like our own where the dead were laid reverently to rest over a long period. A serpentine amulet is among the many intriguing items found in the Harlyn Bay cemetery. Other objects included spindle whorls and loom weights, slate tools, a dagger, brooches and pins. Two gold lunulae (moon-shaped ornaments) are now in the Royal Cornwall Museum collection in the city of Truro.

When the cemetery was discovered, the locals of Padstow and surrounding areas did not exactly cover themselves in glory. The following is from *A Book of Folk-lore*, by the Reverend Sabine Baring-Gould, published in 1913:

In September 1900, I received a summons to go to Padstow in Cornwall, as at Harlyn Bay near there a prehistoric necropolis had been discovered in blown sand that had been carried some way inland and was hard compacted. A gentleman had bought a field there, and was about to build a house. I found that he was impatient to get his dwelling ready before winter, or, at all events, have the foundations and walls got on with, and he would not allow a slow and careful exploration. It had to be done in a hurry. What was more, and even worse, the fact of the discovery got into the Cornish and Devon papers. The season was that of tourists. The owner charged sixpence a head for visitors, and they came in swarms, pushing everywhere, poking about the skeletons and skulls with their umbrellas and parasols, scrabbling in the graves in quest of 'finds', and from the moment this rabble appeared on the scene no work could be done save protection of what had already been uncovered. A more distressing and disappointing exploration could not be imagined. However, some points were determined.

After this less than flattering description of the local populace, Sabine Baring-Gould went on to describe the finds:

More than a hundred graves were uncovered; they were composed of boxes of slate in which the skeleton sat crouched, mainly, but not exclusively, on the right side. Some were of females, some of mothers with their infants in their arms. No skull was discovered that indicated death through violence, and all skeletons were complete. Some of the coffins were in layers, one above another; rudely speaking, they pointed east and west, the heads being to the west; but what governed the position seemed to be the slope of the hill, that fell away somewhat steeply from the south to the north.

Some bronze fibulae were found, finely drawn armlets of bronze wire making spiral convolutions about the wrist, a necklace of very small amber and blue glass beads strung on this bronze wire; a good deal of iron so corroded that, what with the friability and the meddlesomeness of the visitors, who would finger everything exhumed, it was not possible to make out more than that they did not represent fragments of weapons.

There were found at the time a great many needles and prongs of slate, which were afterwards exhibited on the spot and sold to tourists as stone spearheads. They were no such thing. They were splinters of a soft local slate that had been rolled by the wind and grated by the sand into the shape they assumed, and such are found all through the district.

Dr Beddoe came down and examined the skulls and skeletons. He considered the interments to be late, and of a race somewhat short in stature, with dolicho-cephalic (long and thin) skulls, not prognathous (jutting jawed). 'We may conjecture with some confidence that it was after the Gallo-Belgic and before the Roman Conquest.' There were marked peculiarities in the skulls, distinguishing them from those of the Aryan Celt and from those of the men of the Bronze period. It seemed to me that a necropolis of an intrusive people, peaceable, who, whereas all around them burnt their dead, continued religiously to inter theirs.

The main road from Padstow along the coast cuts through this ancient cemetery. It is interesting to note that this portion of the road has ever been dreaded by passengers at night as haunted. On the right hand of the way, coming from Padstow, probably more of the necropolis remains, and it is earnestly to be desired that it may at some time be scientifically examined, without the intrusion of the ignorant and vulgar being permitted. The digging proceedings at Harlyn, as soon as the season was ending, were broken up by a storm and change of weather. The tent was blown down and utterly wrecked. In the following year no opportunity was accorded for the prosecution of the researches.

I think that the Harlyn exploration affords sufficient grounds to make antiquaries careful in examining graves, and cautious in classification in the broad categories of prehistoric, Celtic, Saxon and Roman.

To what stock an intrusive people – widely dispersed and never collected into towns, villages, or hamlets, but migrating through the land, like the gipsies – belonged is what cannot yet be determined

The burial mounds are today covered in grass but the coast path runs right through them. Perhaps it is better that they are not open and exposed for all to see. It would be nice to think that we would behave better than our Victorian forebears but I wouldn't put money on it.

The little village of Harlyn has another interesting tale attached to it. Mother Ivey was a seventeenth-century wise-woman and 'white witch' who lived in a cottage a little way down the coast. In 1997, it was reported that the landowner of a field above Harlyn Bay had asked the local priest to lift an ancient spell put on the 'Curse Field' by Mother Ivey. She resorted to this after the local landowner had ordered that unsold pilchards should be ploughed into the soil rather than given to starving local people in Padstow. Mother Ivey had appealed to the Hellyer family to donate the fish but they refused and instead the pilchards were used as a fertilizer. An angry Mother Ivey cursed the field: 'If ever its soil is broken, death will follow'.

The family continued to use the land until the Hellyer's eldest son was thrown from his horse and killed. Ever since then the field has remained fallow and there are claims that every time someone has attempted to break the soil the curse has struck again.

Ownership of the estate has now apparently passed from the Hellyer family but it is believed the curse lives on. Luke Richards wrote in *The Guardian* that: 'In the 1970s a group of metal detector enthusiasts started digging and within days one suffered a fatal heart attack. Ten years later when a water company disturbed the soil to lay pipes the foreman died the following day.'

▲ Trevose lighthouse

Peter Maxted

Past Mother Ivey's cottage and the bay also named after her, the prominent headland at Trevose Head offers views up and down the coast, westward towards St Ives and north-east as far as Morwenstow when the weather is clear. The lighthouse at Trevose Head was the last to be run on compressed air and paraffin; it was modernized in 1913 when a new fog horn was installed that took the form of an enormous trumpet. At over 200 feet above sea level, its light has a range of over 20 miles and the beams of 4 other lighthouses can be seen from it.

Trevose lighthouse was badly needed for prior to its erection in the nineteenth century, the area was deadly to shipping. This is from the *West Briton* local newspaper (still going strong) of 1811:

In the gale of Monday evening last, HMS Bloodhound, Lieut. Bray, ran on shore in Harlyn Bay, by mistaking Trevose-Head for Stripper [presumably Stepper Point] the western entrance to Padstow Harbour, where she intended to go. This is the third vessel stranded near the place in the short space of a month, by which eleven lives were lost entire for the want of the proposed light-house on Trevose-Head, which clearly proves the great necessity for the immediate erection thereof.

South of Trevose Head lie the sandy bathing beaches of Constantine Bay, with its typical AONB village of discreet houses with gardens of tamarisk and lawns, and a small hotel. The village was a favourite retreat of Margaret Thatcher in the 1980s. Inland here is a (fairly secluded) golf course with the remains of an ancient church and holy well near its southern perimeter. Like others at Polzeath and Perranwell it was built in a hollow in the sand. Underneath the ruined tower is a large boulder of Cataclew stone weighing, apparently, nearly a quarter of a ton. This may have been a sacred object around which the tower was built. The name

Dave Matthews

'Constantine' is an interesting one and almost certainly does not relate to the Eastern ruler or city. Another Constantine village sits in the South Coast Western section of the AONB (see Chapter 9).

Next lies Treyarnon, with its extensive youth hostel sitting just above the beach. If you stay there in winter it is quite something to wake up in bed and see the storms sweeping up the beach just below your window. Both Treyarnon and Constantine Bays are popular with surfers, these days all year round.

Above both these coves the headlands are made of igneous rocks known collectively as 'greenstone' or to local quarrymen as 'blue elvan'. Most of the greenstones are harder and more resistant to erosion than their slate hosts, so they tend to form positive features and stand above the level of the fields on the inland plateau. Most of the buildings are made of granite and slate (slate is the predominant underlying rock so this is an abundant resource).

There are few trees in this section of the AONB due to the exposed nature of the landscape. The few hardy thorn trees that do survive are sometimes bent almost double away from the wind. The wooded river valleys of the northern sections are conspicuous by their absence here.

The herringbone 'Jacks and Janes' pattern of stone walls is typical of the area – the stones are laid diagonally first one way, then the other. Many of the walls sprout bracken, ferns and brambles and more attractive grasses and wildflowers. Thrift grows in surprising, football-sized clumps even on the most exposed banks and walls.

This whole section of the AONB is particularly popular with tourists. Between Trevose and Bedruthan there are at least seven camping sites but fortunately all are of the small, secluded variety that fit in acceptably with the AONB. Inland, there are several larger ones. Although there are few other manmade settlements here, it was not always so. There are the remains of Bronze

Peter Maxted

Age barrows, Iron Age cliff castles and a nineteenth-century iron mine.

At Porthcothan beach the river drops from the high plateau above with surprising speed. There is an old pack bridge over the stream just above the beach.

Many a mention is made around the Cornish coast of the practice of smuggling. Occasionally an eyewitness account survives. Just inland from here is Trevethan Farm, which has also been known in the past (erroneously) as Trevethan Manor. There are a number of mentions here of a fougou – an Iron Age underground passage or chamber. Of course, as with any 'secret' passage, there are stories of smuggling.

In 1899 the Reverend Sabine Baring-Gould wrote:

There are around the coast a great number of what are locally called Vougghas, or Fogous (Welsh Ogofau) caves that were artificially constructed for the stowing away of 'run' goods....At one of the wildest and most rugged points of a singularly wild and rugged coast, that of the north of Cornwall, are two tiny bays, Porth Cothan and Porth Mear, in the parishes of St. Merryn and St. Eval. At Porth Cothan the cliffs fall away and form a lap of shore, into which flows a little stream, that loses itself in the shifting sands. A manor-house, a mill, a farmhouse or two are all the dwellings near Porth Cothan, and of highways there is none for many miles, the nearest being that from Wadebridge to St. Columb. About a mile up the glen that forms the channel through which the stream flows into Porth Cothan, is a tiny lateral combe, the steep sides covered with heather and dense clumps and patches of furze. Rather more than half-way down the steep slope of the hill is a hole just large enough to admit of a man entering in a stooping posture…the height is 3ft.6in. and the width 3ft. But once within, the cave is found to be loftier, and runs for 50 feet due west, the height varying from 7ft.6in. to 8ft.6in., and the width expanding to 8ft.3in.

Immediately within the entrance may be observed notches cut in the rock, into which a beam might be thrust to close the mouth of the cave, which was then filled in with earth and bramble bushes drawn over it, when it would require a very experienced eye to discover it. As it was, though the mouth was open, my guide was in fault and unable to find it and it was by accident only that I lit upon it.

At 7 feet from the entrance a lateral gallery branches off to the right, extending at present but 17 feet, and of that a portion of the roof has fallen in. This gallery was much lower than the main one, not being higher than 3 feet, but probably in a portion now choked it rose, at all events in places, to a greater height. This side gallery never served for the storage of smuggled goods. It was a passage that originally was carried as far as the little cluster of cottages at Trevethan, whence, so it is said, another passage communicated with the sands of Porth Mear. The opening of the underground way is said to have been in a well at Trevethan. But the whole is now choked up. The tunnel was not carried in a straight line. It branched out of the trunk at an acute angle, and was carried in a sweep through the rocks with holes at intervals for the admission of light and air. The total length must have been nearly 3500 feet. The passage can in places be just traced by the falling in of the ground above, but it cannot be pursued within. At the beginning of this century [in around 1800] this smugglers' cave was in use.

There is still living an old woman who can give information relative to the use of this cave.

'Well, Genefer, did you ever see smugglers who employed the Vouggha?' [Vouggha, as already stated, is the old Cornish word for cave.] 'Well, no, sir. I can't say that; but my father did. He minded well the time when the Vouggha was filed [sic] with casks of spirits right chuck-full.'

'But how were they got there?'

'That was easy enough. The boats ran their loads into Porth Cothan, or, if the preventative men were on the watch, into Porth Mear, which is hidden by the Island of Trescore, drawn like a screen in front. They then rolled the kegs, or carried 'em, to the mouth of the Vouggha or to Trevemedar, it did not matter which, and they rolled 'em into the big cave, and then stopped the mouth up. They could go and get a keg whenever they liked by the little passage that has its mouth in the garden.'

'Did the preventative men never find out this place?'

'Never, sir, never. How could they? Who'd be that wicked to tell them? And they wasn't clever enough to find it themselves. Besides, it would take a deal of cleverness to find the mouth of the Vouggha when closed with clats of turf and drawn over with brambles; and that in the garden could be covered in five minutes – easy.' After a pause the old woman said, 'Ah! it's a pity I be so old and feeble, or I could show you another as I knows of, and, I reckon, no one else. But my father he had the secret. Oh, dear! oh, dear! what is the world coming to – for education and all kinds o' wickedness? Sure, there's no smuggling now, and poor folks ha'n't got the means o' bettering themselves like proper Christians.

Taken from *A Book Of The West*, by S. Baring-Gould, 1899

Back on the beach, in winter the rocks and pools here and at nearby Porth Mear are great for mussel picking. The whole area is also rich in biodiversity with two prominent SSSI areas at Park Head and Trevose Head.

Away from the high cliffs and sandy bays, the inland landscape pattern comprises mainly medium-sized fields of mediaeval enclosure, supporting a mix of arable land and pasture. Much of the farmland here has benefited from agri-environment schemes supported and, in some cases, part funded by the Cornwall AONB Partnership. These are voluntary schemes – highlighting the fact that many farmers are taking steps to actively conserve the landscape of their own volition. These schemes have led to a range of improvements in the landscape including reversion of arable areas to grassland, retention of grass margins, the encouragement of farmland birds such as the corn bunting, coastal grazing and provision of open and disabled access – the latter allowing some circular trails from the Coast Path. The challenge is how to maintain these improvements in the long term. Demands on the money available for agri-environment schemes are

▲ Food for free

Debbie Ashton

many and Natural England and Defra have the unenviable task of determining priorities for the schemes. There is a real concern that many of the improvements to the landscape of this area, and many others in Cornwall, that have been brought about over the last ten years will be lost if the grant schemes are not continued. Yet money, as we know, is very tight and environment improvement schemes are often sacrificed to short term expediency. We shall see.

The Cornwall Wildlife Trust Nature Reserve, Downhill Meadow at Downhill, lies just outside the AONB boundary. This AONB section ends at the National Trust haven of Carnewas, above the world famous Bedruthan Steps. Bedruthan became a popular destination when

Dave Matthews

▲ Bedruthan at high tide

Newquay developed as a holiday resort a hundred or so years ago. And the 'legend' of the giant Bedruthan and his stepping stones probably dates from this time.

The cliffs here are slumping into the sea and even the famous cliff steps are often closed. The footpath too is constantly having to be re-routed due to landslips. A type of netting, used to secure broken rock on motorway embankments, has secured some of the cliff face, fixed by rock bolts. If the possibility of landslides were not enough, when you traipse down the steep steps to the rocky beaches exposed at low tide, you will pass signs warning visitors not to risk swimming in these waters due to heavy rips, fast tides and submerged rocks.

Whether the name refers to the steps, the rocky 'stepping stone' stacks or the whole area has long been debated. J.R.A. Hockin, in his book *Walking in Cornwall* written in 1936, wrote: 'There is no general agreement as to what Bedruthan Steps actually are, whether the name refers to the great stacks of detached cliff – the giant's stepping stones – or to the older and damper of the two rock stairways down to the beach.'

Bedruthan Steps looks pretty special from the coast path. But In order to fully appreciate the beauty and importance of the protected landscape, it is necessary to leave it. Less than a mile to the south, the coast looks very different. The five or so miles on to Newquay are a random mess of holiday bungalows, guest houses, surf shacks, gift shops, pubs, chippies and even quite large hotels and timeshare blocks. A couple of the hotels are not unattractive (for modern buildings) and of course once you are inside you have an unrivalled view of a lovely seascape but, while the sea is as beautiful as ever, the landscape reminds one of the eyesores on the Costa del Sol. If ever there was any doubt as to the importance of designating and protecting much of Cornwall's coastline, then take a boat out from Newquay to the north and contrast the built-up and the unspoilt coast!

Newquay itself is Cornwall's premier tourist town. Full of clubs, pubs, cafés, bars and surfers and with good beaches, it is brash, lively, full of young people, colourful, noisy and not one of our naturally beautiful places. Fun, yes, beautiful, no.

St Agnes

It's a cold, blowy Boxing Day with the wet sand glinting in the wintry sun. Trevaunance Cove hosts happy children, splashing in their wellies in the rock pools. Dogs rush madly through the shallow surf and up the beach. A kite flies overhead. We breathe the clean air, take a final look at the lowering cliffs and sea cave, send a silent message of sympathy to the mad winter surfers paddling furiously away in the waves, and head for the pub, for local ale, fish and chips and a roaring fire. Not everything that is beautiful in Cornwall is outside.

St Agnes is the smallest section of the AONB at just 6.3 square kilometres, yet it contains a wealth of interest. It runs from the southern edge of Perranporth to the northern tip of Porthtowan and inland to include St Agnes Beacon.

The Beacon, *Bryanick* in Cornish, meaning 'pointed hill', is part of the chain that carried the news of the approaching Spanish Armada in 1588. From the top, at 192 metres (629 feet), the views take in St Ives to the south, Trevose Head near Padstow to the north and the white peaks of the china clay district near St Austell inland. On a clear day you can see for the best part of thirty miles and, it is said, make out thirty-two different church towers.

There are Bronze Age barrows at the summit and the remains of the long (nearly two-mile) Bolster Bank earthwork is evidence of early Iron Age settlement. Bolster, according to Cornish legend, was a giant, the second most famous after Cormoran of St Michael's Mount fame and one of the largest (he could step from St Agnes Beacon to Carn Brae hill – over two leagues away as the chough flies). He treated his wife cruelly, making her carry boulders up the Beacon (many fell and can still be seen lying around) so that he could indulge his second favourite pastime of chucking stones at other

Dave Matthews

▲ Looking up to The Beacon

giants across Cornwall. His favourite one was eating local villagers. Naturally his wife became bent from all this labour and he cast around for another wife, his eyes eventually falling on the beautiful, chaste village girl Agnes. She agreed to marry him on the condition that he completed a number of tasks, which he agreed to and undertook successfully. At some point he also seems to have defeated a local knight, Sir Constantine. The final task Agnes set Bolster was for him to prove his love by filling a hole near the cliffs above Chapel Porth with his own blood. He cut his wrist and waited for the hole to fill. But Agnes had found a hole with an outlet on the cliffs and eventually Bolster bled to death. The red stain on the cliffs can still be seen.

Agnes was canonized for her deeds (coincidentally there is a Roman martyr of the same name) and is now the patron saint of teenage girls. Let's hope they don't follow her example every time they meet some gullible bloke.

Geologically the Beacon is a metamorphic batholith (a large blob or dome of intrusive or plutonic igneous rock that forms from cooled magma deep in the Earth's crust) with rich mineral veins below. Try saying 'batholith' to someone and then try to convince them that you haven't got a lisp. Much of the rest of this section of the AONB is geologically made up of underlying slate *killas* (a Cornish mining term for metamorphic rock strata of sedimentary origin which were altered by heat from the intruded granites) that form an undulating plateau about 91 metres (300 feet) above sea level.

This is cut through by short streams flowing to the north coast along with outcrops of ragged, greyish cliffs that slant backwards from the sea.

Industrial heritage

Perhaps more than any other part of the AONB, save some of West Penwith, the landscape of the St Agnes section has been shaped by its recent industrial past. It is impossible to walk down to Trevaunance or Chapel Porth without treading amongst the ruins of mines and the ghosts of miners.

Although now a rural tourist idyll, the St Agnes area was perhaps the densest industrial area in Cornwall during the late eighteenth and nineteenth centuries. It once produced the highest quality tin in the world, and copper, lead and iron were also mined. Many ruined engine houses can be seen along the cliffs and the valleys are full of shafts and adits. St Agnes forms part of the Cornwall Mining World Heritage site and parts of

▲ Wheal Coates mine

Dave Matthews

Neil Keen

historic interest include the converted Wheal Kitty and the preserved Wheal Coates mining areas.

At Blue Hills, in nearby Trevellas Coombe, tin is still streamed as it has been in the valley for centuries. Shallow pits around the Beacon supplied candle clay for miners and fine sand was quarried for use by plasterers. The area was once nicknamed 'The Badlands' for the Wild-West feeling that the mining industry encompassed here and the general lawlessness that prevailed 200 years ago.

A report from the local council – the Cornwall Industrial Settlements Initiative – prepared as part of the Cornish Mining World Heritage site bid, has the following to say:

To the west the skyline is dominated by St Agnes Beacon, a granite intrusion that is highly visible for many miles around; it forms an effective barrier to the hinterland of St Agnes in this direction. Closer to the village, to the north and north-west are the former mining landscapes of Polberro, Bal, Wheal Coates etc., and to the east those of Blue Hills and Wheal Kitty; here low heather and gorse scrubland predominate amongst the scattered cottages, small-holdings and rock-strewn mine remains. Beyond Blue Hills lies the dramatic scenery of Trevellas Coombe and the grassy plateau that forms the Trevellas airfield and grazing land. To the south, the land is a maze of small fields and scattered mining remains.

The topography of the St Agnes area meant exploitation of mineral resources was relatively easy: the mineralized zone was cut through with deep valleys and sea cliffs, often exposing seams. The granite mass of St Agnes Beacon is equally exposed but on all sides. The valley streams were an early source of tin ore themselves and later provided power for processing. There were few settled areas; the surrounding land was mostly unenclosed

▲ Miners' small-holdings near St Agnes

Cornwall Council Historic Environment Department

85

moorland and rough ground so there were few restraints on surface working – not that a mediaeval farmstead or two would have stopped a mine being sunk anyway.

Worked probably from prehistoric times and through the medieval period, the St Agnes area remained a copper and tin producer until the early twentieth century. There was stream-working in the local valleys, especially in Trevaunance which began to be deep mined in the eighteenth century. There were three other principal tin grounds. The oldest were on the north and east slopes of St Agnes Beacon, at Bal and Polberro. These were already well established by the beginning of the sixteenth century when Leland travelled through Cornwall. The second major area was to the east of St Agnes (Goonlaze Downs, later the Wheal Kitty and Blue Hills group); this is known to have been active by the seventeenth century. The third area, containing the lodes to the south of Churchtown (Polbreen, Rosemundy and later Wheal Harriet), were mostly eighteenth-century workings.

Scattered around these main areas were numerous small and relatively poor mines, lifting small amounts of tin, copper, lead and other minerals and worked intermittently throughout the eighteenth and nineteenth centuries. Copper mining was concentrated in a circle around St Agnes itself, whereas tin extraction was mostly at some distance from the village – around Chapel Porth and Porthtowan to the west and south and Perranporth to the east. Tin mines are recorded in these areas from the seventeenth century, but by the mid-eighteenth century they had switched mainly to copper, become major producers and were amongst the first mines in the area to use steam power (from the late eighteenth century onwards).

The St Agnes tin mines and, from the mid-eighteenth century, copper mines, were amongst the most prolific in Cornwall in the seventeenth, eighteenth and early nineteenth centuries. They were numerous and, for the most part, small – an advertisement in an 1817 *West Briton* lists over a hundred tin mining 'bounds' in and around St Agnes. However, Polberro was an exception – by 1750 it was one of the largest and richest tin mines in

Dave Matthews

the county – so much tin was produced in that year that there weren't enough pack horses locally to transport it, and the first recorded use in Cornwall of wagons to transport ore was at Polberro. The quality of the tin was of the highest order – *'Stean San Agnes an gueall stean in Kernow'* or 'St Agnes tin is the finest tin in Cornwall' was a traditional local saying.

In 1785, Rudolf Raspe discovered stannite, also known as bell metal ore, in one of the old mines, which was to become West Kitty – this became very important for specimen collectors.

Rudolf Erich Raspe, who wrote *Baron Munchausen,* was a German writer, philosopher and scientist with a particular interest in tungsten. From 1782 to 1788 he was employed by Matthew Boulton as assay-master in the Dolcoath mine (near Carn Brae, it was Cornwall's deepest mine). The Trewhiddle Ingot, found in 2003, is a 150-year-old lump of tungsten found at Trewhiddle Farm near Pentewan (see Chapter 10). It may predate the earliest known smelting of the metal (which needs extremely high temperatures) and it's been suggested that it was found during a visit by Raspe to Happy Union mine nearby.

The earliest known use of gunpowder for mining in Cornwall around 1670 was in the St Agnes area though steam power came later than to many Cornish mines as the relative shallowness of the lodes meant that it was not needed to begin with. Both of these improvements probably owed much to the initiative and investment of the Tonkin family of Trevaunance, who also tried repeatedly to build and develop the harbour and settlement at St Agnes.

The old pattern of small scattered mines did not survive the economic slump following the end of the Napoleonic Wars, which saw falling tin prices and mass unemployment. The first great exodus of Cornish miners began during this period. Revival came in the second decade of the nineteenth century with a renewed phase of huge capital investment and the consolidation of many of the small sites into about fifteen large ones, such as Consolidated Tin Mines, formed in 1815 from four others and made possible by a Boulton & Watt steam engine which carried out the pumping work. This was later to become the great complex of Blue Hills.

The peak period of development came in the 1830s, with many of the principal local mines coming into full production (Wheal Coates, 1815; West Kitty, 1834; Wheal Luna, an open cast mine, which was operating adjacent to the harbour, 1838). In 1837 Royal Polberro entered into its main period, which was to continue until 1895, employing 450 people in 1838. During this time it sold an average of 30 tons of tin a month and the sheer physical scale of the operation is described by the *West Briton* in 1843: 'A surface of upwards of 200 acres, and 24 shafts, 9 of which are now in full working, with 3,000 fathoms of levels'.

After the 1870s crash in tin prices, there was a gradual decline in the scale and output of the mines. In 1896 H. Thomas in his *Cornish Mining Interviews* said: 'I can remember about 14 or 15 mines at work. But after tin fell seriously in 1874 the number began to diminish. Now the only mines at work are West Kitty, Wheal Kitty, Polberro and Blue Hills. Wheal Friendly cannot battle

▲ Engine house near St Agnes

Dave Matthews

with hard times any longer and is about to be wound up…..'

By the 1920s, only Wheal Kitty, West Kitty, Polberro and Wheal Friendly (which was on its last legs) had survived, because they were run as a single concern, with re-investment in 1926 on a new shared dressing floor (where the tin ore and waste rock were separated). The mines have all been closed since the 1930s, despite some small-scale tin streaming, exploratory and speculative works up to the 1950s and, of course, the very small scale streaming at Blue Hills, which comprises all that remains of this once phenomenal industry.

The land around here has changed constantly. Some 2 million years ago the Beacon was an island. Yet 7,000 years ago, Mesolithic hunter-gathers would have looked out from the Beacon or high cliffs over a very different scene. They would have been surrounded by oak forest with the sea many miles away to the west. The remains of this submerged forest are sometimes exposed at low tide just a little further along the coast at Portreath. Flint arrowheads and prehistoric tools are still sometimes found in the heather and gorse on the Beacon.

Below the mine-strewn cliffs lie several large sandy beaches. Trevaunance Cove has good swimming and surfing and excellent fishing at Trevaunance Point around high tide. Just inland from the cove is the seventeenth-century Driftwood Spars inn, with many of its timbers reclaimed from shipwrecks. All the way up the tranquil valley are the remains of mining activity. Today you may hear the cry of seagulls and the shouts of children on the beach; 150 years ago the valley would have echoed to the sound of beam engines, pumps and winches.

Further west is the beautiful beach at Chapel Porth, with its expanse of sand and strange sea caves. It is popular with surfers but needs a permanent lifeguard presence as it can be treacherous, especially at low tide when the sea comes in astonishingly rapidly. A favourite sport of some locals is to watch tourists amble back from the outlying parts of the beach and then increase their pace, sometimes desperately, as the tide sweeps in.

From the National Trust car park you may take the coast path west along the cliffs then cut inland through a quiet landscape that has, like all this area, been shaped by industry. Don't go off the tracks; there are shafts and adits galore amongst the gorse and brambles. Some of the land (as on the eastern side of the valley around

Bob Mitchell

Wheal Coates) is almost bare of vegetation; this is usually because arsenic was dug out here. The local wildlife doesn't seem to mind, however, and these are great places to see lizards and sometimes adders sunning themselves in summer. At the top of the valley there is a great view down Chapel Coombe to the beach and sea.

Within the AONB a number of old mining tracks and roads connect hamlets and villages. The Beacon itself is open-access land with few trees. Much of it (and the cliffs nearer the coast) is heather-clad heathland, with the heather seemingly enjoying the poor, mine-waste-polluted soil. The surrounding land shows field enclosures of former miner's smallholdings. The villages that once housed mining families are mostly of traditional granite with a smattering of modern white bungalows.

There are a few non-mining ruins on the Beacon. The trig point at the top stands on stones that were once part of a white painted tower, variously known as St Ann's Summer House or the Pleasure House. It is interesting to find that vandalism in rural areas is not a modern phenomenon. In 1812, after an incident at the Pleasure House, the *West Briton* printed a request for information (with a ten guinea reward) on 'persons who broke and carried off the window frames and broke floors and doors'. There was a radar station on the Beacon during World War II but hardly a trace now remains.

The coast path from Porthtowan runs past Chapel Porth and Wheal Coates mine (with evidence that this area was worked back in mediaeval times) and on to St Agnes Head. Inland here the fields and heath were covered with buildings as recently as sixty-five years ago – this was the site of an American army base during the war. The path runs down to Trevaunance Cove, where centuries of history are observable, especially to the trained eye. I was taken there recently by a landscape architect who pointed out many features that the casual observer might pass over. For example, the jumble of stones on the beach takes on the outline of an old jetty and the holes in the cliffs are not random but once held wooden hoists and cranes. You can see where steps were once and where darker patches of rock show evidence of blasting.

There are not many harbours along the north Cornish coast compared with the south and the history of St Agnes harbour at Trevaunance Cove explains why. The Tonkins attempted to build a harbour from 1632 onward, finally succeeding in 1710 but almost bankrupting themselves in the process. It was washed away just twenty years later! A boom in copper and tin half a century later meant a new harbour was constructed in 1798. Copper ore was exported to the new industries in South Wales and in return coal from South Wales was brought in for the smelters at the mines. In 1802, a pilchard fishing industry was established from the harbour, reaching its peak in 1829 before declining. The harbour itself was affected by the coming of the railways and not kept in good repair. It was finally destroyed in the storms of the winter of 1915 although parts of it can still be seen. Enormous blocks of stone which were once part of the harbour wall are strewn around and even now regularly move or even disappear – a testament to the power of the sea. Recently restoration work on the slipway and the jubilee gardens above has greatly improved the character of the cove.

The coast path then runs on past more mine workings and the Trevellas airfield to Cligga Head then on to Perranporth. Trevellas was first used as an airfield in 1924, when a surplus World War I training biplane, called an Avro 504k, piloted by Captain J.V. Holmes, used to take local residents and visitors up for 'aerial joyriding'.

In World War II, convoys in the English Channel found themselves under regular attack from the Luftwaffe. German aircraft taking off from occupied France also had plenty of range to reach the UK's coasts, and by early 1941 were bombing ports and factories including those in Exeter, Falmouth, Plymouth and Bristol.

Between 1941 and 1942 a dozen Spitfires (complete with long-range fuel tanks) from 66 Squadron were rushed to Trevellas. The pilots and crews were at first living and eating in tents which frequently blew down in the Atlantic gales. From 1942 onwards, Spitfires from Perranporth were also used in bomber support missions, protecting British and American bombers from German fighters. At the height of the war, the airfield was home to Spitfire squadrons (and wings) from Australia, Canada,

Poland, France and Czechoslovakia as well as the English squadrons.

The airfield is now, as it was in 1924, a private flying club. You can do a parachute jump there and if you ever want the most spectacular view of Cornwall, try the one from a couple of thousand feet – you can see all the way from the Tamar to the Scillies.

Not far away, just beyond the AONB boundary, lies Trevellas Manor, once home to the Donnithorne family who owned nearby Polberra, which, as mentioned previously, was one of the richest mines in Cornwall, producing profits of £100 a day and employing hundreds of workers in the eighteenth century. The most well-known member of the family is the Rev. Isaac Donnithorne whose portrait by Thomas Gainsborough hangs in Falmouth Art Gallery in its original frame chosen by the artist and recently restored after 200 years.

Isaac's father, Nicholas Donnithorne, was High Sheriff of Cornwall in 1731 and was married to Johanna Prideaux so there is a connection with Prideaux Place

(see Chapter 3). The family lived at Trevellas Manor near St Agnes and it is likely that this painting was commissioned to hang there.

The large portrait was one of Gainsborough's most expensive commissions. Donnithorne was ordained as an Anglican priest in 1735, but in 1762 he inherited from his brother Joseph the Donnithorne family interests in the county. It is likely the painting by Gainsborough was part of the gestation of an artist almost as famous. John Opie, the 'Cornish Wonder' was born nearby, the son of a mine carpenter. He may well have seen the Gainsborough painting andeven been inspired by it.

Opie's first recorded sketch was made at the age of ten and his work eventually came to the attention of local physician and satirist, Dr John Wolcot (aka the poet Peter Pindar), who visited the teenager and became Opie's mentor, buying him out of his apprenticeship and eventually taking him to Truro and then London. Wolcot introduced the 'Cornish Wonder' to other artists, including Sir Joshua Reynolds. George III purchased one

▲ The Gainsborough painting that may have inspired John Opie

▲ Underwater at Bawden Rock, Trevaunance Cove

of his pictures. He became a full member of the Royal Academy in 1788.

Opie is perhaps the most notable Cornish painter ever. He painted most of the great and the good of his day including Mary Wollstonecraft, Samuel Johnson, Charles James Fox, Edmund Burke, Robert Southey and Mary Shelley; over 500 portraits in all, most in oil, and 252 other pictures. He died in 1807, aged just forty-six and was buried in St Paul's next to Joshua Reynolds.

There is a Voluntary Marine Conservation Area between Trevaunance Cove and Trevellas, safeguarding life underwater and on the seashore.

Sea birds are prolific and there are often sightings of seals, dolphins and basking sharks nearby. Many of the coves are brilliant for collecting mussels (be careful of the tide) and inland, around the Beacon, there are a number of badger sets and a plethora of rabbits and other small mammals that may explain the birds of prey – especially buzzards – often to be seen wheeling in the sky above.

The other SAS

St Agnes is also home to the campaigning group Surfers Against Sewage (SAS) which was started, after a public meeting in 1990, by a group of surfers who were literally sick of surfing in the sewage-polluted waters of the local beaches including Trevaunance Cove and Chapel Porth. Over the next twenty-two years they were to influence policy and instigate clean-up campaigns around the UK. The fact that the waters around Cornwall are now almost all safe to swim and surf in nearly all of the time is largely due to the endless hard work of SAS and the pressure they put on South West Water. More recently they have turned their attention to the ever-worsening issue of litter on our beaches and shallow waters with clean-up and awareness-raising campaigns as well as longer term political projects. If there is one group that is more dedicated to preserving the natural beauty of Cornwall than any other, it is SAS.

Dave Matthews

Portreath to Godrevy

The ship's timbers are shrieking almost louder than the wind. The cold rain is horizontal in our faces, making it impossible to see clearly. We are bucking on the waves as if a crazed horse is trying to hurl us into the water. Salt spray. Wet canvas. Ropes running wild. And now, below the noise of the elements but clear to the terrified ear, the awful sawing sound of wood grating on rock. Out of the rain and mist, a huge figure emerges. Tall as a cliff, it is looming down over our stricken craft. Vast jaws open and all we can see is darkness and teeth, teeth, teeth.

The Cornwall AONB section that runs from just outside Portreath to Godrevy beach is a small narrow stretch of land that nevertheless offers a noticeable land-scape contrast. The coast itself is dramatic, not to say fearsome, with high cliffs and rocks that are a wrecker's dream (assuming wreckers ever existed, of course) and a sailor's nightmare. Just inland, however, the country turns from heath to farmland and then quiet wooded valleys.

Portreath is not a pretty village. The beach is good and popular with surfers but the place itself is a jumble of holiday flats and scattered bungalows. Fortunately the AONB starts just to the west of the settlement area, so things improve quickly. The path west from Portreath winds up and down past the evocative Deadman's Cove, Hell's Mouth and the collapsed sea cave known as Ralph's Cupboard. Legend has it that this was once home to the giant Wrath, probably an imaginative corruption of Ralph, who would lie in wait for passing ships, especially on stormy nights, wade out and attack them for their treasure and then eat the crew.

The cliffs along the coast, many slumping seawards, are of unstable, soft slates, treacherous in wet weather and especially when the ubiquitous sea mist rolls in. There was a massive cliff fall in 2011 when one of the headlands at Hell's Mouth collapsed into the sea. By complete chance someone was taking a video at the time and the resulting pictures were on all the national news programmes and, of course, a YouTube sensation. Fortunately, the fall was in a National Trust section of the coastline. The Trust spends around £3,000 every year looking after each mile of coast and carries out regular inspections of the sections of coast path it manages, taking action where necessary to divert the footpath inland away from high risk areas. At Hell's Mouth, the local ranger had moved the footpath inland and erected warning signs a week before the cliff collapsed.

Most of this stretch of coast is known locally as the North Cliffs and from the open area of grass and

Dave Matthews

heath-land there are spectacular views inland to Camborne and Carn Brea Hill with its granite monument, prehistoric stone cairns and strange folly of a castle.

Carn Brae is not in the AONB but has a long and fascinating history and rugged beauty. Geologically it is a granite mass connected to the Bodmin Moor granite at some depth, as has been proved by deep lode mining in the area. It dominates the country around, as it has for millennia, towering over its younger cousin Carn Marth and its twin, Carnmanellis. The largest quantity of tin and copper in Europe lay in the vicinity (and to some extent still does). The 'great flat lode' lies on its southern flank and the last mine to close in Cornwall, South Crofty (soon perhaps to reopen) lies just to the west.

Some of the earliest settlements in Cornwall have been found on this still-mysterious hill. Traces of a Neolithic people are to be found; historians believe they are relatives of the 'Windmill People', known to have migrated across from the continent and named after Windmill Hill near Avebury. Bronze Age remains have been found too and a series of stone walls date from the early Iron Age. Druids Way leads up the hill from the north. There was a hermitage on the top from the Middle Ages to the nineteenth century and, of course, the hill itself is a pin-cushion of mine chimneys. The castle on the eastern end of the ridge is a nineteenth-century folly, and the great granite Basset monument towers above everything. It is safe to say that Carn Brae has been occupied continuously for over 4,000 years.

Just inland from the cliffs, a narrow strip of heath-land, dotted with heather and wild flowers in summer, gives way to open arable fields. There are very few dwellings here, apart from some typical Cornish farmhouses, yet four miles south is Cornwall's most densely populated region. There are several footpaths inland, though, and it is possible to take a circular walk to the Red River and back to the coast. The Red River forms the southern boundary, running through a valley of deciduous and mixed woodland; much of it is a nature reserve.

The Red River itself, little wider than a stream in parts, rises on the granite batholith of Carnmanellis inland. It then meanders down, bisecting Pool and Camborne until it follows the valley westwards towards Hayle. The river's gradient is relatively steep; it falls 170 metres from its source on Carnmanellis to the sea at Godrevy. It gets its name from the mining waste, rich in iron oxide, that was washed into it over centuries, turning it a rusty red colour. When the mines finally closed, the water cleared but you can still see the orange ochre on the river bed.

The Red River Nature Reserve is a fine example of natural regeneration. Once one of Cornwall's most industrialized valleys during the mining period, the reserve is now a partially wooded valley, with areas of heath and some beautiful lakes and ponds along the way. Some great wildlife has been spotted on the reserve, including badgers, foxes, otters, woodpeckers and a whole array of butterflies and insects. Some of the plants are very special too. The reserve is still regenerating and lots of conservation work goes on to clear areas for habitat improvements and to create better access to previously hidden places. As I walked its length recently, on footpaths and bridleways, the air was thick with bird-song even in October.

▲ The Red River

Peter Maxted

One interesting question that I pondered while walking through the nature reserve by the river last year was: what constitutes 'natural' beauty? Here is the council's Historic Environment Service's comment on the river: 'As a result of past mining activities the river has undergone many modifications and for significant parts of its course the river has been diverted, canalized, and, in places, embanked. Very little, if any, of the river can be considered to be in a truly natural condition.' Yet it flows clear and beautiful through new 'natural' forest with an abundance of nature swimming in it, snuffling its banks and hovering over it. However manmade its course, I would still describe it, as so many Cornish industrial landmarks, as 'naturally beautiful'.

Although the river's colour and name are legacies of the mining era, its history stretches much further back as is shown in the names of the farms and small communities along the valley. Gwealavellan – from the Cornish *gweal an vellin* meaning open field by a mill, refers to a long vanished mill at Reskajeage, traced back to 1382. Menandarva, meaning the hillside of Derwa, refers to a legendary saint and the tale of 7 bishops and 770 religious men from Ireland, who, in 450 AD, came ashore in West Cornwall, were attacked by Chief Teudor and all killed in a single day. Roscroggan means the Heath of Shells. This may refer to bones from a long-past battle, maybe that of 450 AD, or sea-shells often found in the river bed nearby. Kehelland comes from the Cornish *kelly hellan,* meaning copse by an old enclosure or encampment. Roskear – camp by a ford – refers to an Iron Age fortified 'round' destroyed in the nineteenth century by mining activity. Finally, Carlean may come from *kel leghen*, meaning a religious cell made of slate, or from *kelli-en* or small woodland referring to the copse behind Hell's Mouth. Also, it may come from the Latin *legionum castra*, meaning 'camp of the legions' – though no legions are known to have penetrated this far.

Camborne

Once the richest town in Cornwall, Camborne now has a reputation for poverty and is the butt of many a joke. It reminds one of some of the depressed mining and mill towns of the north of England. There is high unemployment, poor prospects for young people, low house prices, vanished industry – and it always seems to rain.

Yet it was not always a bleak and dreary place. An inscribed altar stone now in the town church dates back to the tenth century and shows there was a settlement here then. Of course, the hill that towers to the south-east of the town, Carn Brae, has, as we have seen, an even longer history.

Camborne came to prominence and, for a time, to prosperity, during the great years of mining. The town is literally ringed with engine house chimneys. South Crofty to the east still has its gear – and may yet begin to work again, perhaps even quite soon. Dolcoath Mine in the nearby Tuckingmill Valley started to be mined for copper during the 1720s and became one of the leading Cornish copper producers before the end of the eighteenth century. Copper subsequently declined but around 1850, at a depth of 210 fathoms (1,260 feet), the

▲ East Pool mine near Camborne

Ainsley Cocks

mine reached the tin zone and the output of black tin rose steadily to over 2,000 tons a year. At one stage Dolcoath was Cornwall's deepest mine.

The mines were served by related industries, including the once world-renowned foundry of Holmans, which for many years was Cornwall's largest manufacturer of industrial equipment. During World War II it manufactured the infamous Sten sub-machine gun, and at its peak employed some 3,500 men. Today the skeletal, windowless walls of the old Holman's complex dominate the drive into the town.

Nearby Pool was, for over 180 years, home to the world-renowned Camborne School of Mines – it was for a while the only specialist hard rock education establishment in Britain, until the Royal School of Mines opened in 1851. CSM retains its name, which is still recognized as a badge of excellence around the globe, even though it has relocated and now forms part of the Combined Universities in Cornwall complex some fifteen miles south in Penryn.

TREVITHICK

By far Camborne's most famous son and one whose statue stands in the town centre outside the library is Richard Trevithick. Born just to the east in Pool, where a stone near the leisure centre commemorates him, he was the son of a miner and worked for a while down the mines himself. He began to study engineering and developed steam engines to rival Watt's. His most famous feat was the very first steam carriage on both road and rail (preceding Stevenson's Rocket). In 1801 he demonstrated a horseless carriage's ability to go uphill, resulting in one of the most famous of all Cornish songs, 'Going Up Camborne Hill, Coming Down'. Trevithick worked all over the world and died in Kent, but he remains one of Cornwall's most famous exports.

TEHIDY AND ONWARDS

North of Camborne, part of Tehidy Country Park lies in the AONB, with lakes, woodland walks and excellent bird-watching. There is a thriving wildlife community including butterflies, badgers, weasels, dragonflies, bats, foxes, shrews, otters, rabbits and (incredibly tame) squirrels. Bird life comprises numerous waterfowl, kingfishers and a range of woodland birds. If you go in the spring you will see ducks mating on the lake – not a pretty sight.

Tehidy is a 250 acre estate that was once owned by the Bassets, a hugely wealthy and influential mining family. They came to prominence in the early seventeenth century when Francis Basset, who married into the wealthy Godolphin family, was a prominent Royalist. He was Sheriff of Cornwall and for a while owned St Michael's Mount. A hundred years later, another prominent Basset, also named Francis, made a fortune from mining. Interestingly, he was educated at both Eton and Harrow and had a distinguished military career. He owned Dolcoath Mine among others and lived through the greatest and richest period of Cornish history. He is the Basset who is celebrated in the (extraordinarily ugly) monument on top of Carn Brae, which can be seen for many miles around.

Adrain Langdon

Dave Matthews

▲ The Basset Monument on Carn Brae

Wendy Allard

▲ Ducks on the lake in Tehidy Park

Tehidy Manor stood for 600 years until the 1850s when it was rebuilt to reflect the family's huge wealth and prestige. Then in 1917 the mansion and its 250 acres of land were bought (for the sum of £10,000) to be used as a hospital. It was badly damaged by fire a few years later but rebuilt in the same style. The estate was purchased by the County Council in 1983 and turned into a recreational country park for the local community to enjoy. The house and surrounding buildings have now been subdivided into a number of private homes. At both eastern and western entrances to the park stand large attractive thatched houses – a real rarity in this part of the world.

The woodland at Tehidy is composed of ash, alder, oak (there is a large oak wood), beech, sycamore, birch, conifers and chestnut interspersed with a number of lower growing shrubs including holly, hazel and many different varieties of rhododendron. Typical woodland plants such as bluebells (particularly in the North Cliff Plantation), wild garlic, primroses, daffodils and a range of native ferns can also be found.

There are a number of prehistoric remains on the site including an ancient earthwork. Magor Farm, with the remains of a Roman villa, the furthest west in Britain, is just outside the AONB boundary to the south-west of Tehidy. This Roman villa is the only one in Cornwall and until very recently (see Chapter 14) the only substantial Romano-British building found in the entire peninsula west of *Isca Dumnoniorum* (Exeter) almost

Dave Matthews

ninety (Roman) miles away. The Cornish word *magor* actually means ruined walls.

Back on the coast, the path from the northern gate into Tehidy takes you onto the coast path then west to the Knavocks, a rocky promontory, and then Godrevy Beach, which runs into Hayle Sands. The west-facing beach is reputed to be one of the best surfing beaches in Cornwall. Certainly the number of surfers to be found at any time of year attest to its popularity.

Guillemots, razorbills, fulmars and cormorants are among the many seabirds that nest on the cliffs around the headland. Winter is a particularly good time to see them and many others that are attracted to the estuary below.

Above the beach are the grass-covered dunes of Godrevy Towans, which support rare wild flowers. Further inland a dozen small pastures surround Godrevy farm and the remains of a manor house. The stone walled fields are evidence of a landscape character of mediaeval origin.

Out to sea, Godrevy Lighthouse, on the offshore island and above the treacherous Stones Reef, was built in 1859. The decision to build it was made when the SS *Nile* was wrecked in 1854 with the loss of all hands. In 1934 the lighthouse was made automatic and currently flashes every ten seconds with a range of twelve miles. The tower and nearby coast were the inspiration for Virginia Woolf's book *To the Lighthouse* – although the actual novel is set in Scotland.

While there are very few buildings or homes here, the coastal resorts of Hayle and Portreath flank the AONB and, inland, the conurbation of Camborne/Redruth is close by. This means that a greater number of visitors, both local and tourists, tend to flock to this area than to many others in Cornwall, putting considerable strain on the natural environment.

The headland at Godrevy is not necessarily going to be there for long. In 2005 the National Trust published research showing that nearly 300km of coastline in the south-west could be affected by erosion. A number of high-risk sites were identified, including Godrevy, Mullion Harbour and St Michael's Mount. At Godrevy the continued erosion of the cliff will eventually sever the road providing access to the headland, car park and farm.

From Godrevy you can look down onto the Hayle estuary and the ancient town of Hayle itself, the western gateway to this part of the AONB.

▲ The cliffs at Godrevy

Dave Matthews

Hayle

Like Bude, Hayle seems to be town with a confidence problem. The official web site reads: 'Find out what's going on around Hayle', and 'Have a look at the cool attractions close by'. Yet Hayle is possibly one of the earliest settlements in Cornwall, perhaps in the whole of mainland Britain. There is evidence that it was the northern point of a Neolithic trade route and there have been a number of Bronze Age and Roman finds in the area. It would certainly be logical for it to have been one of the earliest trading ports.

Two millennia ago the estuary reached inland as far as St Erth bridge. A port here would have traded goods from Ireland (then more advanced, economically and culturally, than mainland Britain) and Wales. Rather than take the treacherous sea route around Land's End,

merchants would put in at Hayle and transport their goods by land across the narrowest part of Cornwall – just six miles to Marazion. Here, from another relatively safe harbour below the Mount, they would take ship for Brittany and the Mediterranean shores beyond.

There is a strong likelihood that this trading route was used in Neolithic, Bronze Age, Iron Age and Roman times – in other words for the best part of 4,000 years. Goods also went the other way, of course – with wine and glass travelling back from the Mediterranean to the Celtic lands. Once the east–west route became more travelled, Hayle declined until the Industrial Revolution, when it once again became a pre-eminent trading post.

The beginnings of the renaissance were in the export of tin and copper ore and the import, from Wales, of coal. Tin smelting began nearby and the finished products

Peter Maxted

were exported from a new quay. Foundries followed, then beam engines, which were sent all over the world. The two main foundries were the Cornish Copper Company and John Harvey and Sons. In 1840 Harvey's built the largest engine in the world. It was shipped to Holland to help in a draining operation behind the famous dykes.

The railway came to Hayle as early as 1837 carrying both passengers and goods but the later nineteenth century was a period of relative decline, interrupted in the early twentieth century by the development of the nearby gunpowder works, which were at their busiest during World War I.

Black's Guide in the 1870s was not wildly complimentary: 'A dirtier, squalider, less interesting town than Hayle is not to be found in all Cornwal.' But today the town is reinventing itself as an industrial heritage centre. A sign states: 'Hayle – Birthplace of the Industrial Revolution', a claim that may just be disputed in South Wales, Manchester and elsewhere but is certainly attempting to put Hayle on the map.

Much of the area around the river has been restored and there is a 'memorial' walk offering views over Copperhouse Pool. The black bridge at the far end of Copperhouse Pool has different sized arches. Apparently one arch had been built when a certain Parson Hocking of Phillack complained that it was too low, citing an ancient law which entitled him right of passage to row under the bridge. The second arch was then built large enough to let his rowing boat pass. The area is a site of special scientific Interest (SSSI) and Copperhouse Pool is also an RSPB Nature Reserve.

Dave Matthews

West Penwith

I was patrolling the boundary, rather hoping that the ball wouldn't come flying my way accompanied by (highly optimistic) shouts of 'Catch it, Pete,' and spoil my contemplation of the view. For I was at the little cricket ground belonging to the Nancledra Hillbillies, representing the mighty Seaview Old Boys of Falmouth. The Hillbillies' ground is high up on the West Penwith peninsula with a spectacular vista of pale green hills topped with granite mines and cairns, and with the blue Atlantic glittering in the distance. The day was sunny but to the south-west a great bank of silvery-grey sea mist was approaching. The weather changes quickly at the very tip of Britain.

Many of the Cornish call this area 'Far Penwith', especially and unsurprisingly those from the Tamar Valley.

Carew concluded his mammoth *Survey of Cornwall* here in 1602 and wrote: 'My laste laboure for closing up this wearisome survey is bonded with Penwith hundred.' (A hundred is Saxon measurement of land retained by the Normans and throughout the Middle Ages. It is composed of a hundred 'hides', a hide being the amount of land needed to support a peasant family).

This sizeable section of the AONB runs from the western edge of St Ives on the north coast right round to Mousehole near Penzance in the south, and includes the coast, the high uplands, heaths, moors and villages such as Sennen and Zennor, as well as the small granite town of St Just.

Penwith is named after one of the ancient administrative hundreds of Cornwall and derives from two

Philip White

100

Cornish words, *penn* meaning 'headland' and *wydh* meaning 'at the end'.

Farming the uplands

The upland areas of Cornwall, notably West Penwith and Bodmin Moor, were heavily forested in the two or three thousand years after the Great Thaw at the end of the Ice Age. Perhaps the very tops were still clear – the tors where we can see the great granite outcrops today – but even they were probably mostly scrub-covered at least. The earliest hunters probably used fire to clear some of the forest, forcing deer and other animals out into the open where they would be caught more easily.

As, over the millennia, the hunters turned to farmers, they cleared larger areas of forest to create grazing for cattle, sheep and goats, giving us largely open landscapes of grass and heath – so the upland landscape we are looking at, minus the power lines and mine chimneys, might be very similar to that observed by Stone Age man.

The first stone monuments were built during this period, including the chambered structures we know as 'quoits' such as Zennor Quoit, Lanyon Quoit (between Madron and the coast) and Chûn Quoit above Pendeen.

Originally what we see today would have been underground with only the mighty capstone visible but as the soil has been washed away or removed for crops so the great skeletons' tombs have been revealed. During the Bronze and Iron Ages standing stones, stone circles, barrows and cairns all followed. According to Cornwall's Historic Environment Service, 'It is clear from the siting of these monuments that their builders gave importance to views to, from and between them, and to features of the natural landscape such as hills and rocky outcrops. This is a clue to the openness of the landscapes in which they were built.'

More land was enclosed as settlements grew and crops such as grain became important. Livestock was wintered in the valleys and let out onto the uplands for rough grazing in summer. This practice continued until at least the later mediaeval period and the pattern of mixed farming, with cultivation and enclosed pasture in fields near settlements, and fine-weather grazing on the heaths and moors, continued with relatively little change. Mediaeval farmers used strip farming and had common land for summer grazing and fuel. Even in the nineteenth century, with the landscape utterly transformed by

▲ Lanyon Quoit

Peter Maxted

industrial mining, farming was relatively unchanged. Bronze Age farmers would have recognized and understood the methods of a Victorian farmer 3,000 years later and vice versa.

For several reasons this type of farming declined from the mid-1800s onwards. The railways brought larger quantities of cheap coal so the moors were no longer regularly cleared of grass and bracken for fuel. Grazing on rough ground declined as dairy cattle were introduced – they need richer lowland pasture. The slopes of the moors became overgrown and in many parts of West Penwith only a small coastal strip is still farmed. One farmer told me, 'Our job is to stop the tops reaching the cliffs,' by which he meant that they were a buffer zone between coast and the rapid takeover of the high ground, particularly by gorse and bracken.

Between the uplands and the coast is a patchwork of small, stone-hedged fields, many prehistoric in origin and managed from ancient granite farmsteads. Farming here is mainly arable with some pasture and small herds of livestock. Much of the distinctive pattern of enclosure around farmsteads has existed almost unaltered for at least 2,000 years and in some cases back to Neolithic times.

In the twentieth century, mining and other industries faded. As a result, the downs and moors, which had been the focus of human activity for so long, became near-deserted. Without grazing or fuel gathering many areas have become densely overgrown, especially since World War II.

The Historic Environment team work hard to keep the landscape well managed: 'To maintain and enhance its unique historic, wildlife and scenic value, heath-land needs to be actively managed; in particular scrub and bracken need to be controlled. These can be cut by hand or machinery over small areas and small controlled fires can also be used. The best solution for long-term care, however, is to restore the low-intensity livestock grazing which for so long was the major use of these areas.'

As mentioned in the introduction, and in spite of some Council assistance, the Cornish uplands face the loss of grazing animals and therefore a dramatic change to the landscape. If the hill farmers are not supported in

some way they will decide that working their socks off, for around £10,000 a year if they are lucky, is simply not worth the effort. Then we will not only see the demise of a traditional way of life that dates back millennia but a change to the landscape we are used to. First bracken, then bramble and gorse and finally stunted hardy trees will cover the hills. The ancient monuments will disappear as will all but the tips of the rocky tors.

In Penwith, ESAs (Environmental Sensitive Area schemes) were introduced in 1993 to reward farmers for appropriate land management. Of the hill farmers surveyed in 2007, 80% were in an agri-environment scheme and keeping much of the upland areas managed but since then ESA has been phased out and support to hill farmers reduced.

The mining story

The north-west coastal section, particularly around St Just, was extensively mined for centuries and many mine buildings and shafts remain. If I close my eyes I can imagine what the landscape must have looked like 150 years ago. The Atlantic would have been the same pristine blue on sunny days but the land itself would have been dominated by smoke. Smoke from the mine engine house chimneys, smelters and foundries, smoke from the miners' cottages, smoke from the trains that carried the coal in and the ore and tin out. Grey-faced miners, blackened and coughing like the land itself, trudged to and from work or on Saturdays to and from the pub. The great antiquities, Men an Tol, Lanyon and Chûn Quoit, as well, no doubt, as many stone circles, lay under sooty gorse or bracken or, if exposed, were largely ignored as a statue or old house might be in a town. This was a working, industrial area. Grey would have been the predominate colour, green only in small valleys away from the lodes or on smallholdings and tiny farms. It would have been noisy too with the pounding of beam engines, the roar of black powder explosions, the clatter of trains, the whinnying of horses, the shouts of men.

Today the landscape is clean and quiet with the jumble of old mine buildings having no more (though no less) weight in landscape terms than the mediaeval farms or Neolithic stones. Where there once was a

Peter Maxted

▲ West of St Ives

cacophony of industrial noise, only the distant hum of light traffic, the song of birds and the sound of the ever-present wind punctuate the silence.

St Ives

The gateway to the protected landscape at the north-eastern edge is the little fishing port of St Ives. Well, I say little, it actually receives more visitors, year round, than any other place in Cornwall. It has also just been nominated as the favourite tourist destination in Britain for the umpteenth time. St Ives was a fishing port in at least the fifteenth and sixteenth centuries when, just as today, it had a problem with wind-blown sand, for Leland writes in 1538 that the houses and pier were: 'Sore oppressid and coverid with sandes that the stormey windes and rages castith up there'.

Like Looe in the opposite corner of the county, St Ives is best approached by train. The track follows the route which was once a broad gauge railway line – the last stretch ever made. It snakes along the estuary mouth skirting mud-flats teeming with bird life and arrives in the centre of this bustling port and art-lover's paradise.

The story of St Ives is intricately bound up with fish and art. Two centuries ago it was the most important fishing port on the north coast. Vast quantities of pilchards were caught annually – at one stage nearly a billion fish a year!

With such piscine wealth naturally came a price. *Black's Guide* from the late nineteenth century does not mince its words: 'The shops are mean and squalid and everywhere pervades an intolerable fishy smell.'

The aforementioned railway came in 1877, bringing many new visitors, and the Victorian and Edwardian houses and hotels that spill up the slopes were built to accommodate them. The lower reaches of the town remained as fishermen's cottages but gradually began to transform into artists' homes and then studios.

In the twenties the 'St Ives School' included the potter Bernard Leach, followed over the next couple of decades by painters Alfred Wallis and Ben Nicholson, sculptor Barbara Hepworth and many others. In 2010, a BBC4 film *The Art of Cornwall,* presented by James Fox, claimed that the St Ives artists' colony went on to produce some of the most exhilarating art of the twentieth century, 'And for a few dazzling years this place was as famous as Paris, as exciting as New York and infinitely more progressive than London.'

Today St Ives rests on its artistic celebrity, with the new(ish) Tate Modern gallery overlooking Porthmeor beach and more studios and shops than anywhere of comparable size in the world. Be warned though, it doesn't half get busy in the summer. Much the nicest time to visit is in spring or autumn and in September there is an excellent music festival.

> I gradually discovered the remarkable pagan landscape which lies between St. Ives, Penzance and Land's End; a landscape which still has a very deep effect on me, developing all my ideas about the relationship of the human figure in the landscape – sculpture in the landscape and the essential quality of light in the relationship.
>
> Barbara Hepworth, 1952

Trencrom

If Cornwall is the land of giants, Trencrom Hill is their legendary home. A single granite hill, not especially high by Penwith standards, but surmounted by jagged granite pillars and giant boulders, it seems to dominate its taller neighbours. This was the capital of the giants who ruled the region and were constantly at war with those of Carn Brae to the east and The Mount to the south.

In actuality Trencrom Hill is another Iron Age hill fort but one that is, for once, easy to make out. Ramparts and towers can be identified as can a gateway. It is a truly delightful; a place reached by a winding footpath through the heather and gorse (there is a holy well hidden in the undergrowth). The whole hill is owned by the National Trust.

Zennor

The beautiful old church of Zennor was built in the fifteenth century and has many interesting features, including Norman stones set in the wall. There are two old cross-heads, believed to be Saxon, over the vault in which Admiral Borlase is buried. But the feature that attracts most attention is the wooden figure of a mermaid carved on the end of a pew. She carries a comb and a glass and is about a metre in height. It seems that everyone who comes to look round the church is

Dave Matthews

▲ Porthminster Beach, St Ives

compelled to stroke her, and the wood is shining and worn by centuries of hands. Legends abound in this part of Cornwall, and the tale of the Zennor Mermaid is a famous one.

Fishing was the main occupation of the villagers in Zennor and after a good catch they would go up to the church to give thanks, led by a fine choir. In the choir there was a very good singer, a handsome young man called Matthew Trewella. His voice soared above the rest, and one day a mermaid rose from the waves to listen. She was enchanted by the singing and came up again and again. Finally, she slithered up to the church, wearing a long dress to cover her tail. (The legend does not say where she got the garment.)

Whenever Matthew sang she was there at the back of the church. Matthew saw her and fell in love. When the mermaid felt his eyes on her she became afraid and left

▲ The Zennor Mermaid

Peter Maxted

the church. But he pursued her and caught her as she tripped on a stone. Her dress tore and he saw her tail. He begged her to stay with him, but she said she could only live in the sea. 'Then I will live there with you,' he said. And he picked her up and carried her to the water. Neither was ever seen again.

Apart from the church there is a lovely old pub, a backpackers' hostel and an interesting little museum. A short walk takes you out to remote Zennor Head – it is particularly wild and remote in the winter months. According to local folklore, from Zennor Head you can sometimes hear the beautiful voice of Matthew Trewella, drifting back across the waves.

There wasn't much mining around Zennor; most of the mining activity took place on the coast further south. But there was some experimental mining on Trewey Hill and today a small group of ex-miners spend their free time excavating and restoring the old mine of Wheal Chance. You can only visit by invitation, as it is on private land with no footpaths, but I was lucky enough to be taken on a tour recently with the AONB team. The underground experience was both fascinating and salutary. The minerals seeping through and sitting in the granite are striking but there is an astonishing beauty too in the tunnels, the trucks, the beams and props, the tools and pumps – all the paraphernalia of mining past. The mine drips water constantly and a visit there is, I think, the closest you can get to the actual experience of working underground.

Tony, one of the leaders, showed us a bit of old hollow tree trunk during the trip. This was the all that remained of an ancient chain and rag pump, dating, perhaps, from as early as the sixteenth century. Rags and strips of leather were attached to a circular chain, which was then lowered into the water at the bottom of a shaft. When the rags reached the surface they were squeezed out. I can imagine something remarkably similar being used as an all-purpose pump in the very earliest times (this being the sort of technology I can understand!).

Altogether our trip down the mine was an extraordinary experience. It is the closest I and many others will ever get to understanding the conditions our Cornish miners worked in a century or two ago. Hard would

▲ The AONB team about to go underground

have been the work and proud the men who undertook it. I can see why.

On the other side of the valley there is a path marked 'to Zennor Quoit'. This leads to the largest antiquity in the area – indeed, it is the largest Stone Age burial chamber in the UK. Seven uprights are topped by a massive granite capstone. For something so large it's not easy to find, however. On my first visit, the signs ran out fairly quickly and then so did the path. Optimistically following animal tracks through the gorse and heather and climbing steadily, we eventually found ourselves on completely the wrong hill and looking down on a ruined farmhouse. The sky had gone a threatening dark grey and although we could see the Atlantic behind us, we were pretty well lost. A local man walking his dog (called *Sterran* – the Cornish for star) put us back on track. He also told us about the farm.

Aleister Crowley was a notorious researcher into the dark arts; some called him a sorcerer early in the twentieth century. He was named 'The Wickedest Man in the World' and 'A Monster of Depravity' (probably by the *Daily Mail*) – titles that simultaneously titillated and petrified the public. Towards the end of his life he spent some time in Cornwall.

The farm at Higher Tregerthen, near Zennor, had been occupied, in 1916, by D.H. Lawrence, Katherine Mansfield and John Middleton Murray, who tried to found an ideal community there called 'Rananim' – a kind of early kibbutz maybe or perhaps closer to a hippy commune. Crowley and Lawrence were acquaintances and he and Mansfield may have been more than that, but if Crowley was ever in Cornwall it was quite a while later.

There are, however, many rumours and tales of Crowley staying at the Carn (or Carne), another farm near Tregerthen. From the Ordinance Survey map of the area this is certainly the ruin that we saw. Tales in the area and elsewhere of murder and ritual sacrifice at the Zennor Quoit and nearby Trencrom abound, as do salacious stories of naked dancing at midsummer. No doubt if Crowley did stay here the locals would have had a field day and fact and fiction would have been intertwined dramatically. One thing I can tell you is that none of the three of us wanted to go down and explore the ruin.

Dave Matthews

▲ The rocky river valley at Zennor

Monuments and Mines

At Gurnard's Head and Bosigran on the coast, there is evidence of Iron Age cliff castles. Inland from here the high moor and heath is dotted with antiquities – quoits, carns and stone circles. You actually cannot walk far without stumbling on (or over) an ancient monument. Penwith contains the highest concentration of Iron Age archaeological remains in Europe including well-preserved hut circles and even villages, as well as a number of important hill forts.

John Borlase

▲ Gurnard's Head

Vegetation on the hills is mostly heather, gorse, rough grass and the ubiquitous bracken. One word of warning: the dense bracken and gorse often hide open mine shafts or adits. Many of these have still not been capped. Stick to the footpaths.

There are several nature reserves within the Penwith upland area. A mile west of Nancledra by footpath is the Baker's Pit Nature Reserve. This area of heath-land with some pasture, managed by local farmers, was once a china clay works and this has left its mark. Old buildings are returning to nature and the large flooded clay pit supports aquatic life. Wet willow woodland and scrub are also prominent. One important plant is western gorse, which flowers in late summer. It is a dense, spiny, ever-green shrub with characteristic yellow flowers and is generally smaller than the ubiquitous common gorse. The whitethroat is a regular summer visitor here. It lives in scrub and overgrown hedgerows but the colourful male may perch on an exposed bough, showing his white throat, blue-grey head marking and reddish-brown back and wings. Merlin, hen harrier and peregrine all visit this reserve too during the winter months.

About two miles inland from Pendeen is the Chûn Downs nature reserve. Cross-leaved heath is abundant here as are blooms from June until October. The delicate, rose-pink flowers are oval to urn-shaped and the grey-green leaves are held in whorls of four. This downy plant thrives in damp, boggy areas.

The focal point of the reserve is Chûn Castle, a prehistoric hill fort. Chûn is from the Cornish *chy-an-woone*, meaning 'the house on the downs'. Close by to the west are the remains of Chûn Quoit, an ancient burial chamber. This atmospheric monument consists of four huge upright slabs, topped by a massive capstone and it is the only example of its type that is still perfectly preserved.

Also inland from Pendeen, on the top road to Madron and Penzance, there is a smashing little walk that takes you to several ancient sites in the space of a couple of hours. Travelling inland from the coast, half a mile before Lanyon Farm there is a track to your left going north-east past a derelict farm and some mediaeval walled fields. Soon you see the sign on the right for Men an Tol ('stone of the hole'). The site consists of two standing stones and the central holed stone (big enough to crawl through, especially if you need to cure your rickets, scrofula or bad back or become particularly fertile). Around are the remains of other stones, suggesting that the Men an Tol was once at the centre of a late Neolithic or early Bronze Age stone circle.

In another hundred yards you see the Men Scryfa ('written stone') – not signposted – in a field on your left. Sometimes there are cattle in the field and the area round the stone can be muddy enough to prevent you reaching it. The Latin inscription translates as 'Rialobran, son of Cunoval', a local prince from around the late fifth century. The stone may mark his grave. The stone itself is almost certainly a menhir from a much earlier period.

Travelling on you reach the Nine Maidens (*Nomer Mis*) stone circle. There are currently eleven stones that have been recently restored, with some re-erected, although the original structure may have contained as many as twenty-two uprights. From the circle there are any number of tracks, through the gorse and heather, to the bulk of Ding Dong mine about 600 yards further on. The mines in this area are reported to be the oldest in the UK and of course tin was streamed on these moors in prehistoric times. Richard Trevithick worked as an engineer of the Ding Dong mine in 1796.

Once back on the road you come to Lanyon Quoit. It's quite easy to miss as the Cornish hedge behind which it lies is often overgrown. Originally the eighteen-

foot capstone sat on four pillars but in 1815 it collapsed in a storm (probably having been weakened by years of people digging for treasure). It is now on only three uprights and these have been shortened and squared off so it's much lower than before.

A mile further south again is the Bosvenning Common Nature Reserve which remained undisturbed for many years. From its carpet of lowland western heath and different species of wild heathers, one may look down-land towards Carn Brea in the east and Mounts Bay in the south.

Birds abound in West Penwith, gulls on the coast, curlews over the moors and, interestingly, still flocks of starlings at the edge of villages and towns. Once these were our most common bird but they are becoming increasingly rare in much of the country. It is a testament to the area's remoteness and lack of agri-business farming that the great black flocks can still be seen here.

Back on the coast, the path runs from Zennor to Gurnard's Head, site of yet another Iron Age fort; a sling-shot from around 200 AD has been found here. There is also a ruined coastguard hut abandoned rather more recently. The rocks are an interesting mix of slate, green-stone and, of course, granite. This is part of the Land's End granite, from a later period than that of Bodmin Moor and central Cornwall and comprising two distinct types, the Zennor lobe to the north and the St Buryan lobe to the south (the latter is a mere 3 million years younger).

Past Pendeen lighthouse, beaming out across the Atlantic four times every minute, we reach one of the great mining areas, comprising Levant, Botallack and Geevor. Levant was both a copper and tin mine (it is likely that copper was taken from exposed cliff seams back in the Bronze Age). The mine ran down then out far and deep under the sea – at the beginning of the twentieth century it was 1,500 feet below the sea bed.

Botallack, to the south, seems today almost a part of the cliffs themselves, the twin engine house chimneys being among the most photographed scenes in the county. Here too the mine stretched out under the sea.

Between Levant and Botallack lies Geevor tin mine, which closed as recently as 1986 – some of the miners

Peter Maxted

▲ The Men an Tol

Amy Lyle

▲ Botallack Mine

from that time still work there, for Geevor has been turned into a Cornish Mining World Heritage visitor attraction, telling the tale of Cornwall's tin and copper mining through the ages.

Now most of Cornwall's 'tourist attractions' are, I feel, necessary evils (I exclude Eden) – good for children, somewhere to go when it rains and often a bit tacky. But Geevor is a proper grown-up experience. Aside from the exhibits (of which 'the dry' almost brings one to tears) you can also experience underground conditions for yourself as you squeeze through Mexico shaft (not for the claustrophobic). *The Guardian* called Geevor 'Quite simply the most evocative industrial heritage site anywhere.' I agree.

St Just

The town of St Just is Britain's most westerly town and is a bit of a mixture, comprising clusters of old miners' cottages and newer art and craft galleries, some modern buildings (mostly quite sensitive) and a couple of cottage industries. It has a marvellous *plein an gwarry* (place of plays) where performances are often staged.

Wesley preached often in the area. You may say 'well, where didn't he?' but St Just seems to have had a special

resonance for him: 'Between eight and nine I preached at St Just on the green near the town to the largest congregation I was informed that had been seen in these parts. I cried out, with all the authority of love, "Why will ye die, oh house of Israel?" The people trembled and were still. I have not known such an hour before in Cornwall.'

From St Just it is an easy stroll out to Cape Cornwall. This is the point at which Atlantic currents split, either going south up the English Channel or north into the Bristol Channel and Irish Sea. Around Cape Cornwall (which the Cornish call the 'true' Land's End) there are more mining remains and on the cape itself the engine house chimney has a plaque to Heinz (yes, the baked bean people) who bought the cape in the 1980s and then gave it to the National Trust. Below the mining remains in a little walled field are the ruins of St Helen's Oratory – a Christian chapel dating from before the Norman Conquest.

Now the coast path takes you to the mouth of the Cot Valley, one of several deep coombes that cut through from the high hinterland to the coast. This was once thick with mining buildings; today it comprises a quiet narrow road and a gurgling stream. Higher up there is an ancient youth hostel perched on the hillside – it can be hired by groups in the wintertime and we've been to many a good party there.

The Cot Valley is glacial – not on a huge scale like the drowned rias further east but with one fascinating feature that I have seen nowhere else. There are strange glacier-formed round boulders on the beach washed pale by the tide – 'dinosaur eggs' our children called them. But look up and you will see where they come from. The stark vertical edge of the cliff has masses of round stones sticking out from it – these have been rolled down the valley by the melting glaciers and now stand frozen in time above the beach.

Not long ago the valley was choked from head to toe with one of Cornwall's most pernicious invasive plants. A successful Japanese knotweed eradication programme has recently taken place – removing this threat to landscape and other plants with considerable success, but at vast expense.

The walk to Sennen can take you along the coast and across sweeping Whitesand Bay or inland across Nanquidno Downs with many hut circles (but also quite a few shafts – keep to the footpaths). If you take the inland route you will skirt the little airfield from where you may take a flight to the Isles of Scilly. At Sennen there are several watering holes and a very pretty circular art gallery in the old lifeboat capstan house. Onwards to Land's End itself, the coastal path twists past the Irish Lady rock formation.

Land's End

Well, what can you say about this most iconic of places? What will you take away? The grandeur of the views? The vast sweep of the Atlantic as it carries your imagination across to the Americas? Or a sad ache at the way the nearest buildings have been turned into a tacky theme park?

Richard Carew in the 1602 *Survey of Cornwall* wrote:

'... you who have vouchsafed to travel in the rugged and wearysome path of mine ill-pleasing style, that now your journey endeth with the land; to whose promontory (by Pomp. Mela, called Bolerium: by Diodorus, Velerium: by Volaterane, Helenium: by the Cornish, Pedn an laaz: and by the English, The Lands [sic] End) because we are arrived, I will here sit me down and rest.'

It seems that Carew may have had access to some long disappeared texts or perhaps a fertile imagination. Bolerium and Velerium do not seem to have any direct translation, although the former is the name of an American bookstore and velerium is mined in the Dungeons and Dragons fantasy world. Helenium is a North American plant, a member of the aster family.

In 1870 a later visitor, one Francis Kilvert, recounts his experience of Land's End in 'A Cornish Diary':

Captain P took Miss Lewis and me down to the Land's End, a little triangle of rock reached by passing round to the seaward side of a tall upright shaft of cliff. The accomplishment of an old dream. The rocks at the Land's End are lower than the cliffs on either side and they eventually run out to sea below the triangular standing place in a low broken range of reef. But they are very strangely fantastically shaped and some of them are exactly like long, thin square baulks of timber reared up and leaning against each other. One thing wanting – a rougher sea. The sea was very calm but had the water been broken we should have missed its splendid colour. Under the captain's guidance I went down a long narrow winding passage in the rocks on the north side of the Land's End and kneeling on a flat piece of rock like a table which hangs over a horrible chasm by craning over the abyss I could look through the great cavern which perforates the cliff, and see the sea rushing through the cavern from the north to the south coast. It is said that a boat can sometimes pass through. Coming back we met a noisy rabble of tourists, male and female, rushing down the rocks towards the Land's End as if they meant to break their necks – and no great loss either.

Horse-drawn carriages took the first organized tourist excursions from Penzance in 1873. In 1981 the National Trust offered £1 million for Land's End, but lost out to a higher bidder – a reminder of the sums involved in coastal protection (that £1m would be worth ten times that today).

And here is a comment from a recent visitor (taken from TripAdvisor)

Whoever built this tat should be shot. I was sad and angry in equal measure to see the truly vile 'attractions' despoiling Land's End. Who on earth was responsible for this violation of such an iconic and magnificent natural site? If I'd walked from John o' Groats (unlikely ever to happen!) I'd have taken one look and turned straight round and walked right back. Make the effort to ignore, as best you can, the hideousness of what man has done to this place, and marvel at its natural beauty.

Early travellers, merchants and saints avoided Land's End if they could, as it was notorious for shipwrecks. In the last few centuries there have been some major ones. In 1797 the *Nereid* was wrecked in a fierce December storm, in 1809 the *William* and her cargo of rum sank in January and in 1884 the *Balbec* was lost. The Longships Lighthouse was built to protect shipping from this fate, although the *Bluejacket* foundered on the rocks on a clear night in 1898, nearly demolishing the lighthouse in the process.

The lighthouse stands on Carn Bras, the highest of the three rocks (the others are Tal-y-Maen and Meinek) on the site of the original light built in 1795. The present-day one dates from 1873 and since 1988 has been unmanned. Its light has a range of eleven nautical miles.

Two brothers, John and Robert Naylor, are reported as having undertaken the first recorded 'end-to-end' walk from John o' Groats to Land's End in 1871. Today, the most popular way to do it is by bicycle but be warned, the first stretch through Cornwall is by far the hardest, as you switchback the seemingly endless series of river valleys.

Out to sea on a clear day, the sharp-eyed can see the Isles of Scilly on the horizon. Under the sea, according to legend, lies the lost land of Lyonesse. Inland wild Cornish heath-land is festooned with vivid heather and populated, in warmer summers, with hundreds of butterflies.

The coastal route takes you down to Porthgwarra, also known as Sweethearts' Cove after two lovers who drowned there, and then Porthcurno. This is where the first transatlantic cables linked Britain with the Americas – an engineering feat celebrated in the Telegraph Museum housed in World War II bomb shelters and bunkers.

The village is perhaps even better known for the world-famous Minack Theatre. In 1932, Miss Rowena Cade and two gardeners, Billy Rawlings and Charlie Angove, began to carve out the amphitheatre from the cliffs. Today the theatre is a venue quite unlike anything else you will ever see. Productions run through the summer months – visitors and locals bring picnics and cushions and settle down to watch. Even during the most gripping plays you can sometimes be distracted by the backdrop of the ever-changing colours of the vast sea and sweeping sky.

A cliff-top stroll brings you to Treen and the Logan Rock. This is the most famous of many such 'loggin'

▲ Sunset at Land's End

▲ Porthgwarra

Jonathan Jenkin

▲ The Minack Theatre

Dave Matthews

▲ Treen and the Logan Rock

rocks – they are so finely balanced that you can move them a little, sometimes with no more than the push of a finger, even though they weigh many tons. The one here at Treen is said to have been raised up by a giant and legend had it that only a giant could take it down.

The nearby pub, also called Logan Rock, tells the tale of a naval officer, one Lieutenant Goldsmith in the early nineteenth century, who obviously took this tale as something of a challenge. He, with some of his men, tipped the Logan Rock from its perch. The hue and cry this aroused locally was such that Goldsmith was then forced by local pressure to reinstate it at his own expense – which the locals made sure was considerable! It is possible for the fairly able-bodied to climb to the Logan Rock and even up onto it. A friend and I did this a few years ago and sat triumphantly on top, using it a little like an enormous, albeit gentle, see-saw.

The beach at Treen is one of Cornwall's most delightful with an ever-shifting sand bar and a turquoise sea. Before you rush down there, however, there are two caveats. First there is a steep path and a tricky scramble down a rock face to reach the beach – anyone with vertigo will struggle. When you do get down, you'll find it is popular with nudists – mainly male and elderly, a sight which is not to everyone's taste.

There is a clearly identifiable Iron Age fort above the Logan Rock itself, and from there you may walk to picturesque Penberth Cove with its small fishing fleet and working capstan. A little up the road that runs down

to the cove, there are some impossibly pretty cottages and, at the gateway to a (private) manor house, the stream opens into a small pool. Here I saw my first wild otter a few years ago. A dark, sleek shape climbed the little weir, slid gracefully across the pool and slipped into the woodland beyond. Magical.

There is strenuous up-and-down section of coast path that then pushes on to the smuggling cove of Lamorna. The Lamorna Wink pub is supposed to represent the local landlords' attitude to the smuggling process.

Lamorna is now a popular spot for tourists and a small fishing cove (it is quite exposed and boats must to be dragged up the slipway during storms) but it was once a thriving industrial centre. Lamorna granite was quarried here and shipped all over the world. It was used to build the Thames Embankment and many other landmarks. Quarrying for the high quality granite began in 1849 and a stone quay was built in 1854. However, stormy seas often delayed the loading of the stone and threatened moored ships. This raised the price of Lamorna granite and sea transport was abandoned in favour of difficult but regular transport overland to Penzance and then on by train. The quarries ceased production in 1911.

Another steep valley runs down from the heathland above, wooded and warm with a plethora of wild flowers. Inland there is a network of country lanes linking farms and hamlets. Above Lamorna on the little back road to Penzance are the 'Merry Maidens', a Bronze Age ring of stones, guarded by the two

Dave Matthews

▲ Fishing boats at Penberth

their fields, by then already many centuries old, continued to be used. It is quite likely that Chysauster, like many settlements in the area was fairly close to the original trade route overland from Hayle to the Mount.

Between Lamorna and Mousehole lies the Kemyel Crease Nature Reserve. This, unusually, is a conifer plantation, sloping down to the sea; a small, sheltered woodland in a windswept area. The site is split in two by the Coast Path but there is little other access. Monterey pine is the main species, although not native it has been widely planted in the south of Cornwall as a shelter-belt tree due to its rapid growth and salt tolerance. Up to twenty metres tall, and with widespread boughs, its dark green needles and rutted bark make it a very distinctive part of the local scene. Monterey cypress is here too, a beautiful tree with a lemon scent. Another fast-growing evergreen, the cypress was also originally introduced here as a windbreak. Triangular in shape when young, this species spreads as it ages. Under the trees, Kemyel Crease is rich in fungi and, in summer and autumn, the unusual earth star fungus is to be found. It is pale brown but darkens with age, the outer layer peeling back to form the distinctive star-shaped pattern on the ground.

The West Penwith AONB section ends above the small fishing harbour of Mousehole. In this little village, the quaint cottages and narrow winding streets would give it a timeless air – were it not for the endless demanding cars trying to force their way through. Try Mousehole on an August day, then tell me about the motor car as a great liberator.

The village is famous for its light decorations in winter when not only the houses but also many of the boats in the harbour are decorated. The lights are turned on just before Christmas and people come from far and wide to see them (parking outside the village of course).

Mousehole is also the home of a famous Cornish dish – starry-gazey pie. Now I like pies (rather too much, my wife says) and I like fresh sardines, but put the two together, especially with the fish heads poking up through the pastry (star gazing) and you have a fairly unattractive prospect, even to me. No wonder starry-gazey pie has not caught on worldwide in the way that the Cornish pasty has.

upright 'Pipers'.

Inland from here, a form of settlement can be seen of a kind not found elsewhere in Britain, developed in west Cornwall and the Isles of Scilly in the second century AD. Perhaps influenced by early Roman design (they mirror in a ruder fashion the dwellings in some Mediterranean areas of the time), courtyard houses consist of round and oval stone dwellings. They are adjacent to byres and other farm buildings that look onto open, partly paved farmyards (courtyards). Around the houses are sizeable stone walls (making them an early gated community, perhaps). Indeed, there are the remains of substantial gates too.

Each unit was a self-contained farmhouse. Quite a number of courtyard house settlements have been found in West Penwith but the biggest and best-preserved is here at Chysauster above Penzance. Many developed from open settlements of Bronze Age round houses, and

South Coast Western

A blustery, sunny day in early spring and the first ride of the New Year. Up onto the undulating back road that runs from Penryn to Gweek, climbing steadily past the rippling reservoirs on my right, past ancient brooding farmhouses, moss-covered granite Celtic crosses, ancient woodland and rich ploughed fields behind Cornish hedges where the first wildflowers are raising their heads. Through Gweek Woods with glimpses of secret muddy creeks and tiny stone bridges and then, after less than an hour's riding, up onto the great, flat expanse of the Lizard, wheels spinning, wind in my hair, a song on my lips. Could there be a bike ride of greater contrasts or greater joy anywhere in such a small area and short space of time?

This is the second largest section of the Cornwall Area of Outstanding Natural Beauty, at 192 square kilometres, running from Marazion all the way to the outskirts of Falmouth and taking in the unique landscape of the Lizard Peninsula. It has a particularly splendid coastline with more variety than almost anywhere, running nearly fifty miles from end to end.

Penzance

The gateway to two sections of the Cornwall AONB, Penzance/Newlyn lies on the western side of Mounts Bay overlooking St Michael's Mount itself and on eastwards to the Lizard beyond. It is half a mile from the western edge of Newlyn to the beginning of the Penwith AONB.

The name Penzance comes from the Cornish *pen* (meaning head or headland) and *sans* (meaning holy), believed to refer to the rocky point south of the present harbour. A chapel is known to have stood there, approximately on the site of the present church. This was still intact in the eighteenth century (inside a fish shed, appar-

ently) but the only remaining object from this chapel is a carved figure, now largely eroded, in the present churchyard.

There have been many Bronze Age and Roman finds in the area, unsurprisingly as the Hayle to Ictis (St Michaels Mount) overland trade route was well established by Roman times.

Wikipedia in 2012 has Penzance as 'the most westerly town in the country', a claim that may have the good folk of St Just marching the seven miles eastwards with pikes and muskets.

The town was granted a market charter in 1404 by Henry IV and, by Henry VIII in 1512 the right to charge harbour dues. Until the time of the Armada, the little village of Mousehole to the west was the principal harbour on Mounts Bay, though both it and the small community at Penzance were largely destroyed by a Spanish raid in 1595. By the beginning of the seventeenth century Penzance was the larger port and in 1663 Charles II made it a new coinage town for the tin industry.

Penzance marks the end of the railway, some five hours from London Paddington. It is a working town as well as a popular tourist destination; its adjacent sister Newlyn is Cornwall's main fishing port. Newlyn also has a thriving artists' community and was, of course, home to the original Newlyn School – many paintings from its heyday can be found in the Penzance art gallery.

Sir Humphry Davy is the town's most famous son – his statue stands in Market Jew Street. He was described by A.L. Rowse as 'the Cornishman of genius par excellence'. His father was a humble woodcarver, so Davy's rise to scientific fame, and eventually to being created a baronet at the age of fifty, is all the more surprising.

Davy is of course best known for his development of

Sara Erith

▲ Out from the Mount

the miners' safety lamp. Prior to this, mine working was undertaken by the light of exposed candles. The build-up of gas, particularly methane, meant that explosions were unpleasantly common. The 'Davy lamp' dramatically increased safety, as well as the miners' lifespan and Davy was feted by miners and mine-owners alike.

He also is credited with the discovery, through electrolysis, of sodium, potassium, calcium, magnesium, strontium and barium. It is fair to say Davy is one of the most important chemists of all time – not bad for a woodcarver's son from little Penzance.

The Golowan (Cornish for midsummer) festival is held in Penzance each year in June. A very ancient traditional festival, it was banned in the 1890s by the town council due to ever-increasing insurance costs (a highlight of the festival was a parade with lighted tar barrels!). It was revived in 1991 and is now ten days long, culminating in Mazey Day with an ''obby 'oss', music, dancing and a fair amount of drinking.

Penzance is also the departure point for the Isles of Scilly (note *not* 'the Scilly Isles') with the *Scillonian* leaving daily for St Mary's. It can be a rough crossing and an alternative is to take the helicopter from the base just east of the town. Further along the sea front from the Scillonian berth is a splendid outdoor lido, the Jubilee Pool, a seawater-fed art deco extravaganza dating from 1935.

There was a significant Jewish community in Penzance for many years but one of the town's best known streets, Market Jew Street, actually takes its name from the Cornish *marghas Yow*, meaning Thursday market. Another landmark is the amazingly eccentric Egyptian House in Chapel Street, built in 1830 as a museum and geological repository. It is now, appropriately, owned by the Landmark Trust.

The Mount

The spectacular bulk of St Michael's Mount dominates the bay. It is linked with Marazion by a granite causeway passable only at mid to low tide. Its Cornish name, *carrack looz en cooz,* interestingly means 'the grey rock in the wood' – suggesting a time when it sat among trees – possibly as a part of the lost land of Lyonesse extending further west to the Scillies.

115

Whether or not it formed part of Lyonesse, it is more than likely that the Mount was *Ictis*, the first known mention of which was by Greek geographer Pytheas, who visited the island in the fourth century BC. The original text containing the mention has been lost but Pytheas is quoted by Ptolemy and by later Roman historians including Pliny, and he seems to have mentioned the tin trade that we know was taking place during this late Bronze Age/early Iron Age period.

Diodorus, a Greek historian writing around the time of Christ, had this to say:

The inhabitants of that part of Britain which is called Belerion [Land's End] are very fond of strangers [much like today then] and from their intercourse with foreign merchants are civilised in their manner of life. They prepare the tin, working very carefully the earth in which it is produced. The ground is rocky but contains earthy veins, the produce of which is ground down, smelted and purified. They beat the metal into masses shaped like astralgi [knuckle-bones] and carry it off to a certain island off Britain called Ictis. During the ebb of the tide the intervening space is left dry and they carry over to the island the tin in abundance in their wagons....Here then the merchants buy the tin from the natives and carry it over to Gaul, and after travelling overland for about thirty days, they finally bring their loads on horses to the mouth of the Rhone.

There is a legend that Joseph of Arimathea visited the area, trading for tin, and that he brought the young Jesus with him before going on to Glastonbury. 'And did those feet…?'

No visitor to Cornwall should leave without seeing this marvellous place. A vast rock, surrounded by water at high tide but accessible by a causeway at low, is crowned by a granite castle, parts of which date back to the twelfth century. In turn it has been a church, a monastery, a fortress (including a prison) and the private home of the St Aubyn family.

The monks who lived there first were of the Benedictine order, and the church was first consecrated in 1144 by the Bishop of Exeter. (It is still open today for services and private prayer.) It was destroyed by an earthquake, of all things, in September 1275 but was rebuilt during the fourteenth century. The Mount became a place of pilgrimage in the Middle Ages, the main highway through Cornwall leading directly to it. It was captured by one Henry de la Pomeroy in 1193 and he fortified it and lived there for some time until it was besieged by King Richard's army and eventually surrendered. But its position was of such military and strategic value, over the turbulent centuries that followed, that it was forever being attacked, and more often than not surrendered. The threat of a Spanish or French invasion was always present. In 1647 Parliament decreed that Colonel St John Aubyn should be captain there. There was a great deal of restoration to be done, and the fine living quarters that can be seen there today were developed.

Such a magical place would never lack for legends. The Archangel St Michael was reported as having appeared to some fishermen there as early as 495 AD, giving the place the name it bears today. Earlier still, a terrible giant, named Cormoran, was said to live there, bringing terror to the locals on the mainland and wading ashore to steal their livestock. The giant was eventually killed by a local Cornish boy called, predictably, Jack. Jack crept to the Mount under cover of darkness and dug a huge pit. He then blew his horn as morning was breaking and the giant, rushing to get him, fell into the pit and was killed. A well is still shown to children today as part of the pit. On top of the church tower is a stone chair said to have been used by St Michael – it is difficult and dangerous to get to, and legend has it that the first person in a newly-wedded couple to sit there will be 'top dog' in the marriage.

Miracles were believed to have been performed in the church; notably a lady pilgrim, who had been blind since she was six years old, was said to have recovered her sight there through intercession to St Michael. One of the relics kept there is reputed to be the jawbone of St Appolonia of Alexandria, martyred for her faith after first having all her teeth pulled out.

Today the visitor to the Mount has a steep climb up a path through a fine garden. The St Aubyn family still

Dave Matthews

▲ Praa Sands

live in the house, in private quarters, but many of the main rooms are open to the public. In 1954 the family decided to make over the entire Mount and buildings to the National Trust and they are now one of the main tourist attractions of Cornwall and probably its most photographed scene. The view from the top is spectacular, the fine sandy beaches very clean, and the surrounding coastline very beautiful.

Not many visitors to the Mount take in the amazing gardens on the southern side. There have been terraces there since the eighteenth century but most of the design and planting dates from the early twentieth century. It is astonishing how many plants not only survive but flourish on this exposed patch of rock.

When the causeway is inaccessible, and rising sea levels may make that ever more frequent, there are regular boat trips available run by weather-beaten locals who know every ebb and eddy of the seas.

Just inland a few wetlands still exist in the Marazion Marshes nature reserve, which has Cornwall's largest reed-bed. More than 250 bird species including bitterns, warblers, egrets and heron, as well as 500 plant, 500 insect and 18 mammal species have been recorded here.

Along the coast, the land ascends and falls – Perranuthnoe, secretive Prussia Cove, fast-eroding Praa Sands, spectacular Rinsey Head, all the way to the old pilchard-fishing port of Porthleven.

Prussia Cove was named after the 'King of Prussia', the self-styled moniker of one John Carter who effectively ruled the area for thirty years at the end of the eighteenth century. He was perhaps the most famous smuggler on the coast and there are many stories about him and his exploits.

Baring-Gould, in his *A Book of Cornwall*, saw Carter as something of a Robin Hood figure:

On one occasion, during his absence from home, the excise officers carried off a cargo that had lately arrived for Carter from France to the local custom house store. On his return, Carter summoned his men, and they broke into the stores that night and carried off all that he held to be his own, without touching a single article to which he considered he had no claim.

In the 1780s it was estimated that 160,000 people, a fifth of the nation's horses and at least 300 vessels were involved in smuggling. As much as a quarter of the whole export/import trade of the country was conducted illegally. A quarter of all smuggled tea and half the smuggled brandy entered Britain by way of the coasts of Devon and Cornwall. In Cornwall 'legal' tea, spirits, fine cloth and, a century or so later, tobacco, were almost unknown. There were King's Pipes in many coastal towns where Revenue men burnt contraband tobacco – the one in Falmouth can still be seen by Custom's House Quay today.

A Smuggler's Song

If you wake at Midnight, and hear a horse's feet,
Don't go drawing back the blind, or looking in the street,
Them that asks no questions isn't told a lie.
Watch the wall, my darling, while the Gentlemen go by!

Five and twenty ponies,
Trotting through the dark –
Brandy for the Parson,
'Baccy for the Clerk;
Laces for a lady, letters for a spy,
And watch the wall, my darling, while the Gentlemen go by!

Running round the woodlump, if you chance to find
Little barrels, roped and tarred, all full of brandy-wine,
Don't you shout to come and look, nor use 'em for your play.
Put the brishwood back again – and they'll be gone next day!

If you see the stable-door setting open wide;
If you see a tired horse lying down inside;
If your mother mends a coat cut about and tore;
If the lining's wet and warm – don't you ask no more!

If you meet King George's men, dressed in blue and red,
You be careful what you say, and mindful what is said.
If they call you 'pretty maid', and chuck you 'neath the chin,
Don't you tell where no one is, nor yet where no one's been!

Knocks and footsteps round the house – whistles after dark –
You've no call for running out till the house-dogs bark.
Trusty's here, and Pincher's here, and see how dumb they lie –
They don't fret to follow when the Gentlemen go by!

If you do as you've been told, 'likely there's a chance,
You'll be give a dainty doll, all the way from France,
With a cap of Valenciennes, and a velvet hood –
A present from the Gentlemen, along o' being good!

Five and twenty ponies
Trotting through the dark –
Brandy for the Parson,
'Baccy for the Clerk;
Them that asks no question isn't told a lie –
Watch the wall, my darling, while the Gentlemen go by!

Rudyard Kipling

▲ Off the coast of the Lizard

Dave Matthews

▲ High seas at Porthleven

Smuggling and piracy was rife all along the coast. Pirates (or, to be polite, privateers) sailed from Falmouth (usually employed by the Killigrews), Fowey, Mevagissey and Penzance on a regular basis. But the Cornish were not the only pirates; it was reported, in 1536, that sixteen fishing boats were seized by North African pirates off the Cornish coast in one month alone.

There is not much evidence of actual 'wrecking' as in boats being deliberately lured onto rocks and the crew being killed, as opposed to folk looting wrecks that were driven ashore, of which there is considerable documentary evidence. Wrecking seems to have been a figment of the Reverend Baring-Gould's imagination, just as the legend of the north coast smuggler 'Cruel Coppinger' was nearly all made up by Parson Hawker (what is it about these nineteenth-century clergymen?).

At Praa Sands a short trip inland brings you to one of Cornwall's best-kept secrets, the tiny (and haunted) Pengersick Castle. Angela Evans, who owned Pengersick

for many years, was a friend of my family, particularly of my mother and brother Alan. To say she was eccentric would be to give understatement a bad name. Pengersick was her passion; she looked after the castle, excavated the grounds (it is a very ancient site), restored the gardens (notably the mediaeval herb garden), built a visitor centre, ran the Pengersick Trust, to whom the castle now belongs, and lived in two rooms in a crumbling shack attached to the rear of the castle with an elderly greyhound and, at one counting, *eighteen* cats.

Unlike her slightly less than salubrious living quarters, Angela kept the castle in tip top condition – filling it with Jacobean furniture, armour and weapons. The second floor bedroom is a favourite with ghost hunters.

I loved castles as a boy and still do but it seems Angela took her obsession a stage further and actually bought one. I remember her telling me, 'When we saw Pengersick in the 70s it had bats and jackdaws' nests, the garden was overgrown and there was no heating in the castle or

119

Dave Matthews

▲ The beach at Porthleven

the annex – still isn't really, only a wood stove. The bank manager said only a lunatic would buy it, so I did.' Angela died a couple of years ago but would be pleased to know that restoration continues and that the Pengersick Trust is looking after this jewel of a site very well.

From Pengersick you can walk the coast path or take any number of inland trails to Porthleven. This is a pretty tourist town in summer, with a particularly good ice-cream parlour and many craft outlets. A double harbour protects its little fishing fleet from the worst of the weather in winter and it is much needed – the storms here can be as ferocious as any in Cornwall.

Inland, across the AONB's northern boundary, lie the estates of Godolphin and Trevarno. Why the stunningly beautiful countryside around here is not designated is something of a mystery. It may have to do with the pressure that some of the great landowners put on Cornwall Council in the 1950s *not* to be designated, maybe in fear of what they might or might not be permitted to do within their own land. This is, of course, a concern that persists today, but one that has little cause – *sympathetic* development in the AONB is not only allowed but encouraged.

Godolphin

Godolphin House dates from Tudor times with the façade, side and rear of the house all being built in different periods. The family were enormously wealthy and influential – in the sixteenth century Leland wrote: 'There be no greater tynne works yn all Cornwal than be on Sir Wylliam Godolphin's ground', the ground in question being the tin rich Godolphin Hill that towers above. One Sidney Godolphin, a poet of some note, died fighting for the King in the Civil War. Another, the first Earl, was a Privy Councillor under Charles the Second and Lord High Treasurer under Queen Anne. The Godolphin line disappeared in the early 1800s when the Duke of Leeds married a daughter and inherited. Nearby Leedstown is named after him.

I visited the house on a spring day a few years ago when it was first opened to the public. I remember that Angela Evans, of nearby Pengersick Castle, was one of the guides showing us round. In the stables were vast numbers of old coaches, wagons and farm carts in various different states of repair. And in the woods nearby was the most astonishing carpet of bluebells that I have ever seen, testimony to the totally untouched

▲ The Loe Bar

Dave Matthews

nature of the woodland. The house and grounds are now in the hands of the National Trust.

Trevarno, an estate just a couple of miles east, has an enormous and diverse plant collection, a sunken Italian garden, a yew tunnel and an especially beautiful lake with an elegant Victorian boathouse. In spring when flowers are many and visitors are few, it is a delightful place. There was once a railway station at Trevarno and the old railway line to Helston is also being restored.

Both Godolphin and Trevarno are within one of the ten sections of the Cornish World Heritage site and, in my humble opinion, should also be part of the AONB (all right, I'll stop saying it now).

Just to the east of Porthleven lies Loe Pool, held back from the sea by a shingle barrier, Loe Bar. Before this was formed (from a mixture of sand, silt and flint) in the thirteenth century, it was the mouth of the river Cober, allowing ships inland to Helston, then a port exporting tin and copper. Today Loe Pool is Cornwall's largest freshwater lake, teeming with wildlife. There are excellent walks around either side of the pool, the one on the westward side taking you up through the ancient Penrose Estate.

In 1948, Ewart Jones produced one of the very first 'pocket sized' guides of which I still have a yellowing, dog-eared copy. He writes: 'This walk around Loe Pool is undoubtedly one of the most beautiful obtainable, not only in Cornwall but in the whole of England. Yet in spite of its close proximity to Helston, very few visitors bother to try it.' (He should see it today on a summer Sunday!)

The landscape now rises to the Lizard Peninsula – an exposed upland with open grassland and maritime heath. This is interspersed with intricately patterned fields, many mediaeval and some prehistoric. Ewart Jones wrote of the 'basic, lovely loneliness of the countryside here', a rurality that cannot have changed appreciably since the Domesday Book was written. No other agricultural district in England imparts quite the same aura of unchanging continuity. Please note, Cornish readers getting hot under the collar at the reference to England, that I am *quoting* and from an author writing some sixty-five years ago, before the main revival of Cornish nationalism..

On the western and southern sides of the Lizard there are intimate coves and high cliffs – Kynance Cove is

Joanne Clement

▲ The western side of the Lizard

Small fishing villages such as Coverack and Cadgwith are part of a particularly picturesque built landscape. At Lizard Point (the most southerly place in Britain) the lighthouse, first built in 1619, now has a range of twenty-five miles.

This is just as well, for offshore here are the dreaded Manacles, 1.5 square miles of jagged rocks just beneath the waves, also known locally as the 'graveyard of ships'. The old Lloyds signal station on the cliffs, though not the most attractive of buildings, was well sited – at one stage it monitored every piece of shipping entering or leaving the English Channel.

On the western side of Lizard Point is the old lifeboat station with its slipway still (relatively) intact. Launching a lifeboat into the full force of the prevailing westerlies was never easy and in the 1960s the station was moved further east to Church Cove.

Lizard Point, like Gwennap Head near Land's End, is a great place for whale-watching. Groups of long-finned pilot whales are sometimes seen offshore, particularly in November and December along with white-beaked dolphins. Minke whales are often seen with fin whales known to pass through in the winter months. Basking sharks are now common in summer.

especially well known, with its white sand, turquoise water and, in high summer, its thousands of tourists. Managing tourist pressures is a particular challenge for the tourist board (Visit Cornwall), the National Trust and other members of the partnership that administers the Cornwall AONB.

Peter Maxted

▲ The Lizard lighthouse

Colin Speedie

▲ Basking shark

Dave Matthews

The geology of the Lizard takes in granite, slate, gabbro (which is extensively quarried near Porthoustock turning the coast path briefly into a moonscape), hornblende schist and, of course, the famous serpentine rock (the church of St Peter at Coverack has a pulpit constructed from serpentine).

On the coast between Lizard and Mullion you will find the monument to Marconi near the point from where he sent his message across the Atlantic (although he actually sent his first messages, to the Isle of Wight, from further east at Housel Bay). He sent the letter 's', in Morse code all the way to Newfoundland in 1901.

Also on this coast you may, if you are lucky, catch a glimpse of the rare Cornish chough – the red-legged member of the crow family that is Cornwall's 'national' bird. According to one legend (of many), King Arthur was transformed into a chough when he died.

Inland on the Lizard there are small farms, Bronze Age barrows and standing stones as well as visually domi-

nant later structures such as Goonhilly Earth Station and Bonython wind turbines. Both of these features are out of place on the flat landscape of the Lizard but the satellite dishes of the earth station predate the AONB and the wind turbines, recently replaced with even higher ones, are a visible reminder of the tension between the desire for a an uncluttered landscape and the need for clean, green energy. In an ideal world we'd have both these structures elsewhere, but you hardly need me to tell you that we don't live in an ideal world.

A part of the peninsula is known as the Meneage (land of the monks). There is a Meneage Street in Helston and a St Antony-in-Meneage on the north-east tip of the Lizard. Much of the central area is exposed heath-land with a rare type of heather, known as Erica Vagans, found nowhere else in Britain. Also inland is the disused World War II airfield at Predannack Downs with its strange helicopter graveyard.

Nearly all of the area is a nature reserve of one kind

or another. The National Nature Reserve (NNR) on the Lizard, one of only three in Cornwall, is made up of numerous isolated sites. The area around Predannack has two main habitat types – coastal grasslands and heath and inland heath. The whole Lizard is a wonderful mixture of habitats, just crying out to be explored.

There are two wild features of the Lizard NNR that have a national profile. The chough is the avian star of the area, mostly to be found between Lizard Village and Kynance. You generally hear their characteristic call before seeing them.

Last year the RSPB's Claire Mucklow told me:

Three pairs of wild chough have successfully raised nine youngsters this year. Other young pairs have attempted to nest too, making 2010 a very exciting year for Cornwall's special bird. The returning choughs first nested on the Lizard where the first chough chicks to hatch in more than 50 years made Cornish history.

It is testament to the pioneering pair on the Lizard and their healthy offspring that we now have a burgeoning population, steadily increasing in numbers and expanding to reoccupy some historical nest sites along the coast of the Lizard, Penwith and the north coast of Cornwall. Having nine youngsters

▲ The chough, Cornwall's national bird

Paul Gillard

fledge from the three nest sites is excellent news. We are also hoping that the young pairs that are busy 'practising' will settle down and make their own little bit of history.

The success of choughs, following their natural re-colonization, is helped enormously by good habitat management at many sites around the Cornish coast. Grazing of the cliffs and slopes keeps these areas in good condition for choughs, which depend on a mosaic of habitats and access to the soil for their invertebrate food.

Cornish heath, the other wild feature of national importance, only occurs naturally in this country on the Lizard and was first mentioned as growing there by John Ray in 1670. It is an attractive shrub, found plentifully on the dry heaths of the Lizard 'Downs'. The narrow, dark green leaves sprout in fours or fives. The long, dense flower spikes have leafy tips and the bell-shaped flowers occur in shades of pink or lilac and sometimes white.

On the western side of the Lizard, much of the heath is in the National Nature Reserve as is some of the coast. To the centre the whole of Goonhilly Downs is protected whilst in the east much of the Helford Estuary is also part of the Lizard NNR.

Just to the north of the national reserve is another small local one. Windmill Farm is made up of grassland and heath together with scrub, bog, swamp, hedgerow and some crops (not bad going for such a small piece of flat land). There are two ponds as well, teeming with aquatic life.

The adult marsh fritillary may be seen on the wing here during spring and early summer. The colony on the reserve is one of the very few on the Lizard. The name derives from the Latin word *fritillus* (dice-box) because of the butterfly's spotted markings.

The barn owl, with its heart-shaped face, quietly swoops and glides in its quest for prey at twilight. One swooped close in front of my car once as I was driving down a back road – a thoroughly unsettling experience. Its wingspan is more than twice its height. When barn-owl chicks are demanding food, or in the dark winter months, you may see the adults during the day especially when the weather is overcast. Fossil records show that the creature appeared on earth around 2 million years ago and, unusually, this owl does not hoot, it gives out a strange, sibilant hiss!

Predannack Airfield separates the western section of the Lizard NNR from the smaller North Predannack Downs reserve run by the Wildlife Trust. This reserve is mostly prime Cornish heath with pools and wet willow woodland. Early Bronze Age barrows are reminders of the distant past and there are several ancient 'turf-hut' circles. There are also remains of buildings from World War II, rapidly returning to nature. On Goonhilly Downs, with its huge satellite dish structures and wind turbines, are also the remains of a World War II radar station; German bombers heading for Falmouth or Fowey would be identified and fighters scrambled from nearby Predannack.

Wildlife around here includes the adder with its characteristic thick body and triangular head with v-shaped mark and often also with zigzag markings along its back. It feeds on small mammals and lizards but is a shy animal rarely seen except sometimes on paths and rocks on sunny summer days. It will not attack, only defend itself if cornered. The adder is the only poisonous snake found in Britain but, although its bite is unpleasant, it is unlikely to cause you serious harm. Often the shock of a snake-bite in the UK is worse than the bite itself.

John Borlase

▲ Stonechat

The male stonechat is also found here, unmistakable because of its tri-coloured plumage of black head, orange breast and white neck patches. The female is similarly marked, but with brown rather than black. The majority of stonechats are resident in Britain, feed mainly on insects and are likely to be seen near gorse, which the male may use as a launch-pad for his characteristic dancing flight.

On the edge of the nature reserve, the village of St Keverne is where blacksmith Michael An Gof led the Cornish uprising protesting against the punitive taxes levied by Henry VII. Not far from here, the Reverend William Gregor, in 1791, first discovered titanium which he named manaccanite after the nearby village of Manaccan. I first visited this pretty little village some twenty-five years ago. In those days the local pub, the New Inn, was run by a marvellously eccentric Irishman. By nine o'clock in the evening he was usually so 'relaxed' that he let the locals help themselves from the barrels behind the bar and put their own money in the till!

A couple of miles to the north of St Keverne the landscape changes again to a gentler aspect with wooded valleys falling down to the Helford estuary. This secluded Cornish landmark is a ria, or drowned river valley, the result of the rise in sea level shortly after the last Ice Age. It is broken by many quiet inlets including Daphne du Maurier's famous Frenchman's Creek.

Across the river from Helford village runs a small passenger ferry to the Ferryboat Inn on the northern side. A ferry has been running continuously here since the Middle Ages and was once a vital link for the communities on the Lizard, linking them with the markets in Truro, Penryn and Falmouth. In centuries past, the cart and driver would travel on the ferry while the horse swam along behind. Today coast path walkers take this route (aboard the ferry) to avoid a long trek inland.

From the far reaches of the Helford estuary at Gweek, the land rises again to farmland, small woods and the villages of Constantine and Mawnan Smith. The latter used to be famous for its smithy and the ancient craft of metal-forging has recently been re-introduced to the village. Gweek itself is an ancient tin mining port,

Peter Maxted

▲ The Helford river

Wendy Allard

▲ Seals are rescued and looked after at Gweek

possibly used during the early Iron Age – there are stories of trade with the Phoenicians. When the River Cober was no longer able to serve Helston as a port in the Middle Ages, Gweek had a new lease of life. Apparently its (self)-importance was such that the citizens erected a gallows on the quay to show that they had the right to hang criminals. Today it is a quiet backwater with a boat-building business and the popular Seal Sanctuary which rescues sick and injured seals from around the coast and helps them convalesce until they are ready for re-introduction to the wild.

Constantine is not unattractive, with some quaint cottages, most near the church or ranging up the little main street. The village, like the bay on the north coast, is probably named after the Iron Age Cornish king rather than the Roman Emperor. Constantine was a kinsman of Arthur's, possibly another nephew like Mordred. He is supposed to have been Arthur's successor and to have been converted to Christianity by St Petroc. He is also supposed to have done battle with the giant Bolster in St Agnes (see Chapter 6). In the centre of this village is an unprepossessing grocery shop. Walk in and past the chocolate bars and frozen peas and you are suddenly

Peter Maxted

confronted with an Aladdin's cave of fine wines and rare spirits. There is a malt whisky, in a locked case, priced at several *thousand* pounds.

Below the village, Constantine Woods stretches from Polwheveral Creek up a steep valley with a disused quarry at the top. This was once heavily industrialized but is now very tranquil with huge moss-covered boulders, gnarled trees and a rushing, foaming stream, which, for my money, is almost as attractive as Golitha Falls.

The woods on this northern side of the river gradually give way to settled land with a number of large, and not always attractive, houses owned by the rich and famous. This is not a recent phenomenon for there are several significant older houses and, more importantly, gardens, on this side of the Helford.

Glendurgan Garden

Cornwall abounds in superb gardens and Glendurgan is a marvellous example. The mild climate of this part of the south-west coast is undoubtedly a factor in its success. Like many others the garden has been created using the natural landscape – in this case a wooded valley running down to the estuary.

Glendurgan was started in the 1820s by Charles Fox,

one of three brothers, all devout Quakers. They were fascinated by horticulture – indeed, Charles's brothers created two other gardens in the region, Trebah and Penjerrick. Glendurgan was given to the National Trust in 1962.

During the 1820s a cottage was built at the head of the valley and later a fine house, as the cottage was destroyed by fire in 1837. Descendents of the Fox family live there still.

The garden itself has many magnificent trees, among them the handkerchief tree, the Californian redwood, the Maidenhair tree, the whitebeam, the Chilean fire bush and the tulip tree. There are also many magnolias and camellias. But one of the most unusual features is a large maze. Originally laid out in 1833 but later neglected, its restoration was begun in 1991. The early laurel hedges were reduced to ground level and new shoots broke through. In the centre of the maze is a summer house: when visitors reach it they shout triumphantly that they have 'solved' it. But then comes the problem of how to get out again....

This superb garden ends in the little hamlet of Durgan, by the sea. There are few places in Cornwall that could truly be described as 'quaint' – Durgan is one of them. The whole hamlet is owned by the National Trust and nearly all the little cottages are available for rent. There are no shops or other trading; it is an aspic place indeed.

Peter Maxted

▲ Helford gate and stile near Constantine

Trebah

Next door, Trebah is one of the few privately owned gardens that is open to the public in this part of Cornwall, and it was originally laid out by the same Fox family who were responsible for its near neighbour, Glendurgan. In 1981 it was bought by the Hibbert family. They developed it, and in 1990 both house and garden were donated to the Trebah Garden Trust, an independent registered charity.

Of all the gardens in Cornwall, Trebah is arguably the one best suited to families and, in particular, children. From the first notice: 'Dogs please keep your owners on a lead', to the lovely private beach at the end, very clean and safe for swimming and with fascinating rock pools, you feel that this is the place for your family. There are adventure playgrounds, childrens' trails, creative workshops, outdoor theatre and many other special events for Christmas, Easter and Halloween.

But that is not to say that Trebah is not primarily a magnificent garden. Huge and unusual trees line each side of the valley – the Chusan palm is the highest in the country – and there are two acres of hydrangeas, a forest of gunnera well above an adult's head and many rare plants that normally only flourish in the southern hemisphere.

If you stand at the top of the garden and look down that beautiful valley to the strip of blue at its end, you can only marvel at the vision of its early creators, faced with just a bare rocky ravine. And if this is a mental contrast, imagine the scene in 1944 when the garden was crawling with American troops as they disembarked from the little quiet beach for the noisier, deadlier ones of Normandy.

I spoke last year to ex-paratrooper Major Tony Hibbert who, at the age of ninety-one, is still going strong and talks of his garden with undiminished enthusiasm. I mentioned the village of Flushing a little further along the coast past Falmouth. 'Ah yes, Flushing,' he said. 'I've been keeping my eye on a very interesting rare tree there for the last twenty years.' He wouldn't, despite my prompting, tell me what or exactly where.

There is yet another garden just along from Glendurgan and Trebah on this stretch of the Helford, making this area something of a horticulturalist's paradise. Carwinion is also owned by the National Trust – the garden not the house, which is private. It is most unlike a National Trust property, more like the jungle garden at Heligan, wet, wooded and relatively unmanaged. A footpath runs alongside the garden to the estuary and in the summer plays are performed on the lawn outside the house.

Turn left at the water below Carwinion and you climb around to some ancient woods clinging to the cliffs. A path up through here leads to tiny Mawnan Church, surely one of the prettiest in Cornwall. Further on is Rosemullion head, once an Iron Age fort though you have to look hard for evidence amongst the turf, rock and grass. In the autumn this area is one of my favourite places for mushroom hunting.

From here you may look back across the water to Nare Point to the south. This totally unspoilt headland hides an interesting wartime tale. Worried by the continued bombing of Falmouth Docks a few miles to the east, the Government asked Ealing Film Studios to create a counterfeit docks at Nare Head. A huge wooden structure, complete with lights and sound effects, was built, even down to the moving lights and noises of trains. It is not known how many German sorties were fooled but it surely ranks with any number of creative British ideas from the war.

The coast path twists around to the beach at Maenporth, with its ugly holiday complex (designed and built when the AONB designation meant less than it does today) and Swanpool where this lengthy section ends on the edge of Falmouth. There is another interesting nature reserve on the AONB boundary here – Swanpool itself. As the name suggests, it is home to a number of swans (for years a single old cob and his mate ruled the pool but now there are two pairs and eight signets) as well as geese, mallard, moorhen, coots and many others living in the reeds. Under the surface of this unique water, for it is partially saline depending on the tide coming up from the beach below, lies the rare and protected 'trembling sea mat'.

Falmouth

I'm not going to write too much about the delights of this gateway town – for one thing it is my home and I

Peter Maxted

have been known to be both biased and boring on the subject. But, more importantly because, if you want to know about Falmouth's fascinating history, you should get hold of a copy of Philip Marsden's marvellous book *The Sheltering Sea*.

Falmouth is a maritime town at the mouth of an estuary that has seven rivers running into it. Henry VIII's Pendennis Castle gazes out to sea and across to its twin sister at St Mawes.

For a long time Falmouth was just a little cluster of fishermen's cottages at Smithwick, as well as the castle on the headland and the manor at Arwenack, home to the notorious Killigrews. Leland met John Killigrew on his journey through Cornwall and may have been instrumental in persuading Henry to build the castle (though its sister at St Mawes had already been started). The construction of Pendennis was much to the benefit of the Killigrews who owned the land. Up until the eighteenth century, the important, and much older, port was upriver at Penryn – hard to believe these days as you look at the silted-up route with just a tiny channel at low tide.

The town began to grow just before the Civil War

(the Parliamentary forces burnt down Arwenack House and besieged Pendennis Castle for nearly six months) before taking off in the latter part of the seventeenth century. This was largely because Falmouth became the base for the mail boats – known as the Packet Service. This in turn led to the growth of the docks, especially as ships got bigger, for Falmouth has an unusually deep harbour – the third deepest in the world.

The town had an eventful war – older people still remember the docks being bombed – and in 1944 it was a major embarkation point for the D-Day landings.

Today it is still an important ship repair centre so is very much a working town in spite of the large number of tourists who come in the summer (and have, latterly, began to visit during much of the rest of the year). The National Maritime Museum is a major visitor attraction.

Falmouth is also now very much a university town with an abundance of (mainly) art students bringing their own brand of eccentric beauty to the streets, not to mention the pubs. It has some splendid gardens and small parks and architecturally is largely unspoiled (though there is some grottiness around the edges).

South Coast Central

With the salt tang of a sea breeze in my face, I'm sitting in the stern of the Falmouth to Flushing ferry as it chugs across the calm(ish) half mile of sea between the two. To the south the bulk of Black Rock marks the entrance to Falmouth harbour. There is a seal sunning itself there, oblivious to the busyness all around. Sunlight glistens on the water as we weave between moored yachts, avoiding gigs, dinghies, kayaks and small fishing craft, dancing round buoys and markers, across the cluttered harbour to the seaweed-clad granite wharf.

Step ashore (carefully up the uneven slippery steps) and you are in the South Coast Central section of the Cornwall AONB. This takes in the land around the nine creeks of the Carrick Roads, the ridiculously pretty Roseland Peninsula and all the coast from Penryn to St Austell. It stretches inland up-river almost to Truro and the ancient silted-up port of Tregony. As well as being part of the AONB, the Fal estuary is also a Special Area of Conservation, or SAC, designated under the EC Habitats Directive and providing protection for specific

Dave Matthews

▲ A traditional sailing craft in Falmouth Bay

habitats and species. Two offshore Marine Conservation Zones (MCZs) have recently been suggested, which would provide the undersea area with a similar level of protection as the designated areas on land.

If you do arrive by water your first landfall will be the picturesque village of Flushing. Cottages line the shore and stretch back up the valley to the border of the Trefusis Estate. Lord Burghley's map of about 1580 shows the beginnings of the village as just a couple of houses – the fortified home of the Trefusis family on the hills behind and a house labelled Nankersis in a valley to the south-west. Falmouth, mind you, is no larger at this time, consisting of just the Manor of Arwenack and the castle at Pendennis.

Flushing village began to take shape in the late seventeenth century when Dutch engineers arrived to build a sea wall and quays for shipping on the south-western shore. They also built themselves a few houses and called the hamlet 'Nankersey' or 'the valley of the reed swamp'. In time, it appears they got permission to re-name it Vlissingen (or Flushing) after a village in the Netherlands. Both names appear to have been used for the better part of a century, but finally it became Flushing. Besides the Dutch, local people – nearly all fishermen – built their cottages close to the shore. The main catch then was pilchards, and on the old maps a pilchard factory is shown (it was named Pilchard Palace!)

In the eighteenth century fleets of Packet boats, in the service of the Post Office, would anchor in the bay, and their captains and officers built elegant houses in Flushing, nearly all of which are there today. Many naval officers, some of high rank, also owned properties there, and so the village grew. Its mild climate attracted visitors and some large houses on Trefusis Road were built – this is known locally as 'Millionaires' Row'.

Today, in spite of some of the prettier cottages being holiday homes, it is very much a living village, with a church, a chapel, two pubs, a village shop and a primary school. The latter was threatened with closure in the 1980s, but the decision was reversed in the face of furious opposition from the whole village. Flushing is also a centre for yachting and has a small yacht club.

Penryn

If you don't want to make the trip to this section of the AONB by water from Falmouth, then you can travel inland up the creek to the much older port of Penryn. This gateway town has a long history, being founded in 1216. At least a century earlier, Glasney College had been established there. According to Leland, 'In a marshy area called Glassiney, a certain Bishop of Exeter, Walter Bronescombe, founded a collegiate church with a provost, twelve prebendaries and other clergy. This college, which lies in the valley of the bishop's park at Penryn, has fortifications and strong walls, with three strong towers and guns at the end of the creek.' Certainly the fortifications were needed for the area was continually subject to pirate activity but I suspect the 'guns' may be a little fanciful.

For nearly four hundred years the College was an internationally respected place of learning until it was demolished during Henry VIII's dissolution of the monasteries. Most of the stone went to build or extend other houses in the town and what relics are left are now in the local museum. Penryn still retains its mediaeval street plan and many of the houses date back to the sixteenth and seventeenth centuries.

Despite gradually being superseded by the port of Falmouth, its brash, new neighbour, Penryn had a second heyday in the eighteenth century when granite from the quarries above the town was exported from the quay all over the world. Harbours in Singapore and Gibraltar were built from it as were several London landmarks including London Bridge.

The harbour at Penryn is all but silted up now, although fishing boats can still navigate the channel through the mud at high tide. But the town has come full circle and is again a seat of learning. A new university campus has been built on the site of the old Tremough Convent on the town's western edge. It is run jointly by the University of Exeter and University College Falmouth and, with now over 10,000 students, it means that sleepy old Penryn is very much on the map once more.

The AONB comes right up to the town's perimeter at the beginning of the footpath by St Gluvias Church.

A small wharf and scruffy foreshore with several derelict boats make an unprepossessing start to a lovely walk alongside the creek's northern edge to Flushing. From St Gluvias churchyard with its ancient lopsided gravestones, the path passes through the deep reed bed at Gorran Gorras (often flooded in winter), past Trevissome House and Sailor's Creek and into Flushing by way of the boatyard at Little Falmouth.

From Flushing the footpath runs round the coast to Mylor Churchtown (there is also an alternative, shorter walk inland across fields). Here is a new marina and sailing school, a couple of restaurants and one of the oldest churches in Cornwall – it has been here since 511 AD. It is believed to have been founded by a Breton abbot and missionary, Mylor or Melor – later St Mylor. He and his monks would have settled there no doubt because there is a freshwater spring in what is now in the churchyard. The first church would originally have been made from wattles and mud: the present building

dates in part from Norman times, though it has been much altered and added to over the centuries. Outside the south porch is a Celtic cross. Made of granite, it is the largest Celtic cross in Cornwall – seven feet of it extends underground. The first recorded priest there was one Walter Manclere (1199–1216). Thirty-five vicars later the church still flourishes and, unlike most churches now, is always open in the daytime for anyone to come in.

The lower edge of the churchyard is just a few feet from the harbour. Thirty years ago this was quite small; today it holds a vast collection of yachts, walkways and jetties. Yet the extension has always been seaward. On land there is only the Yacht Club, a few houses, a restaurant and a café, and, of course, the old church. All around is farmland and a wonderful view of the Carrick Roads.

Mylor Church and Mylor Harbour lie so close together that if you come down the churchyard from the

Dave Matthews

▲ Falmouth from Flushing

lychgate, facing the sea, it is difficult to distinguish which are the trunks of trees and which the masts of yachts!

High Water

There are ships in the churchyard
Tangled in trees.
Blossoms fall from their masts,
Signals from leaves.

Moored by the ark
Tombstones like rafts
Float on brown water,
While far below
The pink fish swim slowly
From wreck to wreck
Seeking old bones, old treasure.

Eleanor Maxted

You may now take the route back inland to Flushing or Penryn or continue on to Mylor Bridge along a quaint, quiet little creek-side road known to locals as 'the under-road'. The centre of Mylor Bridge is pleasant as is the nearby Enys Estate with its abandoned manor house, lake and bluebell woods. Much of Mylor Bridge, however, is modern bungalows set back in unobtrusive estates perhaps as a sop to AONB status. They are not actually ugly, but perhaps somewhat unlovely.

From here the coast walk continues around through oak woodland to the ancient Pandora Inn where you can look across the creek to Feock, Point and Penpol. Once perhaps the most scenic pub in Cornwall, intensely patronized by wealthy yachties in summer, the thirteenth-century thatched building was ravaged by fire in 2010 and is slowly being rebuilt. Past the Pandora the path eventually peters out (following the coast path proper involves a ferry trip from Falmouth to St Mawes).

Vince Hawthorn

All the villages mentioned (and a number of others) nestle by the shore of one of the nine creeks that run inland from the open expanse of the Carrick Roads – known as one of the best waters for sailing in the whole of Europe.

As you look out from the village at small farms and woodland, stretching in places down to the water's edge, it is rare not to see the billowing sails of yachts large and small at pretty much any time of the year. If you are lucky you might catch a glimpse of one of the ancient working boats – the last fleet of oyster boats still operating under sail.

The Carrick Roads part of the Fal estuary is particularly deep and large ships often lie at anchor here, up to and past the crossing point for the King Harry ferry, which takes you from Feock parish across to the Roseland. There has been a ferry crossing here at least since mediaeval times, though the present chain ferry began in 1888. Above the ferry sits the splendid house and grounds of Trelissick, with its parkland and attractive formal gardens.

Trelissick

Trelissick house, its gardens and adjoining grounds, looking across the Fal estuary to the open sea, are arguably the most beautiful in the county. The house is privately owned, though open twice a year for exhibitions, but the 376 acres of park and gardens were given to the National Trust in 1955 by Mrs Copeland, who inherited them in 1937 and did much to restore and enlarge the existing gardens. Although the first house, a simple villa, was built there in 1705, subsequent owners improved both house and gardens, notably one Ralph Daniell whose father, as with so many other landowners, had made a fortune in tin mining, and who lived there from 1805 to 1844. He created new pleasure grounds and a kitchen garden, and built the remarkable Water Tower (Rapunzel's Tower to the locals) – now available to rent as a holiday home.

The gardens are spectacularly beautiful from early spring to late autumn; they include magnificent rhododendrons, camellias, magnolias, azaleas and hydrangeas, and many rare and exotic plants and trees. Though, as

Neil Keen

mentioned, the gardens are owned by the National Trust, meaning you must pay an admission fee if you are not a member, anyone may walk freely in the superb parkland which runs down to a small beach and has wonderful sea views. The small road that runs beside the gardens, down to King Harry Ferry, is spanned by a wooden bridge leading from the main part of the garden to another, which contains an orchard. The grass there is left uncut so that wild flowers flourish. Further on, amongst the creek-side woodland, is the remains of an Iron Age fort suggesting there may have been a river crossing here for a lot longer than originally thought.

There is an art gallery, representing some of the best in Cornish painting, glassware, sculpture and crafts, a shop, a restaurant and a second-hand bookshop. Open-air theatre is also performed there during the summer and an ancient barn has been converted into an interesting conference space – the Cornwall AONB

Dave Matthews

Partnership held its fiftieth anniversary conference there in 2009.

Above Trelissick the creeks and inlets stretch further still inland and one can travel up to Malpas, Tregony and Ruan Lanihorne – if you have the right craft.

Tregony is a pretty place on the upper reaches of the Fal with a thirteenth-century bridge across the river but its history reads like a mini disaster movie. Tregony, like Gweek further west, was an important port in Roman and mediaeval times and a centre for tin trading. Although the village is nearly fifteen miles from the sea, the river was then both tidal and navigable. However the Fal silted up sometime in the seventeenth century. The town declined rapidly thereafter. There was a church in Tregony until the sixteenth century when it was flooded, abandoned and then looted for stone. No trace remains. The Methodist church building is still there but is now a private house. There was also a large public school there in the nineteenth century, destroyed by fire in the 1890s. Tregony sent two MPs to Westminster until 1832 when the Reform Act got rid of rotten boroughs (constituencies with very few voters and those usually in the pocket of the local MP). As I said, one thing after another.

Because of the gradual silting up of the river, the only really satisfactory way to explore the labyrinth of creeks

Dave Matthews

all around the River Fal is from a small boat, with a shallow draught, on a high tide. A canoe is ideal. Traversing the creeks is like stepping back in time; largely undeveloped and unspoilt, they are enveloped in a cloak of woodland adding to their sense of remoteness. They are home to many different birds – herons abound, as do divers, guillemot, razorbill and long-tailed ducks, shags and cormorants, black-necked grebes and, most recently, white egrets. These were a rare sight just ten years ago, now they are commonplace. Badgers and foxes prowl the shore and otters slide silkily into the water.

Truro

Truro is Cornwall's capital and only city, thanks to having a cathedral, but it is not the largest urban conurbation – it has a population of just over 22,000. It has been a port and a stannary town and has a wealth of fine Georgian architecture – Lemon Street was once described as 'the finest Georgian street anywhere in England'. It hosts the

courts, the main museum, Cornwall Council's offices, the Hall for Cornwall and may soon have a sports stadium on the outskirts.

There was a castle there in late Norman times (there is still a Castle Street and Castle Hill) but it had gone by the time Leland visited in 1538: 'The castell was clene down and the site used for a shoting and playing place'.

Truro, it seems, has been a prosperous town for most of its eight centuries partly, perhaps, due to its central location or maybe due to its usefulness as a safe port – for it stands upriver on the Fal away from the dangerous coast. The channel is still deep up to and past King Harry Ferry but the approach to Truro is greatly silted up and boats now only come right up at high tide; otherwise they stop at Malpas.

The cathedral, though fine, is a late building created in an older Gothic style. It was not completed until 1910. There is an ancient Celtic cross outside, predating the cathedral by over 1,000 years.

Near the top of Lemon Street there is a tall monument to Richard Lander, who deserves to be as well known nationally as Livingstone or Burton. He discovered the source of the River Niger in Africa and was the first person to be awarded the gold medal of the Royal Geographical Society.

Truro has a few of the usual chain stores but quite a number of small independent shops especially in the narrow streets radiating out from the cobbled centre of Boscawen Street. The city is busy in the daytime but tends to go quiet at night. For nightlife, Newquay or Falmouth are much livelier.

One of the lovely things about Truro is how easy it is to get out of! To the north-east and north-west the Allen and Kenwyn rivers bring their wooded valleys almost to the centre of the city. To the south the AONB begins at Malpas on one side of the river and flanks Calenick creek on the other. A major housing development adjacent to the AONB was recently proposed but refused after a fierce campaign by local people who valued their landscape and the proximity of Truro to such beautiful countryside. Away from the protected areas, however, to the east and west, large and controversial developments are in the pipeline.

Dave Matthews

▲ Truro Cathedral

Roseland

Cornwall Online states: 'Few places in Cornwall can compare with the Roseland – one of the most picturesque and unspoilt parts of the British Isles.' Visit Cornwall, the Cornwall tourism authority, waxes even more lyrical: 'Landscape artists and photographers talk of The Roseland as a grail of unspoilt beauty on the Cornish Riviera, with a variety of scenery unparalleled even on this spectacular coast.'

Believe it or not, they're not over-egging it; the Roseland is truly unspoilt and undeveloped. But it so nearly wasn't so. In the eighteenth century there were plans to take advantage of the deep water anchorage and build a massive docks complex down the side of the Roseland peninsula – far larger than the docks at Falmouth across the bay. It would have extended from Trelissick and perhaps beyond, virtually to St Mawes. Docks, roads, warehouses and railways would have seen the little church hidden in the trees at St Just in Roseland submerged in a huge smoky conurbation – 'a second Southampton'. The plans were revised in the early nineteenth century but were fortunately shelved again.

Now, St Just in Roseland still sits in its tranquil setting and the church is considered to be amongst the most picturesque in the country. It dates from the thirteenth century and the churchyard is perhaps the least bleak you will ever find – it's more like a sub-tropical garden with exotic shrubs, trees and flowers.

The walk from the church to St Mawes is well known but now the National Trust have opened up a new path inland around the tiny creek and then out to Messack Point with stunning views up and down the Roads. The two-mile stretch between St Just and St Mawes was, until recently, somewhat disfigured by overhead power lines. A joint effort by the National Trust and Western Power has seen these lines re-laid underground – to the considerable enhancement of the AONB landscape.

St Mawes

Part sleepy fishing village, part holiday destination and part wealthy retirement centre, St Mawes is bit of a mixture. The town takes its name from the Celtic St Maudez who probably came over from Brittany. Logically, it seems the south coast of Cornwall got the majority of its saints from France while the north coast got them from Ireland and Wales.

St Mawes is hard to reach by road but delightful to visit via the water (by ferry from Falmouth). In the summer another smaller ferry takes you across the Percuil Estuary to Piece, saving coast path walkers an eight-mile detour inland. St Mawes is clearly designed to be seen from the sea, with its quaint cottages, well-designed

▲ Looking towards St Anthony's Lighthouse

Peter Maxted

luxury hotels and little shops. Inland the duller houses are hidden on estates in the folds of the hills.

The small but perfectly formed castle dominates St Mawes – the best preserved of Henry VIII's coastal fortresses (partly because it never saw action). It was built between 1539 and 1545 to counter the invasion threat from Europe, in partnership with Pendennis Castle across the Fal estuary.

A little further on from St Mawes sits St Anthony Lighthouse, built in 1834; it guards the entrance to the Carrick Roads. The lighthouse is open to the public and was the setting for the television series *Fraggle Rock*.

Talking of rocks, the coastal geology around the Roseland is interesting. It consists of killas rocks which form the cliffs and shores of the bays and coves between the heights of Nare Head, Dodman Point and Black Head. According to Colin Bristow, Ordovician quartzites (part of the Roseland breccia formation) are to be found along this coast; dating from the Devonian period, these are among the oldest rocks in the south-west. When they were formed, Cornwall is believed to have been just south of the equator! Great piles of pillow lava (rock that is formed when boiling magma is cooled in salt water (see Chapter 2)) can also be seen on the coast around Gorran Haven and Nare Head.

Below the main promontories, sandy beaches abound, clean, unspoilt and popular with visitors in the summer. The coast path winds on through Porthscatho and Portloe, Gorran Haven and Mevagissey to Pentewan and on St Austell.

It is the inland part of the Roseland that really gives it its charm. The soil is well-drained, fertile and loamy, supporting both arable and livestock farming. Most of the farms are small, though many are owned by the great estate of Caerhays. A predominantly mediaeval field pattern remains, with Cornish hedges often quite high, many better-preserved than elsewhere in the county thanks, perhaps, to the less fierce winds. Roads are mostly narrow country lanes – slow driving but great for cyclists and horse-riders. One of the pleasures of a trip on the Roseland is to see if you can spot a tourist coach stuck down a narrow twisty lane with high stone hedges on

▲ View from Nare Head

▲ A Roseland road

Dave Matthews

Dave Matthews

Courtesy of Cornwall AONB

▲ No room for the devil!

either side. (This is unless you happen to be on it, of course. Or behind it.)

Apart from the coast path there are a large number of inland footpaths, including many 'permissive' ones, by which to explore the AONB. Several of these will take you to one of the most attractive little villages set amongst the farmland – that of Veryan, with its thatched round houses. These were designed, so legend says, to prevent the devil from hiding in the corners.

Caerhays Castle is a private 'folly' (i.e. not an ancient) castle. However, it is still striking and was designed by John Nash at the start of the nineteenth century. The original owners, the Trevanion family, fell on hard times and by 1855 the roof had fallen in and much of the castle was derelict with geese found nesting in the drawing room. It was taken on and refurbished by the Williams family who still own it today. Conducted tours of the house can be booked. There is a simply amazing woodland garden, open to the public, noted for its camellias, azaleas, magnolias and rhododendrons.

Back on the coast, you pass the Iron Age hill fort, Dingerein Castle, where King Gerren of Dumnonia, after whom the village of Gerrans is named and who was killed in the fighting at the Battle of Catterick in 598 AD, is said to be buried. Legend has it that he was the Sir Gerrans who fought alongside King Arthur. Other Iron Age fortifications exist at Dodman Point and Black Head and at Veryan and there is a Bronze Age barrow at Carn Beacon.

Peter Maxted

▲ Caerhays garden and lake

Past Caerhays there is a climb to Dodman Point with its high cliffs, nearly 300 feet above the sea. Further on you reach the village of Gorran Haven, once a thriving fishing village. It is now significant in that it is a prime example of a huge issue for Cornwall – the old fishermen's cottages in the heart of the village are almost entirely given over to holiday homes and, in the winter especially, the place is empty and eerie.

Mevagissey

Mevagissey on the other hand, while touristy in summer, is still a working fishing village and also has a year-round thriving art community and many galleries. Cottages, largely built of cob, overlook a network of narrow streets with gift shops, cafés and craft outlets. One of its quirky tourist attractions is the World of Model Railways which has more than thirty miniature trains travelling through varied and detailed landscapes, including a trip through the Alps.

The town was once a hub of Cornwall's pilchard fishing 'industry' and one of its claims to fame is that it had a power station, built in 1895, powered by pilchard oil! The smell must have been interesting. This provided electricity for the lighthouse and surrounding streets. Local sources claim that 'Meva' was the first town in the country to have electric street lighting. It would certainly have been the first, and only, to be lit by pilchard power.

Mevagissey is not far from the eastern edge of the AONB, but still within the protected landscape lie the old clay workings at Pentewan. Once a busy harbour built for shipping china clay, the dock basin is now separated from the sea by the beach and is filled with fresh water. The beach itself is dominated by an extensive holiday camp.

Heligan

Inland near here are the famous Lost Gardens of Heligan – a thousand acres of ancient estate rescued during the 1990s from their totally overgrown state and gradually being restored to their former glory. The gardens were created by members of the Cornish Tremayne family, over a period from the mid-eighteenth century up to the end of the nineteenth. In the twentieth century Heligan estate came under the ownership of a trust to the benefit of several members of the extended Tremayne family. One of these, John Willis, introduced record producer Tim Smit to the gardens. He and a group of fellow enthusiasts decided to restore the garden to its former glory and eventually leased them from the Tremayne family.

Here is the story, in their own words:

At the end of the nineteenth century its thousand acres were at their zenith, but only a few years later bramble and ivy were already drawing a green veil over this 'Sleeping Beauty'. After decades of neglect, the devastating hurricane of 1990 should have consigned the Lost Gardens of Heligan to a footnote in history.

Instead, events conspired to bring us here and the romance of their decay took a hold on our imaginations. Our discovery of a tiny room, buried under fallen masonry in the corner of one of the walled gardens, was to unlock the secret of their demise. A motto etched into the limestone walls in barely legible pencil still reads "Don't come here to sleep or slumber" with the names of those who worked there signed under the date – August 1914. We were fired by a magnificent obsession to bring these once glorious gardens back to life in every sense and to tell, for the first time, not tales of lords and ladies but of those 'ordinary' people who had made these gardens great, before departing for the Great War.

We have now established a large working team with its own vision for our second decade. The award-winning garden restoration is already internationally acclaimed; but our lease now extends into well over 200 acres of the Wider Estate, leaving the project far from complete. We intend Heligan to remain a living and working example of the best of past practice, offering public access into the heart of what we do.

Our contemporary focus is to work with nature, accepting and respecting it and protecting and enhancing the variety of habitats with which our project is endowed.

Tim Smit has, of course, gone on to greater things with the Eden Project but Heligan remains a magnificent ongoing adventure and one of the Cornwall AONB's real gems.

It is only fair, having mentioned Eden, to offer a little space to this most magical of attractions. It is not in the AONB, indeed it is miles inland, but is an example of how non-protected landscapes in Cornwall could be transformed, 'bringing the rest up to the level of the best'. Take a post-industrial landscape, in this case an enormous, exhausted, china clay pit, and design an iconic set of buildings with a sculpted landscape surrounding them.

You might think there was a fair bit of hubris going on in the decision to name a project after the birthplace of Adam and Eve. You might then think that there was further temptation of fate with the project becoming known as 'the eighth wonder of the world'. Yet the vision of Tim Smit and his co-founders endures, ten years after the building was first opened. It has become an iconic Cornish site and the stunning biomes (enormous plastic greenhouses) have helped with Cornwall's renaissance and its image worldwide. Well over 5 million visitors have passed through Eden's gates.

But Eden is far more than just a well-designed and interesting visitor attraction. It demonstrates the dependence of mankind on plants – something we have been in danger of losing sight of. It is a cultural centre, particularly in the fields of sculpture (check out Tim Shaw's astonishing bull next time you visit) and music – the summer 'Eden Sessions' have brought in a huge, mostly new and younger, audience to the region. It is a major economic success and a large employer – with several hundred full-time staff. It is a repository for rare plant species that may otherwise be lost to us as we destroy our habitats across the globe. And, most importantly, it is an educational experience, projecting a message of interdependence, sustainability and hope to both adults and children. What's not to like?

Hmm, this is beginning to sound like a tourist brochure. Maybe it's time to move on....

▲ The Roseland coast

Dave Matthews

South Coast Eastern

Picture a neatly dressed gentleman walking along a riverside footpath. He wears well-cut tweeds, a hat and stout boots. He carries a shooting stick and is almost certainly smoking a pipe. As he reaches St Winnow Point and the greatwood above Golant, where the rivers Fowey and Lerryn merge, he sits on an old moss-coated tree stump and gazes out over the river towards the dense green trees on the far bank. Long, quiet minutes pass. Then he takes a notebook and a stub of pencil from his pocket and writes: 'When tired at last, he sat on the bank, while the river still chattered on to him, a babbling procession of the best stories in the world, sent from the heart of the earth to be told at last to the insatiable sea.'

The year was 1905, the author Kenneth Graham and the book, to be published three years later, was *The Wind in the Willows*. The story is set on the Thames, but Graham spent quite a bit of time in Cornwall and is known to have written some of his most famous work here near Fowey and along the coast at Falmouth.

One of the great joys of a protected landscape is that, over a hundred years later, one can perhaps find the same spot and look out over the same view. This is true in much of Cornwall (though not the former mining areas, which have a different charm). It is also true of many if not most AONBs around the country. As the head of Visit Cornwall, Malcolm Bell, said to me: 'One of the reasons people come back to a favourite place again and again is if it changes only slowly or not at all. They look forward to sharing the view, and their memories, with children and grandchildren.'

We are in the prosaically named South Coast Eastern section of the AONB, which runs from Par along the coast all the way to Looe and inland up the river Fowey as far as St Winnow. In the context of the Cornwall AONB it is unusual in that it has two sizeable settlements within its boundaries – the town of Fowey to the west and Polperro in the east.

On the map this section looks like a 'thumbs up' with the fore-knuckle on the edge of St Austell and the tip of the thumb almost touching Lostwithiel. To the north-west, the white peaks of china clay country or Cornwall's 'Alps', as they are known locally, stretch into the distance.

St Austell and Par

For one of the oldest and largest towns in Cornwall, St Austell is singularly unprepossessing. Don't take my word for it, here is Leland writing in the sixteenth century: 'At S. Austelles is nothing notable but the paroch chirch.'

St Austell began to grow when William Cookworthy discovered kaolin in the area in the eighteenth century. He was a pharmacist and developed a method of turning it into porcelain. The industry dominates the town to this day with the spoil heaps (somewhat more attractive than coal field ones) soaring above the town, and the docks at Par white with the dust. The name kaolin comes from the Chinese for 'high hill' (no doubt from its first discovery) and thus is better known to us as china clay.

The industry, at its height, employed many thousands of people, quite a few of them former miners – for the rise of china clay coincided with the decline of the tin industry. Most of the clay was shipped from Fowey but now leaves from Par Docks where the 'white river' runs into the sea just as its red cousin used to further north and west.

Par Docks segues into Par Sands from where the next stage of the coast path marks the beginning of the coastal strip of the AONB. It runs round Gribbin Head with its

Dave Matthews

▲ Fowey harbour can get busy

distinctive eighty-foot daymark and past St Catherine's Castle built, like Pendennis and St Mawes further west, by Henry VIII to defend an important harbour. The path then passes above Readymoney Cove, above which is the former coach house, home of author Daphne du Maurier for a few years during World War II, and runs into the port of Fowey. It, and the river that gives it its name, are both pronounced 'Foy'.

Here the town clings to the steep valley sides (as does the village of Polruan opposite). It is the scene for a spectacular regatta every summer and for the Daphne du Maurier literary festival. The river estuary is crowded with boats, many in winter, simply masses in summer. When the Fowey Regatta is on in August, the harbour resembles a nautical Hyde Park Corner. Last time I was there for the carnival procession in the middle of Regatta Week, admittedly a few years ago, they had a marvellous tradition, very close to my heart. As the carnival passed the town's pubs or hotels, each offered free beer to the crowd!

The Fowey River rises some forty miles away in the Bodmin Moor section of the Cornwall AONB (indeed Bodmin Moor was once, before the Normans, known as Fowey Moor). Travelling up river inland past Bodinnick Ferry you pass through dense (for Cornwall) woodland, mostly of ancient oaks. Many of the creeks have become silted up, mainly with tin streaming waste, leaving disused quays, such as that at Lerryn, as forlorn memories of the industrial past.

The oak woods remember an even more ancient history. The forested valley sides hide the legends of Tristram and Isolde, the nephew (or son) and wife respectively of King Mark, who had a doomed love affair. The Tristan (or Tristram – both spellings are used) Stone lies nearby, a seven-foot menhir with the inscription '*Drustans hic iacet Cunomori filius*'; Drustan is the Latin name for Tristan and Cunomorus a Latinization of the Celtic Cynvawr – King Mark's Latin name was Marcus Cunomorus. Mark's castle is supposed to have been the nearby Iron Age Castle Dore, which was first occupied between the fourth and first centuries BC with the defensive walls rebuilt around 50 BC shortly after the first Roman invasion of Britain. So we have 'Here lies Tristan, son of Mark', very near to an important Iron Age castle. There is therefore some substance to the quasi-legendary stories that were embellished later by Geoffrey of Monmouth, Malory, Tennyson and Thomas Hardy. This simple stone is where history and myth intertwine – a fertile ground for storytelling and speculation.

The tale of Tristan and Iseult (or Isolde) is one of the great love stories that comes down to us from ancient days, exaggerated and changed over the centuries but still with the power to be moving and perhaps with a kernel of truth. One other thing is quite interesting; Fowey has never marketed the story (or legend) in the way that Tintagel further north has exploited its (possibly spurious) Arthurian connections.

On higher land between the creeks, the landscape is exposed with far less tree cover. The field pattern is of mediaeval enclosures, although the often convex slopes make the fields appear larger. Land use is arable and pasture, with, somewhat surprisingly, areas of vineyards.

Fowey also lies at the end of the Saints' Way, which begins its cross-country journey on the north Cornish coast at Padstow and was once a route for monks and pilgrims from Wales and Ireland, like its cousin further west between Hayle and Marazion, cutting out a dangerous sea voyage around Land's End. There are a number of early Christian myths around the arrival of Joseph of Arimathea and even Jesus himself, who may have landed on the coast (some say at Fowey, others at St Michael's Mount) before visiting Glastonbury further

Peter Maxted

▲ The Saints Way links north and south coasts

Peter Maxted

▲ Twelfth-century bridge at Lostwithiel

Fowey town

Fowey is one of only two towns in the Cornwall AONB and dates from the early 1300s, though there were earlier manors at Penventinue, Trenant, and a church community at Tywardreath. This mediaeval town was walled on three sides with the fourth bounded by the river with wharves and merchants' houses. Like Falmouth further west, the town has a natural harbour – there was trade there at a much earlier date. Certainly there was a Norman church that preceded the town's charter and there may have been an earlier Celtic one. The present church was built in the early fourteenth century. Also like Falmouth, in the late Middle Ages and on through Tudor and Stuart periods the town developed a reputation for piracy. Sailors from the town and surrounding coastal villages were renowned for their fighting ability and known as 'Fowey Gallants'.

The townsfolk seem to have been a fairly lawless bunch; in 1474, commissioners were sent by Edward IV who took the leaders of Fowey, Polruan and Bodinnick to Lostwithiel, locked them up and executed one – presumably to discourage the others. Goods were confiscated and the chains that protected the harbour were pulled up and given to the rival port of Dartmouth in Devon – surely no greater insult was possible!

Fowey was a focal point of the Civil War in Cornwall, with the king himself visiting and, it is said, nearly being killed by a stray shot from Parliamentary forces. It was the scene of a significant victory when the Parliamentarians, under the Earl of Essex, were defeated as they

north. Certainly some of the Holy Grail stories mention this and William Blake based the hymn 'Jerusalem' on the tales. At St Saviour's Point, to the east of the town, there is an ancient cross to commemorate the supposed visit of Jesus.

Up the Fowey a few miles lies the sleepy town of Lostwithiel, another gateway to the AONB. It was not always so quiet. Dominated by the ruined castle of Restormel, the home of the Black Prince, the first Duke of Cornwall, Lostwithiel was one of the first and perhaps the most important 'stannary towns'. The Coinagehall here formed part of the Duchy Palace which also contained the Shire Hall seat of the county court. Next door was the Stannary Gaol, a place of evil repute for it was said that many prisoners were hanged first and then tried later – if found not guilty a mass was then said for their souls. What an effective way to avoid prison overcrowding!

tried to defend Castle Dore. Six thousand were captured but allowed to retreat from Cornwall. They reckoned without the Cornish (and Devon) peasants, however, who harassed the starving retreat, stealing clothing and valuables. By the time the Roundheads reached Dorset they were reduced to just 1,000 out of the original 6,000.

The aforementioned castle on St Catherine's Point, completed around 1540, was the scene of a successful defence against a Dutch raiding party in 1667.

Fishing, china clay exports and privateering meant the port survived, without really thriving, through Cornwall's boom years. In the late nineteenth century there were rail links with both Lostwithiel and Par but both lines closed in the twentieth century, the last in 1965. Two lifeboats are today stationed at Fowey, one all-weather and one inshore only.

There are two ferries across the river, one in Fowey, which goes to Polruan (foot passengers only) and the other, for vehicles, which is further north on the B road at Bodinnick.

Today, like many Cornish towns, Fowey depends on tourism for its major industry. Much of this is fairly up-market and the hotels and restaurants cater for a quite well-heeled crowd. This is lucrative but not always popular; a recent entry in Wikipedia stated rather curtly, 'A number of wealthy entertainers have second homes around the town, which pushes up house prices to a level that local people cannot afford.'

The town is particularly blessed with literary associations. As well as Kenneth Graham, Fowey was the home of Sir Arthur Quiller-Couch, and, of course, Daphne du Maurier.

Arthur Quiller-Couch

In 1930, the Council for the Preservation of Rural England published *Cornwall: a survey of its coast, moors and valleys,* with suggestions for the preservation of amenities. This was instrumental in Cornwall being put forward as a potential National Park and in the eventual designation of much of it as an AONB. The survey was researched and published by W. Harding Thompson, a member of the Cornwall Town Planning Institute; the

preface was contributed by one Sir Arthur Quiller-Couch.

'Q', as he is better known, was born in Bodmin in 1863 and educated at Newton Abbot Preparatory College, Clifton College, Bristol (my old alma mater), and Trinity College, Oxford – he later became a lecturer there.

'Q' lived in Fowey for over fifty years and adopted the town as it did him. He wrote prose and poetry and in 1900 produced the mammoth *Oxford Book of English Verse, 1250–1900*. He was adopted as a Bard of the Cornish Gorsedd (Gorseth Kernow) in 1928, taking the name Marghak Cough ('Red Knight'). He was a mentor to both Daphne du Maurier and F.R. Leavis, the Cambridge literary critic, and died in 1944.

Daphne du Maurier

Daphne du Maurier was born in London to the well-known theatre actor–manager Sir Gerald du Maurier. She settled in Fowey, at Menabilly, in 1943.

Her novel *Rebecca*, which is generally regarded as her masterpiece, has been adapted for film as has the well-known (but less well-written) *Jamaica Inn*. Other notable works include *Frenchmans' Creek*, *The House on the Strand*, and *The King's General* which tells the tale of Sir Bevil Grenville (see Chapter 2). For several decades she was the most popular author borrowed from UK libraries, taking over from Agatha Christie.

Daphne's home in Fowey was the scene of many parties and was open to a regular stream of guests, both the well-known and the less so. She is rumoured to have had a number of affairs there also.

In the mid-1980s I was lucky enough to get to talk to Lady Carlyon who lived at Tregrehan, a lovely house with an amazing rhododendron collection, near St Austell. She was a great friend of Daphne who often visited Tregrehan (I tried in vain to catch a glimpse of her) and spoke warmly of her generosity, companionship and intelligence. She also mentioned how forceful and uncompromising she could be. Since, as a child, du Maurier knew J.M. Barrie, Tallulah Bankhead, Gertrude Lawrence and many others, this is a cherished link to a bygone age.

Peter Maxted

▲ Evening near Polperro

Daphne was a passionate lover of Cornwall, her book *Vanishing Cornwall* gives a wistful glimpse of times past. She was also a member of the Cornish nationalist party, Mebyon Kernow.

Daphne du Maurier was created a dame in 1969 and died in 1989. Writer Bret Hawthorne recently published a new book, *Daphne Du Maurier's Cornwall*. For those who wish to follow up on the life of this amazing woman there is no better place to start.

Across the river Polruan, with its ruined eighth-century church, is Fowey in miniature. My uncle lived there for a number of years in a beautiful house over-looking the water, now, sadly, a second home belonging to a rich industrialist. The houses of Polruan tumble higgledy-piggledy down the steep slopes, bordering narrow alleys and lanes – it is not driver-friendly (thank goodness). Polruan too comes alive during Regatta Week.

The coastal strip of the AONB runs from Polruan an unspoilt seven miles to Polperro. The land rises steeply

and short streams emerge from the valleys at West Coombe, East Coombe, Porthallow and Portnadler. Road access is limited, so most of this stretch of the AONB coastline is particularly unspoiled. Much of the coast has been bought, piecemeal, by the National Trust, their policy of acquisition piece by piece bearing noticeable fruit, as there is now an unbroken strip of protected land all the way to Lansallos with its quaint church.

Polperro is a thirteenth-century smuggling and fishing village, with steep narrow streets and slate cottages, running down to a small harbour. Some of this is ancient but parts of the harbour were rebuilt after destruction by a violent storm in 1817. Tourism is now the main industry and visitors cannot take their cars into the village; they leave them in the car park outside and walk the remaining half mile to the harbour (if only some other coastal villages in Cornwall would follow suit). There are horse and cart rides and milk floats disguised as trams to help those who cannot manage the steep streets. Attractions include the Museum of Fishing and Smuggling which is housed in an old fish-processing warehouse. Smuggling is ingrained in Polperro's history, Even the Methodist preacher John Wesley remarked after visiting Polperro in 1762: 'An accursed thing among them: well nigh one and all bought or sold uncustomed goods.'

On the path east from Polperro one passes across Talland Bay with its picturesque church nestling in the hills above. The church is interesting. It is dedicated to St Tallanus – the hermit who lived there sometime in the fifth century. The name Talland is probably derived from this name, although it is also possible that it's from the Cornish *tal lan* meaning 'holy place'. The church is unusual in that the bell tower is separate from the body of the building. It is now connected by a fifteenth-century short corridor with ancient beams and, as an added attraction, a set of well-preserved stocks. Outside, the ancient sloping churchyard has a wonderful view of the bay and open sea beyond.

Talland was recently the scene of a planning battle as the local Caradon District Council (now merged into the unitary Cornwall Council) turned down an application for inappropriate luxury homes in the AONB. However, they then approved the building of forty-odd large, luxury holiday homes just above the church. Many of the local people are very angry (there is a website dedicated to promoting the bay area and opposing unwanted development). There are concerns that there may be more housing approved, worries over wind turbines and a debate over light pollution currently running. Some are expressing fears that the suggested relaxation of the planning laws could damage the area further: '[we] are under even greater threat of further urbanisation.'

Above the holiday complex development sits a strange tall structure, visible for miles. This is a marker for ships that shows the distance of one nautical mile from a similar structure just outside West Looe. These towers may be an aid to shipping, but they ain't half a blot on the landscape – you'd think with today's sophisticated satellite navigation that we could dispense with them.

Inland, running for some nine miles from Looe to Lerryn on the river between Fowey and Lostwithiel is the great earthwork known as the Giant's Hedge. This probably marks the defences on the border of an early Cornish kingdom, post Roman and pre-Saxon. Theories suggest that it may have continued on the other side of the Fowey River in which case it may well have been a kingdom with its capital at Castle Dore. And in that case, the ruler may have been Cunomorus, King Mark. In some places it is still twelve feet high, and where it is best preserved, for example, in Willake Wood, it is stone-faced and flanked by a ditch, not unlike parts of Offa's Dyke on the Welsh border. 'Q', in one of his novels, has horsemen riding along the top of it. The Giant's Hedge footpath runs through the nature reserve just above West Looe.

At the end of the AONB section there is a stile and if you follow the hedge to the top of the field, you come to the ruins of Lammana Chapel. This has a sister chapel on St George's Island off the coast, both dating back to the twelfth century.

A gateway to the eastern end of this section of the AONB, the little town of Looe is best reached by train from Liskeard. The railway takes you down the picturesque Looe Valley, following the tumbling river and running, in parts, through quite dense woodland; it arrives in East Looe not far from the Victorian arched bridge. This rather imposing edifice connects the two parts of the town – east and west.

Looe is quite old; the earliest parts date from the late twelfth century. However, there is evidence of earlier occupation from Bronze and Iron Age finds to the west of the town, and the ruined chapel on Looe Island is certainly older than the town. Battleaxe graves, dating from the early Bronze Age, have been found in the area. It was recorded as having been sacked in 1405 by landings from a French and Spanish fleet (nineteen fishing boats were sunk and the crew drowned) and supported Edward II during the Wars of the Roses along with Fowey (somewhat unsuccessfully).

In East Looe a jumble of ancient little fishing cottages are the highlight. Many are now holiday lets or B&Bs, but some are still lived in by locals. It is a little like St Ives only (slightly) less touristy. There is a good beach to the south of the town and a little pier named Banjo (because of its shape) Pier. Fishing is still important and boats moor up the tidal estuary as far as the bridge.

There was a canal linking Looe with Liskeard for thirty years in the first half of the nineteenth century, replaced by the rail link in 1860. The tourist trade came early to the town, even earlier than the railway, for apparently Looe had one of the very earliest bathing machines – set up on the beach in 1820.

Across the bridge, West Looe is a mixture of hotels, guesthouses and some local accommodation. The prettiest cottages climb the steep hill up the valley sides. From the south-western part of the town you look out across Hannafore Beach to St George's Island, also known as Looe Island. This is now owned and run by Cornwall Wildlife Trust. It was presented to them by Babs Atkins in 2005; she and her sister had owned it for many years. It has a tradition of being occupied by strong women; in the eighteenth century a pirate and smuggler known locally as Black Joan had her headquarters there. In World War II the island was bombed by the Germans. Local stories have it that they mistook it for a battleship!

Rame Head

There is something about seeing a wild animal in its natural habitat that makes you feel incredibly privileged; perhaps it is the memory of the hunter within us. Or perhaps it is because, in spite of our thin veneer of civilization, we have not lost that part of us that is deeply connected with the natural world. Either way, if you see a dog fox on Bodmin Moor, an otter swimming the River Camel or, as we did, a wild deer running down the lane from the hamlet of Wiggle to Polhawn Cove, you tend to stop, go quiet and stay still. The deer was a young creature, not much more than a fawn; it jumped down from the hedge and took off up the road. Unfortunately a largish group of walkers was following behind so the deer turned and ran back towards the two of us as the lesser threat. As it passed us at full gallop, it leapt in the air, a good four feet, as if it was safer airborne. It vanished down the hill in flash of brown and white, leaving us speechless for long minutes. Only then did I remember my camera.

Most visitors who whistle through to Cornwall from Plymouth, either on the Tamar Bridge or the Torpoint ferry, miss the Rame Peninsula – Cornwall's 'forgotten corner'. Yet this AONB section, the second smallest at just 7.8 square kilometres, contains the 800-acre Mount Edgcumbe Park, one of the most beautiful in England, as well as the Maker Heights with its military history, the picturesque villages of Kingsand and Cawsand and the striking promontory of Rame Head itself. So much beauty and variety in such a small area.

The western end of the AONB begins at Polhawn Cove on the edge of Whitsand Bay, a haunt of a rare bird – the Dartford Warbler.

We had been staying at a fourteenth-century manor house, much converted, near the nicely named little village of Crafthole. There are many such manor houses dotted right across Cornwall; some are B&Bs or country hotels, some are old people's homes, but many are still lived in.

It was just a short drive or cycle from here to Whitsand Bay, which is enormously popular in summer and easily reached by sail or motorboat from Plymouth, yet can be staggeringly quiet in the wintertime. We had virtually the whole place to ourselves one January day.

Just to the north of the AONB lies Ninney Beach where the wreck of the fishing trawler *Chancellor* can still be seen. Even though the ship ran aground nearly eighty years ago remains can still be found at low tide. Her nine crew were all saved. There is less evidence of an earlier wreck, the schooner *Jane*, which was driven onto the Freathy Cliffs nearby in 1827; its reception was a little different to that of the *Chancellor*. Bill Scolding writes: 'While the stricken crew struggled ashore and the captain clung half-naked to a rock, a gathering crowd plundered the Jane of her cargo of fruit. One passenger, his pockets stuffed with silver, had his coat sliced off by a cutlass-wielding wrecker.' With stories

Adrian Langdon

▲ Red deer hind

Helen Rushworth

▲ Beaches can be very quiet in these parts

such as these no wonder du Maurier allowed her imagination full rein a century or so later.

From Wiggle Cliff the path drops to Polhawn Cove passing above Polhawn Fort, one of several forts built around this stretch of coast (the largest is Picklecombe) by Prime Minister Lord Henry 'Pam' Palmerstone of 'send a gunboat' fame, in the 1860s. This was in the face of the threat of French invasion (later to be found somewhat spurious). The expensive chain of forts, all around Plymouth and elsewhere, were to become known as 'Pam's Follies'.

From here the coastal path climbs steeply to Rame Head. About half way is Queener Point, the scene of another nineteenth-century shipwreck. Scolding again waxes lyrical:

The shelving rocks below were the last landfall of the brigantine Albion, which struck them on the stormy night of 27 September 1839. By the time that the Cawsand coastguard boat reached the scene, one boy had been swept away and the last three men aboard had lashed themselves to the rigging. In the raging surf the rescuers repeatedly threw grapnels and

ropes to the exhausted men, but it was hopeless; Capt Samwells and two crew, and coastguard officer Drew, all perished.

Rame Head is a dramatic conical headland surmounted by the mediaeval (1397) St Michael's chapel, which doubled for a time as a lighthouse (a hermit once lived there and was permitted to stay by the authorities as long as he lit bonfires). During the time of the Armada there was a beacon here, one of a line stretching along the coast. There would have been few other lights, of course, below the stars, so when the great fleet was sighted in the far west, the beacons would have been lit on the Lizard and above what is now Falmouth, perhaps at Nare Head, The Dodman or Pencarrow Head too.

The headland was named in the fourteenth century, probably after its resemblance to the head of a ram. Flint tools found in the vicinity indicate that the area has been occupied from as far back as the Mesolithic period, perhaps as long ago as 5000 BC. During the Iron Age the headland was severed from the mainland by a substantial ditch and rampart stretching across the narrow isthmus to create a cliff castle. It may have been large enough to cover the whole headland area. The rampart is still visible although the bank is very overgrown and the ditch has partially silted up. The landscape on the headland and the coastal strip either side is covered with heather – though this is gradually being overtaken by gorse and bracken.

During World War II there was a radar station here, as there was a little further east, at Kingswear, where my mother served in the WAAF. These provided protection, or at least early warning, for the ports of Plymouth and Brixham. There isn't much trace of the station at Rame today, though you can find mouldering concrete among the gorse if you look carefully.

Rame Head is flanked by two small beaches, Eastern Gear and Western Gear, accessible only by boat (or by rope).

Inland, the coast gives way to heather-clad heath and then small fields. There is a footpath that runs from the coast path to Rame village, barely half a dozen houses but with an ancient eleventh-century church. With some

Paul Gillard

▲ Fulmar in flight

parts from the thirteenth century and some later from the fifteenth, the church of St Germanicus is one of the few in the country to have no electricity – it is still lit by candles and contains the last remaining hand-pumped organ in the UK.

Buzzards, kestrels and peregrines forage inland from their coastal eyries in search of rabbits and other small prey. Back on the coast, gulls and fulmars take wing from the cliffs. Incidentally a seagull in the wild can live to nearly thirty years old. Town birds such as those in Falmouth and Newquay, living on pasties and chips, have a life span only a third of that.

On either side of Rame Head but particularly on the long stretch of path to Penlee Point, you can look down on 400 million years of geology. These rocks are slates from a sequence known as the Dartmouth group from the Lower Devonian period and are some of the oldest rocks in Cornwall. The rocks are usually green-grey with some reds and purples, and are often found in great folds similar to those on the north coast near Crackington Haven. They date from a time when Cornwall was a vast hot and dry plain way to the south, with rivers and lakes but little vegetation. Prehistoric fish swam in the waters – fossils have been found of pteraspids – a heavily armoured fish with no jaw. Soon (in geological terms), the sea would rise and flood the plain leaving Cornwall under water. A later period, the Permian, saw a volcano where Kingsand is now leaving a small intrusion of granite behind. Permian breccia can be seen on the

beach, as can evidence of the lava flow. The granite here at Kingsand may well be older than that on Bodmin, in the centre of Cornwall or in the far west.

There are bluebell woods near Penlee Point, only a small patch but very pretty; they make up part of the Penlee Battery Nature Reserve. The battery was built at the end of the nineteenth century, with a gun reputed to be able to fire seven miles. It was to be used for sea defences in the 1940s against an invasion that never quite came, thank goodness; the emplacements were demolished after the war. Today the Nature Reserve is run by Cornwall Wildlife Trust and has a wealth of wild flowers and rare plants including marsh orchids, bee orchids, wild basil and yellow bartsia. There are underground bunkers below the battery where a colony of bats can be found, and lizards and adders bask on open earth and rock on sunny summer days. Birds spotted here include the green woodpecker and tawny owl. In 1998 the UK's first North American green darner dragonfly was found in this reserve. There is a car park on the edge of the reserve at the end of the little road from Rame.

At Penlee Point, there is a path down to a grotto, once a sea cave but transformed by a couple of royal visitors in 1827 (Prince William and Princess Adelaide), the first sign that you are nearing a great house and garden. This kind of manipulation of wilderness was beloved of the late Georgian and early Victorian gentry. There are some steps back up from here built to raise the great guns from boats up to the battery above.

The path now takes you through the Pierfield Plantation, so from the open cliff top you suddenly find yourself in trees, all the way down to Cawsand.

Walk into the conjoined villages of Kingsand and Cawsand and there is little way of telling one from the other. Yet they are in different parishes and, surprisingly, were once in different counties – you can see the old county border marker on a house in Garrett Street. So the Tamar hasn't always been the county boundary in this southern part – once Kingsand was in Devon and Cawsand in Cornwall!

Cawsand has the honour of naming the bay, where Viking longships once loomed out of the mist in the tenth century. In 1483, Henry VII, whilst still a

▲ Near Cawsand

Lancastrian claimant to the throne, anchored here on his first attempt to wrest the crown from Richard. Thwarted, he succeeded triumphantly two years later at Bosworth and the Wars of the Roses came to an end.

A hundred years later again, the tiny cottages in these narrow picturesque streets looked down on the Spanish Armada. The Armada had been threatening Britain for some time although the original attack was expected from the Spanish colony of Holland on the other side of the country. When it became clear that the west was threatened, Walter Raleigh, with the help of Francis Godolphin, raised levies of farmers and tinners in Cornwall, fortified beaches as best he could and set up a chain of beacons. After a setback in 1587 when a chunk of the Spanish fleet was destroyed in harbour at Cadiz by Francis Drake, the great Armada sailed for Cornwall in 1588. It was sighted off the Scillies and proceeded in a great crescent up the channel constantly nibbled at by a smaller fleet under Drake. The English ships made little headway against the larger Spanish fleet, which sailed serenely past Rame – the Spanish Admiral is reported to have spotted Mount Edgcumbe and decided it would be his once Elizabeth was defeated.

Carew, he of *The Survey of Cornwall* fame, was in command of the militia at Cawsand and saw the great Armada pass by, the greater part of it never, thanks mainly to the weather, to return to Spain.

Above the villages sit the eighteenth-century fortifications of Maker Heights which, like the military forts at

Penlee Point to the west and Fort Picklecombe further east, were built to repel a (never-occurring) French threat in the nineteenth century. Maker Heights is the site of numerous Victorian batteries and the remnants of military building from World War II – a military historian's paradise. Of more interest to the average visitor perhaps are the amazing views and the twelfth-century church. Maker is probably a corruption of the Cornish *magor* meaning ruined walls, so it is likely that the Heights have seen buildings since early Celtic times. Astonishingly, the whole area (all within the AONB) was nearly developed as a posh housing estate in the 1990s. It was saved largely thanks to the Rame Trust, which is gradually restoring some of the old buildings and runs children's events and outdoor festivals in summer.

Maker Church is not especially attractive but has an interesting, and bloody, history. Royalist troops during the Civil War were besieged in the church by Parliamentary forces and eventually captured. In 1763, a dockyard worker, Nicholas Maunder, robbed and murdered a Navy signalman in the church and in 1866 the Reverend Whiddon died while preaching, and crashed through the pulpit rail to the stone flags below. On a happier note, the vicar in the 1720s, Reverend Smart, was the first subject ever painted by Joshua Reynolds – who was just twelve at the time.

Beyond the church lies St Julian's Holy Well and then the land drops away through woodland to the tidal Millbrook Lake. This is actually a tidal creek that runs into the Hamoaze – the estuary where the rivers Lynher, Tamar and Tavy all meet and which is the beginning of the Tamar Valley AONB. A footpath runs alongside the mudflats to the Cremyll Ferry.

The eastern end of the AONB is taken up with the splendour of Mount Edgcumbe House and Park. This is one of a handful of Grade I historic gardens in the country.

The house has been reconstructed in its original Tudor style and the grounds comprise formal gardens, woodlands with wild deer and historic buildings including forts, a temple, a folly and an orangery.

The estate has a long and chequered history. Piers Edgcumbe, whose family estate was the (now National

Trust) property at Cothele further up the Tamar, gained the land on either side of the river by marriage in 1493. However, even prior to that, the Edgcumbes were well-known in the area, with Piers' father Richard doing many services for the new Tudor king, Henry VII.

Henry VIII granted the family a licence to keep deer on the estate and, in 1547, a later Sir Richard Edgcumbe commenced the building of Mount Edgcumbe House. This lasted until World War II, although it had been regularly restored, added to and developed as fashions changed, when it was destroyed by German bombs falling on the wrong side of the river from their target, Devonport Dockyard. The house probably had its heyday, as so many great country houses did, in the late Victorian and Edwardian periods. In the early 1900s there were nearly 200 staff looking after the house and grounds.

In the late 1940s the house was a shell and the grounds and surrounding area were either an army camp or used for food production. The sixth earl, Kenelm rebuilt the house, using the local red sandstone and, in the original Tudor style, keeping what was left of the original Tudor walls and the eighteenth-century octagonal corner towers.

The formal gardens were begun in 1750, designed in Italian, English and French styles. New Zealand, American (1989) and Jubilee (2003) Gardens have been added since.

There are numerous other features, now all open to the public. The Barn Pool is a sheltered deep water anchorage from which American troops embarked for the Normandy landings. Tall trees, many exotic, and a riot of flowers and shrubs are interspersed with fountains and fascinating buildings, such as Milton's Temple, constructed in 1755, a circular Ionic temple with a plaque inscribed with lines from the poem *Paradise Lost* by John Milton.

There are a number of fine garden buildings, but the most beautiful is undoubtedly the Orangery, built in the late eighteenth century by Baron Richard Edgcumbe (note how the family worked their way up through the British aristocracy) with its famous trees looking out over the Italian Garden. The Orangery is now a licensed restaurant (I can recommend the fish and chips).

Just outside the park gates stands the Edgcumbe Arms Inn. Below this is the Cremyll Ferry, in existence since the thirteenth century, which takes visitors out of the AONB and across the water to Plymouth. Generations of Plymothians have crossed on this little passenger ferry (it also carries a limited number of bikes) to enjoy parkland and wild countryside as close, or closer, to a major city than anywhere comparable in the UK.

Dave Matthews

Bodmin Moor

It is easy to be mystical in Cornwall; with the Cornish bards reminiscent of the Druids, the ancient circles and standing stones, legends twisted around facts like ivy – all these pull you back in time. Mostly I scoff at this stuff but I have had one strange experience and, unsurprisingly, it was on that strangest of places, Bodmin Moor.

After about half a mile of steady climbing up a country lane flanked by high mossy hedges, we crested a rise and saw Dozmary Pool in front of us. I wasn't really concentrating, more lost in a reverie, thinking of the stories that surround this legendary deep lake. It was a clear, still day in late summer. As we reached the water's edge an astonishing gust of wind swept from behind us, strong enough to make us stagger. The lake surface erupted in white tipped waves as if it were the Atlantic. Just as quickly the wind disappeared and all was still again. 'The Lady of the Lake,' said my normally down-to-earth wife. 'She was dancing for us.'

Although it comprises just one of twelve sections in the Cornwall AONB, Bodmin Moor, at 21,000 hectares or 80 square miles, is larger in its own right than some of the 45 other AONBs in the UK. A single chapter cannot do justice to such a vast area, so if you want to take a more in-depth look at the Moor and its many facets, I'd recommend *An Introduction to Bodmin Moor* by Mark Camp (published by the Best of Bodmin Moor Association).

Just after the last Ice Age, around 10,000 years ago, Bodmin Moor was mostly covered in forest. During the New Stone Age and the Bronze Age the area was gradually cleared and settlements were built, many of the remains of which can still be seen, in spite of the fact that the Moor was extensively mined and quarried during the eighteenth and nineteenth centuries.

The largest section of the Cornwall AONB is today an expanse of grassland and heather, punctuated by

Dave Matthews

granite outcrops protruding through the thin, precious soil and strewn about with boulders. Evidence of many prehistoric settlements abounds: hut circles, field systems and endless standing stones. In marshy hollows, rivers such as the De Lank and Fowey (Bodmin Moor was originally known as Fowey Moor in Saxon times) rise and in hidden valleys ancient wild oak trees keep a precarious foothold.

Though comparatively small compared with its better-known National Park neighbours in Devon, and although cut almost in two by the A30, the moor retains a surprising remoteness and sense of wildness. Ancient stones such as the Cheeswring and the Hurlers add to the mysterious feel.

Most of the land lies at the comparatively low height (for upland terrain) of 200 metres, rising to 420 metres at Brown Willy, described by a lady traveller of the eighteenth century, Celia Fiennes, as 'a great mountain'. In fact, the moor's overall modest height combined with its south-westerly location means that it is one of the warmest and wettest uplands in Britain – though you wouldn't necessarily think so if you were a hill farmer trying to feed sheep in January.

Very few people live on the high moor but some 20,000 live in the valleys and lowland areas on the fringes and work and farm there; cattle and sheep still graze on the uplands, though perhaps not for much longer. The mediaeval settlements on the fringes of Bodmin Moor

Dave Matthews

were not abandoned as the high ground was and their field systems have remained in use. The form of the boundaries may have changed through time, with some hedges added or removed, but they often follow the layout of the former strip fields. A case in point is the area around St Breward, where the present-day fields clearly show the pattern of former mediaeval strip fields and their boundaries.

The AONB designation means protection of flora, fauna and geological as well as landscape features, so the Moor is home to a plethora of plants and wildlife, some rare and protected, such as otters, marsh fritillary butterflies, bats and songbirds such as the stonechat and wheatear. Bodmin Moor is also the only place in the world where a rare moss, the Cornish Path Moss, grows. On the south-eastern corner, around Minions, the AONB overlaps with the Cornwall World Heritage site.

Other features in this vastly varied landscape include Colliford and Sibleyback lakes, both important reservoirs,

Dave Matthews

▲ How much longer will sheep graze?

and the aforementioned Dozmary Pool with its Arthurian associations; all are significant bodies of water. There are large conifer plantations at Halvana and Small-combe Downs and pockets of deciduous woodland such as that in the south around the especially beautiful Golitha Falls.

Perhaps the greatest threat to the Moor is the loss of grazing animals and the decline in the number of the hill farmers with the necessary skills to manage the land. However, with the onset of climate change, the pressure for wind energy development on or adjacent to the Moor is also a significant threat to the landscape. Just to the north a development of wind turbines at Davidstow, the tips of which would be higher than Rough Tor, is being fiercely opposed. Small scale, sensitively sited turbines, however, are rarely a problem and can contribute to the sustainable communities that Bodmin Moor needs.

There are other tensions. Tourism is essential to the economic well-being of Cornwall and Bodmin Moor is naturally a popular visitor destination. Open Access was granted under the Countryside and Rights of Way (CRoW) Act, which allows considerable access to many areas of the Moor (though not, a common misconception, a complete 'right to roam'). Under the CRoW Act, walking, running, bird-watching and climbing are all permitted but there are some activities that are not allowed to be undertaken just anywhere, for example off-road cycling, camping and horse-riding. The AONB Partnership encourages 'responsible visitors' and seeks to educate them in the knowledge that the land they can walk on is still privately owned, and that the landowner's rights, particularly where animals are involved, need to be respected.

Farming

The small groups of hunter–gatherers who inhabited Cornwall in the late Stone Age, once the ice had retreated, began clearing the area so that animals would be encouraged to graze, and so make hunting easier. During the Bronze Age, much more of the forest was cleared and settlements appeared. Clear evidence of life at this time is to be seen everywhere: fields, farms, burial

Dave Matthews

▲ Bodmin Moor ponies

places, stone rows, circles and standing stones.

These Bronze Age farmers created some of the earliest fields – these were long strips of land with boundaries of low stone walls, probably topped with turves. The walls were a little like Cornish hedges today, and were known as reaves. Animals were grazed within the fields though few crops were grown; the upland soil was thin and poor just as it is today.

For thousands of years the moor has been traditionally used for summer grazing of livestock which has overwintered in the enclosed farms adjacent to the moors. At present, Bodmin Moor contains some 500 holdings with about 10,000 beef cows, 55,000 breeding ewes and about 1,000 horses and ponies (2011 figures). Horses and ponies have always been an important part of farming life on Bodmin Moor, as the only practical way to manage the livestock over such a wide area has been on horseback.

Commoners' rights

Much of the Moor is common land. The origins of common land rights stretch back to time immemorial. In mediaeval times rights were strictly regulated and land-owners appointed officials known as reeves to check abuses.

Common rights today are regulated by The Commons Registration Act of 1965, which requires the registration of all common land nationally and details of the extent and nature of the rights held. Apart from the right to graze livestock some of the more ancient rights still permitted are:

Turbary – the right to take turf for fuel for domestic use

Estovers – the right to take fallen wood or branches for fuel or repairs or to take sand, gravel or stone for use on the commoner's holding

Pannage – the right to allow pigs to eat acorns and beech mast

Many commoners and others have claimed sightings of the famed 'Beast of Bodmin', as mentioned in Chapter 1. Other myths and legends swarm around too in the frequent mists for which the Moor is infamous. Jan Tregeagle, who, as legend has it, sold his soul to the devil, is supposed to haunt the area around Dozmary Pool and a Druid is supposed to have lived on Stowe's Hill near the Cheesewring with a cup that never ran dry. Interestingly, a real gold cup, the Rillaton Cup, now in the British Museum, was found in the 1830s at Rillaton Barrow nearby. It dates from the Bronze Age and similar vessels have been found in graves in Mycenae, the kingdom of Agamemnon.

Bodmin town

There are several 'gateway' towns to this section of the AONB but one, Bodmin itself, actually claims to be the 'Gateway to the Moor'. It is an ancient place and is believed to have had one of the earliest monasteries, already established when St Petroc arrived from Padstow (see Chapter 4) in the sixth century.

In Norman times it was known as Bodmine – probably a Cornish prefix and Saxon suffix, but the original is most likely from '*bod*' (dwelling) and '*meneghy*'

(sanctuary). By the time of the Domesday Book, Bodmin was the largest town in the county, with a market and sixty-eight houses. It was also an important religious centre in Cornwall; the shrine housing the relics of St Petroc was a focal point for pilgrims.

According to the present town council:

Bodmin continued to be a major religious centre all through the later mediaeval period until the Reformation. In about 1136, St Petroc's monastery was re-established as the Augustinian Priory of St Mary the Virgin and St Petroc, with a range of new buildings constructed slightly to the south of the old monastery. In the early 13th century the Franciscan order established a friary in the area of Mount Folly Square. Other religious foundations included two lazar (leper) houses and several chapels: St Leonard, St Nicholas, St Anthony, St George and St Margaret, which have given their names to various parts of the town. The wealth of the town in the late medieval period is demonstrated by the rebuilding of the parish church from 1469-72; it is the largest parish church in Cornwall.

As well as being the religious centre of Cornwall, Bodmin was also an important stannary town and the market place for the tin streamed high up on the moor.

The 1497 the 'An Gof' rebellion against Henry VII's taxes centred on Bodmin, though An Gof (The Smith) himself came from the Lizard (An Gof, now usually written as Angove, is still a popular Cornish surname). In 1549 the 'Prayer Book Rebellion', over the imposition of the Book of Common Prayer in English, was brutally suppressed. The dissolution of the monasteries, including Bodmin Priory, probably contributed to the angry uprising. Defeat led to the Mayor of Bodmin being hanged on his own gallows.

During the Civil War the town was the headquarters of the Royalist army but it declined somewhat thereafter until the opening of the turnpike road to Launceston (now the A30) in the eighteenth century. Then, in the early nineteenth century, Bodmin became the county town just before the accession of Queen Victoria. The county gaol, the infamous Bodmin Gaol, which can be visited today was built, as was the County Lunatic Asylum, in 1820, at Westheath. The phrase 'a bit Bodmin' was, and still is, used locally to describe someone who has mentally gone off the rails.

Other buildings of interest include the Shire Hall, the former courthouse, now a tourist information centre. Built between 1837 and 1838, it features an interesting cantilevered staircase and a typically imposing granite façade. The Regimental Barracks was home to the now disbanded Duke of Cornwall's Light Infantry and is today a museum.

When I first visited the town, back in the early 1980s, it was a bit dilapidated and sad; it had lost most of its major administrative functions to the city of Truro and the courts were soon to follow.

According to a recent statement by the town council:

Over the past few years, Bodmin has enjoyed something of a renaissance with the refurbishment of the Shire Hall and conversion from courthouse to busy heritage and visitor centre and the townscaping of the Mount Folly area. A major Townscape Heritage Initiative has resulted in many of the impressive listed buildings in the town having a 'facelift'. A partnership between Cornwall Council and Bodmin Town Council has enabled the area around the Beacon to be developed into a Local Nature Reserve, providing a vital green space in the town.

From Bodmin much the most attractive route up onto the Moor is not along the brash A30 but either up the Camel Trail (the same one that runs the other way to Wadebridge and Padstow – see Chapter 3) or on one of the two minor roads heading out towards Helland and Blisland.

If you are walking or cycling the path alongside the River Camel is a delight. It follows the river as it skirts the north-western edge of the Moor and AONB for some six miles to the old china clay area of Wenford. The Camel may seem tranquil but a Boscastle-style flood in the nineteenth century destroyed everything in its path including all the bridges. At Wenfordbridge, a road climbs steeply up to the moorland village of St Breward. This sits on the western escarpment, overlooking the Camel. In a former quarrying area above the river, an enterprising local has set up a couple of holiday yurts where you can experience a surprising level of luxury while still staying close to the land – I can highly recommend the experience.

Granite was quarried extensively around St Breward and the village is built largely of the stone – this can give it a slightly forbidding feeling on a wet winter's day. The granite church at the northern end of the imaginatively named Churchtown is reputedly the highest in Cornwall. The Old Inn with its magnificent open fire (you can get too hot at the bar yards away) is ancient – it claims to date from the eleventh century. Around the village are the remains of mediaeval field systems. Just above Churchtown is a tiny hamlet overlooking the Camel with one of my favourite names – it's called Fellover.

From St Breward going east you are almost immediately on truly wild moorland. A footpath from Churchtown takes you north-east through mediaeval field systems. In the distance loom the bulk of Brown Willy and the iconic shape of Rough Tor (by the way, it is pronounced 'row' not 'ruff' – mispronunciation will instantly mark you out as a foreigner or, worse, an emmet). A path to the right takes you down to a lovely little clapper bridge over the De Lank river (well, stream really) then over a down to Shallow Water Common, a vast expanse of open moorland. However, keep straight on and you will pass King Arthur's Hall on your left. It seems expert archaeologists and historians have argued for years over the provenance of this strange structure. It is similar to a stone circle but is rectangular and larger than most. There are (or were) stone circles to the east so there may be a ritual significance, or it was perhaps a fortification or meeting place. It may simply have been a place of shelter for people or animals. There seems to be general agreement that it was nothing to do with King Arthur. It is an evocative place though, especially on a bleak winter's day; be careful for it can get very marshy around and within the 'hall'.

Peter Maxted

Pass Garrow Tor, with its Bronze Age settlements, ancient field systems and hut circles, and you are within striking distance of Brown Willy. At 420 metres this is Cornwall's highest point. It is tempting to try and climb the hill from here but there is a much easier route from the north-west up Rough Tor and over the ridge. To reach it from the south-east involves much scrambling amongst ancient hut circles and scattered stones and, more perilously, through marshy ground where the embryo De Lank meets several other streams.

Camelford

So to climb Cornwall's highest two hills, it is best to start from the little town of Camelford. South of Bude and north of Wadebridge and bisected by the A39 'Atlantic Highway' (ho, ho) this is an ancient market town. There was a settlement in or around here in Bronze Age times, for axe moulds from the eighth or ninth century BC have been found. There was certainly a settlement here during the Dark Ages; King Egbert, the first Saxon King of all England defeated the Cornish here at the aptly named Slaughter Bridge. According to Saxon reports he 'pacified' the Cornish as he did the Welsh – it was in his reign that no Welshman was permitted to cross Offa's Dyke. In the fertile brain of Geoffrey of Monmouth, Camelford becomes Camelot and Slaughter Bridge is the site of Arthur's last battle against his nephew Mordred.

Camelford derives from *cam* (crooked), *alan* (beautiful) and *ford* (a Saxon word for river crossing) and is thus a mixture of Cornish and English. It was a settlement on the old mediaeval trading route between the centre and west of Cornwall and Exeter with one of the few crossings possible of the Camel River. The bridge replaced the ford in 1521 and it became an important commercial centre with the charter granted in 1259 by Richard, Earl of Cornwall. In 1552 Edward VI gave Camelford the right to send two members to Parliament and this continued until 1832, when rotten boroughs were abolished.

The road through the town was given turnpike status during the seventeenth century (some of the milestones date from that period) and was the 'post road' running from Falmouth to London. There are several houses here dating from the eighteenth century, including the Mason's Arms, the earliest part of which may go back to the early seventeenth century. The Town Hall, topped with a golden camel weather-vane, was built in 1806 by the Duke of Bedford. During the same period, French prisoners of war were jailed in the town. Camelford House near the bridge was owned by Thomas Pitt, the second and last Baron of Camelford and cousin of Prime Minister William Pitt.

Today it is a pleasant little market town with some lovely river walks. It is also a true gateway to the Moor. The turning marked Rough Tor is easy to miss (second right after the bridge going north) with a tiny old-fashioned sign attached to an ancient wall your only direction. A narrow lane passes old whitewashed granite cottages, climbs a steep hill then descends dead straight to the car park in a small plantation below Rough Tor itself.

Above loom the twin granite crags at the top, and the path snakes upwards past the monument put up by locals as a memorial to Charlotte Dymond, a Camelford lass who was murdered on Rough Tor in 1884. Her boyfriend Mathew Weeks, a simple farm labourer, was tried, found guilty of the murder and hanged at Bodmin Gaol. There have been doubts as to his guilt ever since.

It is thought that there may have been an Iron Age

Dave Matthews

fort on the summit and possibly defences from an even earlier period; certainly there are the remains of a mediaeval chapel. There is also a memorial to the 43rd Wessex Division who fought in World War II.

The path up to Rough Tor is one of the most popular walks on the moor and many thousands of tourists and walkers visit the area in summer. I prefer it in the winter months when, on a cold clear day, you can climb the Tor, follow the ridge to Brown Willy and survey miles of stunning moorland Cornwall.

Brown Willy is higher than Rough Tor (though not by much, just twenty metres or so) but not as scenically interesting. However, below it are hundreds, if not thousands of ancient settlements, field systems, longhouses and hut circles. You can descend and walk among them – Cornwall's past leaps up to greet you from the stones. More prosaically, this is also a good way to take a circular route back to the car park.

I can't leave this area without quoting Mark Camp. He writes: 'High Moor is the open moorland east of Brown Willy. Very rarely visited, except by those seeking real wilderness…or lost.'

The A30 cuts Bodmin Moor in half like the slash of a knife. For a couple of hundred yards either side, the noise is loud, intrusive and, in such a wild area, inappropriate. But we are all children of the petrol age and well used to it. It is a minor irritation and, anyway, as we move south, soon left behind. Several interesting places and landscape features are within easy reach of the main road. One is the Jamaica Inn, immortalized by Daphne du Maurier, which sits on the last of the old road (and no doubt even older pilgrims' and traders' track) that runs from Bodmin to Launceston. The Inn dates back to the eighteenth century and is a not unattractive low granite building much, though sympathetically, extended. It was a coaching inn and stood alone for more than half a century, served only by isolated local farms until, in the 1840s, the village of Bolventor grew up around it. In the 1840s a local squire bought the land, built a church and school and a community grew up in the middle of the wild moor. It was named, allegedly, because it was a 'bold venture'.

The Inn is now a tourist honey-pot, complete with the obligatory ghost, and best out of season. You can visit the smuggling museum, drink in Mary's bar and marvel at the very spot where Joss Merlyn was shot (there is a plaque on the floor). Jamaica Inn may have had smuggling connections but wrecking, as we have heard, was an invention – du Maurier was as great a fantasist as Parson Hawker, though a rather better writer.

A mile or so inland down either of two narrow moorland roads lies Dozmary Pool. Legend has it that it was bottomless (until it dried up one year, sorry). But the legend persists and it is a truly magical place. I have been there in summer and barely seen another person. You can walk right round (be careful: there are no footpaths in some places, and you mustn't be afraid of large bovines for wild moorland cattle come right down to the water's edge). There have been several claims as to it being the 'dark water' into which Sir Bedivere threw Excalibur as King Arthur lay dying.

Here is how Thomas Malory describes the last of Excalibur:

Then Sir Bedwere departed and wente to the swerde and lyghtly toke hit up and so he wente unto the watirs syde. And there he bounde the gyrdlly about the hyltis and threw the swerde as farre into the watir as he myght. And there came an arme and an honde above the watir and toke hit and cleyght hit and shoke hit thryse and braundished hit and then vannyshed with the swerde into the watir.'

It was Tennyson who later had the arm clad in white samite (heavy silk).

Malory, of course, set the Arthurian tales in the Middle Ages, when the idea of chivalry and knightly virtue was being developed (a concept later to be dashed against the rocks of the bloody Wars of the Roses). A bit further west of Dozmary Pool on the Moor is a little twelfth-century church and some ancient cottages at Temple, founded by a real order of knights, the Knights Templar. These were known across Europe as one of the earliest orders of knights, and like the aptly named Hospitalars (of the order of St John) they built resting places for travellers and pilgrims. One such was here at Temple. China clay was worked here in the late nine-

▲ Colliford Lake

teenth century but the quarries are mostly overgrown and hidden now – gone back to the land.

The road from Temple skirts the A30 travelling back east, and then turns south past Colliford reservoir. The St Neot River was dammed in the 1980s to create this very large body of water. You can park and get to the waterside in many places but the full extent of the lake is best viewed from the high moorland above. Colliford Lake Park is situated at the northern end while there is a fish hatchery that helps to stock the lake below the dam at the southern end.

The road now takes you through the pretty village of St Neot. The church here is renowned for its stained glass. The London Inn is a welcoming old coaching inn (as the name suggests) and there is a holy well north of the village The circular Two Valleys trail from here is, I think, one of the nicest inland walks in Cornwall, taking in as it does village, pasture, woodland and high moorland with many ancient remains.

A detour off this walk (you can also go by bike or car along the road) takes you through Draynes Wood to one of the most surprising sites on the moor, the lovely Golitha Falls. Here the Fowey tumbles over rocks and crashes down in a series of low, white waterfalls. Access from the eastern end (the road runs down from the Jamaica Inn following the river Fowey all the way) is easier than from the west but the paths are not all that clear in places and you find yourself scrambling through mossy woodland on occasion, always with the sound of water in your ears. There are the remains of industry here too – you might spot a water wheel site or some copper mine ruins amongst the trees. They too are gradually heading back to nature. Golitha Falls is one of only three National Nature Reserves in Cornwall (though there are hundreds of local ones). Otters have been spotted in the river; the woodland is mostly of sessile oak and ash – a relic of the ancient woodlands. There are many bats lurking in the old industrial workings and over thirty species of breeding birds and more than eighty species of moth have been recorded here.

Around three miles south-west of the falls is the third gateway to the moor, the town of Liskeard. Liskeard was mentioned in the Domesday Book, its first charter coming a century and a half later. Markets have thus been held in the town for nearly 900 years (and cattle markets are still held on alternate Thursdays). The 'Pipe Well', which can be found in Well Lane, also known as 'the Well of Lyskiret', is fed by four springs and this source of good, clean water is likely to be why a settlement was founded here.

Liskeard was an early stannary town (tin assaying began in the fourteenth century). The church is the second largest in Cornwall dating from the fifteenth century with some traces of the earlier building and a tower that is relatively recent. The oldest well-preserved building is Stuart House, where Charles I stayed in 1644 during the Civil War. It has recently been restored.

Most of the main buildings date from Liskeard's heyday in the nineteenth century. Tin, copper, lead and even silver mining, much of it on nearby Caradon Hill, made the town (and some of its people) very prosperous. Quakers and Methodists both left their mark.

Today, while imposing buildings such as the Guildhall and Foresters Hall remain, the prosperity certainly doesn't. Liskeard is a down-at-heel place, reminiscent of Camborne in the west, with high unemployment and an aura of past and better days. Perhaps they will come again.

Just north of Liskeard sit two interesting ancient monuments. Trevethy Quoit is well over 6,000 years old, dating back, therefore, to the Mesolithic period. It is similar to Lanyon Quoit in the far west and may have been a burial chamber for a number of people. Not far

Dave Matthews

▲ Golitha Falls

away is King Doniert's stone. The stone is actually two pieces, the larger with an inscription commemorating Doniert, a ninth-century Cornish king. The Latin words mean roughly: 'Doniert has asked for this to be for the sake of his soul'. Domiert is probably a Latinization of Dumgarth, who was drowned in around 875 according to a Welsh chronicle of the time. Below the two stones is an underground chamber with a passage about eight metres long.

Caradon Hill sits four miles due north of Liskeard and is one of ten sites making up Cornwall (and, oh, all right) West Devon World Heritage site. There are many Bronze Age and Iron Age burial sites, stones and cairns all over the area but the hill's international status comes from its importance as a mining area. Nearly 5,000 people were employed directly in mining here in the mid-nineteenth century, with most of them working on the rich lode of copper found a few years earlier. Thanks partly to the

Caradon copper mines Cornwall, for a time, produced two thirds of the world's entire copper supply. Around this period of activity in Caradon here in the east, Gwennap near Redruth in the centre and St Just in the far west, Cornwall, if not all of its miners, was rich beyond dreams and the population of the county nearly doubled to 350,000, a figure it was not to see again until the 1970s.

Today the Caradon Hill Project is restoring many of the old mine buildings and improving the landscape setting in which they sit. Sadly, nothing can be done about the dominating radio and telephone structures on the summit.

Just north-west of the hill is the tiny village of Minions, dropping-off point for one of the Moor's most iconic landscape features and one of its best antiquities.

Minions village only dates from the nineteenth century when it was known as Cheesewring village. The Cheesewring itself sits a little to the north on Stowe Hill, its prominent tower of flat stones occurring naturally, as a result of the erosion of softer rock and soil away from the granite layers, though it looks like the hand of man must have had a part. Around the upper parts of the hill are an enclosure and burial sites dating from the New Stone Age. The Cheesewring gets its unusual name from its resemblance to a traditional Cornish cider press. These used to 'wring' the juice from the apples leaving a crushed 'cheese' behind.

On the way to the Cheesewring you pass Daniel Gumb's House. This is actually a restored cave, dating from 1735. Gumb was a stonemason working in the nearby Cheesewring Quarry. More interestingly he was

Dave Matthews

▲ The Cheesewring

also a self-taught mathematician and astronomer; a theorem, said to be Euclid's, can be seen carved in the cave roof. For all of you London Cornish reading this, you may take a nostalgic stroll on Cheesewring granite anytime. Just walk across Westminster Bridge and you will be walking on granite from this very quarry.

The Hurlers, several extant stone circles from Bronze Age times, lie on the path back to the village. They are easily accessible as are the Trippet (or Stripple) Stones on Hawk's Tor further north. Unlike their larger, fenced-off cousin in Wiltshire, you can walk among them and feel the mystery, folklore and legend that has surrounded them for over 4,000 years. In the same way as the Merry Maidens in the far west, the Hurlers were given their names by early Christians keen to debunk pagan sites and stories. Thus they were men 'turned into stone for profaning the Lord's Day with hurling the ball' (hurling being an ancient Cornish sport once described as 'rugby without the rules'). Again, as with the Merry Maidens, there are two standing stones not far away. The circles were probably used long ago for ritualistic purposes. On some moonlit nights they still are.

Both the Cheesewring and the Hurlers are a magnet for tourists. Sometimes it is a tricky job to reconcile the needs of farming and tourist businesses with wildlife conservation and the overriding need to protect the landscape. But Bodmin Moor very often (though not always) gets the balance right – as a beautiful place to visit, a working landscape for the farmers and landowners and an important local and national resource. Above all, it is beautiful, wild and mysterious and we are lucky to have it.

David Raynor

▲ The Hurlers

The Tamar Valley

It is a mild day in early summer. The air is thick with the scent of blossom and alive with the trill of birdsong and the humming of bees. I am sitting on a warm ancient granite step listening to the sound of shears, the genteel murmuring of visitors and watching my son film a fine white rose, which is to form the opening sequence for a Cornish video.

The white rose is firmly associated with Cornwall; a well-known song begins:

I love the white rose in its splendour,
I love the white rose in its bloom,
I love the white rose, so fair as she grows,
It's the rose that reminds me of you.

Yet it is a little ironic to be filming such a flower here, for we are in the grounds of Cotehele, on the banks of the Tamar near Calstock, a pretty village that can trace its own ancestry back beyond the Domesday Book. Now Cotehele is the ancestral home of the Edgcumbes, dating back to the early Middle Ages. So why the irony? Well, here is the tale of one Richard Edgcumbe from the late fifteenth century.

Sir Richard Edgcumbe was a supporter of Henry Tudor's (later Henry VII) claim to the throne towards the end of the Wars of the Roses. And Henry's symbol, of course, was the red rose. In 1483 Richard raised an army to greet Henry's landing at Cawsand, planning to march on London and defeat the Yorkist king Richard III. But a storm damaged and scattered the fleet, Henry returned to Brittany and Richard Edgcumbe had to flee for his life. He was pursued, it is said, by Richard's staunchest supporter in Cornwall, Sir Henry Bodrugan whose fortified home was at Chapel Point above Mevagissey. Bodrugan, as well as being a Yorkist, was a

free-booter, or privateer, one of the first among the gentry on the south coast and preceding the Killigrews of Pendennis by a generation or so.

The story has it that, running through the woods beside the Tamar, Edgcumbe threw his cap, weighted with a stone, into the fast-flowing river. The King's men assumed he had drowned and gave up the chase. (Actually I've always been a bit puzzled by this tale for if the cap was weighted down it would have sunk showing no trace to the pursuers. Much more likely that it bobbed around for a while and was thus spotted. Anyway, Richard Edgcumbe escaped and lived to fight another day.) The story comes down to us from Carew, Richard's great, great grandson.

This was the beginning of the rise of the Edgcumbes for Richard was knighted at Bosworth in 1485 by the victorious Henry and later made 'Comptroller of the Royal Household' with much land and property. His son Piers founded Mount Edgcumbe, as told in Chapter 12, but Cotehele remained the family seat for another hundred years. Incidentally, the tables were turned after Bosworth and it was Henry Bodrugan who was pursued by Richard halfway across Cornwall until he leapt into the sea off the cliffs near his home (Bodrugan's Leap) and escaped. No doubt through all this the Tamar flowed on, indifferent to the human upheaval, as it had for millennia.

'Across the Tamar' is for many of the Cornish what 'Across the Channel' used to be for southern Brits: a strange, alien place, full of arrogant 'furriners' with odd ways, and even odder food. I exaggerate, of course, but not that much, for 'across the Tamar' lies not Devon, for many, but England.

The south-western tribe that the Romans found was the Dumnonii, probably an amalgam of Celtic people that the Romans, with their obsessive need for neatness, lumped together. Their main town was at Exeter and this was really as far as the Romans bothered to penetrate – they were not interested in crossing the wild, granite heights of Dartmoor let alone pushing beyond the Tamar itself. If they needed to trade for tin, the old sea route was still much the best.

The Cornish were, at that time, a branch of the western Celts known as the Cornovii. Gradually the Saxons pushed the Celtic peoples back to the Tamar and beyond where the border remains today. The Cornish were considered a race apart by the English also, and not always in a flattering way. In the nineteenth century, Cornwall was referred to in London as West Barbary. Robert Louis Stevenson famously said of the Cornish: 'not even the Red Indians seem more foreign to my eyes.'

Tamar AONB

The Tamar Valley is a separate AONB to that of Cornwall. It covers about 195 square kilometres (75 square miles) around the lower Tamar and its tributaries the Tavy and the Lynher. It was first proposed in 1963, but was not designated until 1995 making it the most recently designated AONB in the UK. Whilst the AONB comprises both banks of the river and the hinterland, this chapter concentrates mainly on the Cornish side (naturally). I owe some of the information in this chapter to Tim Selman, former Tamar AONB Manager and to Charlotte Dancer, the Tamar Communications Officer.

As well as being designated for the beauty of its land-

▲ The Tamar Valley

Barry Gamble

scape, the Tamar Valley AONB was recognized as an exceptional wildlife area of international significance. The main reason focuses on the estuary and its habitats as a major frost-free feeding area for wildfowl and wading birds in winter. But the geology, clean air and micro-climate also make the valley upstream an important site for lichens and mosses.

Ancient woodland sites still clothe the steep valley sides, and remnants of heath-land still persist on the granite ridge. Layers of history and human exploitation of the land and its minerals have left a legacy of unique habitats such as mine spoil, species-rich hedges, old market gardens and orchards, each of which has its own characteristic wildlife. The majority of the Tamar banks are of farmland or woods but occasionally the river will stream through a gorge with towering granite cliffs for the river has cut its way through lines of weakness in the rock known to geologists as the Tamar Valley fault zone.

Farming and market gardening have been the economic mainstays of the valley economy in the past but now agriculture is becoming generally less and less viable in a fast changing global economy. At the height of the industry, the valley was covered with apple orchards, cherries, strawberries and daffodils that were produced not only for the area but for the rest of the UK. Today many of these soft fruits are flown in from around the world, although this may change in the future as we see in the concluding chapter. The cherry trees may not be as numerous as they once were but around Calstock the spring blossom is still a sight to be seen.

Around 17,000 people live in the towns, villages and hamlets surrounding the Tamar Valley, not counting the conurbation of Plymouth. The challenge, as the AONB team see it, is to evolve systems of working the land that will sustain farm families, supply good local food and other products and provide room for wildlife.

There are a number of ways to explore the valley and its wealth of history and natural beauty. There are good walking trails, an excellent cycle track up the eastern side and some splendid mountain bike trails on the western side. There is also the Tamar Valley railway line and, in summer especially, there are numerous ways to explore by water.

In a recent 'Let's move to' section of the Saturday *Guardian*, the newspaper had this to say:

What's going for it? Cornwall, Cornwall, Cornwall. People are always blethering on about Cornwall. Yes, yes, yes, all very lovely. But while you losers are schlepping down the A30, I'll be turning left around Launceston and heading for the pub.

The Tamar valley is quite the hidden gem. Nobody east of Okehampton seems to have even heard of it which makes it even more pleasurable (and affordable). Steep wooded slopes, orchards, stately homes, an area of outstanding natural beauty [note the incorrect lower-case, typical Grauniad] gorges, riverside pubs, one of the country's best mountain biking trails, the sea a short drive away: and you say you prefer Fowey. Tsk.

Even more miraculously the Tamar seems to have escaped the descendants of Dr Beeching; a single track railway plies from Gunnislake to Plymouth leaping over the Tamar at the awesome Calstock viaduct. Must make for one of the prettiest commutes in the country. The valley is so beautiful that until you see the ruined chimneys it's hard to believe it was once rammed with mines, a hotbed of the Industrial Revolution until the mid-19th century.

From Plymouth, the fourteen mile railway skirts the edge of the Tamar and its estuary before crossing the

Calstock viaduct joining Devon and Cornwall. The journey is full of contrasts, taking in views of the Royal Naval Dockyard in Plymouth and Brunel's famous Royal Albert Bridge over the Tamar before crossing the Tavy viaduct into the quiet countryside of the Bere Peninsula.

As the train climbs towards Gunnislake, remnants of the area's industrial past are indeed visible, together with glimpses of a few slopes and orchards still cultivated by market gardeners.

The valley is quartered by four ancient towns – Launceston in the north, the ancient capital of Cornwall, with its steam railway and Norman castle; Tavistock across in Devon to the east – gateway to west Dartmoor; Callington in the west and Saltash to the south, best known for Brunel's Royal Albert rail bridge, now partnered by the striking road bridge. And always there is the unmistakeable presence of Plymouth, a city rich in history and trying hard to bring itself into the present-day but always stymied by its unlovely post-war architecture.

Mining thrived here from mediaeval times; both silver and tin were significant, but it was copper in the 1800s that made the greatest impact. At the height of the mining boom there were over 100 mines along the river. The chimneys and ruins now sit among trees and tower incongruously above market gardens. Morwellham Quay was the inland port serving the mines, and today it has been brought back to life as a living museum, offering a (reasonably untacky) taste of Victorian life. Until the coming of the railway and its famous viaduct, the quay was the important site for the transport of copper and tin down to Plymouth and beyond.

Morwellham Quay is part of the World Heritage site, which has a number of other visitor attractions such as a copper mine, a working Victorian farm, a narrow-gauge railway, heavy horses and museums of costume and mining.

The narrow-gauge mine railway takes visitors along the banks of the river before heading quite deep underground into the George & Charlotte copper mine. It is a real abandoned workplace, not unlike Geevor tin mine in the far west.

Rosemary Teverson

▲ Quite the hidden gem

Tamar Valley AONB

▲ All quiet today, but the Valley was once a hive of industry

Cotehele

The aforementioned abode of the early Edgcumbes dates from the thirteenth century but little if any of the early mediaeval building remains. The house that I saw on that sunny summer's day was built between 1485 and 1539 by Sir Richard Edgcumbe, of the famous hat, and his son Piers. As Piers and his son, another Richard, then built the new family seat, Cotehele was under-used and perhaps this explains why today it is considered the best-preserved Tudor house in Britain. In 1947 it was accepted by the Treasury and given to the National Trust – the first property in Britain to be acquired by the Trust in lieu of death duties.

Unlike many later houses, Cotehele was a product of the Middle Ages' need to consider defence as well as ostentation; the windows facing outwards are small and high up the walls. The larger unprotected windows open onto the inner courtyard. The house can perhaps therefore be seen as bridging the gap between two eras.

Outside, the formal gardens, where we filmed the 'wrong' rose, overlook the valley below, with a medieval dovecote, a stewpond, a Victorian summer house and an eighteenth-century tower above.

Below Cotehele, on the outskirts of Calstock, a Roman fort has recently been discovered – the largest known Roman site in Cornwall.

The A390 from Liskeard to Tavistock crosses the sixteenth-century 'new' bridge built by the Edgcumbes at Gunnislake. The bridge was painted by Turner and the painting named *Crossing the Brook*. The village was a quiet agricultural place until the dramatic increase in mining and industrial activity in the nineteenth century. Around 7,000 jobs were directly associated with the mining peak in the 1860s and there were brickworks, arsenic mines and quarries too.

To the west, Kit Hill (334 m or nearly 1,100 feet) dominates the area between Callington and the Tamar. It is named after the Saxon word for 'kite', meaning a general bird of prey. Today buzzards and sparrow-hawks are often seen above the hill. It is of the same granite as Bodmin Moor to the west and forms part of the ridge that links it with Dartmoor in the east.

In some ways the story of Kit Hill could be the story of Cornwall itself written in miniature. There are the remains of Neolithic tombs and Bronze Age barrows. It is possibly the site of the battle of Hingston Down when the Cornish Celts allied themselves with an army of Vikings whose fleet had sailed up the Tamar. They were battling, for the second time, against the Saxon king, Egbert, who had subdued the rest of the country and indeed Cornwall too at the Battle of Slaughterbridge near Camelford a few years earlier. Hingston Down was another defeat for the rebellious Cornish and the Saxon king could finally claim to control the whole of 'England'. However, the Cornish were pretty much left alone after that and the Saxon influence is not noticeable in the centre or west of the county. Not until the Normans arrived 230 years later was Cornwall truly subsumed into the rest of the country.

Kit Hill was extensively mined during the eighteenth and nineteenth centuries for copper and tin as well as some silver and wolfram. Today it is a country park, given to the council by the Duchy of Cornwall.

The southern section

A chunk of the Tamar Valley AONB is cut off by the conurbation around Saltash and Torpoint but the southern section at least allows the lower reaches of the beautiful River Lynher and the ancient village of St Germans to be incorporated.

Just above the confluence of Lynher and Tamar rivers sits Antony House, constructed for Sir William Carew between 1711 and 1721. It sits on the site of a much older property, home to Richard Carew of *The Survey of Cornwall* fame in the late sixteenth century. The gardens, landscaped by Repton, include formal courtyards, terraces, ornamental ponds, a knot garden and a number of modern sculptures which blend in superbly.

The house and gardens were donated to the National Trust in 1961, but the house is still lived in by the family (now the Carew-Poles) and the gardens are managed by the Carew Pole Garden Trust. Timothy Mowl in his *Historic Gardens of Cornwall* has no doubts about the their qualities: 'With a baroque landscape to the south and ravishingly picturesque vistas to the north, not to mention terraced French grandiosity east and west, Antony's gardens have it all.'

St Germans

This small village with its colour-washed cottages and gabled almshouse overlooking the small tidal harbour has a long ecclesiastical history. The first Bishop of Cornwall, Conan, was based at the monastery here from 931 (appointed by the Saxon king Athelstan) – the monastic church then became a cathedral. The status was revoked in 1040 when the diocese moved east to Exeter and there would not be another Cornish bishop until Truro Cathedral was finished in 1910.

The priory disappeared with the dissolution of the monasteries but the little church remains on the site of the Saxon cathedral. The stained glass window in the church was designed by Edward Burne-Jones. Outside the village is Port Eliot, the stately home of the Earl of St Germans, in the grounds of which the old priory church still stands. The house itself is a Gothic extravaganza with gardens partly designed by Humphrey Repton who seems to have been a busy bee in this part of the country.

Port Eliot today is home to an annual literary festival and in the early 1980s was for several years the site of the famous (well, famous in the West Country) Elephant Fair – an annual musical event that was the precursor to many of the festivals around the UK today and one that I remember with great affection.

▲ Sunset on the Tamar

The future

The National Association for AONBs (NAAONB) describes the designation's purpose thus:

> We assume that our countryside will always stay the same, but often this is not true. Perhaps the most vulnerable areas are not the wild, open, high places but the gentle, smaller-scale landscapes of England and Wales. These include hedgerows, spinneys and bluebell woods; heath, marsh and meadow. Under pressure for change, much of this traditional countryside has already vanished. AONB status protects the finest examples which remain. AONBs work – with due care for the rural way of life – to conserve the landscape's outstanding natural beauty and ensure its survival for future generations.

So having walked in, cycled through, sailed around and marvelled at the landscape of much of Cornwall, notably the AONB and its gateway towns, and having at least scratched the surface of its geology, history, wildlife, culture and legends, what can we say about, or indeed expect, of the future? Does AONB status really protect the finest examples of traditional countryside that remain? Will the land that so many of us love be the same or, deep breath, perhaps even better in a generation?

If I had been writing this book when I first moved to Cornwall in the early 1980s, I would not have been optimistic. The environmental movement, in which I was active at the time, was in its infancy (sandal and beard jokes were rife) and development, much of it bad, was creeping across the land – a tide only held back by a few far-seeing organizations and landowners such as the National Trust. The AONB designation existed but did not consistently have enough teeth; if you wanted to build a new holiday complex on the cliffs, there were ways around the planning system that was then in place.

Today there is a dramatic change. Environment and conservation is at the heart of policy and is even given lip service by business. Even if many politicians and economic development proponents still don't 'get it', we are light years further forward than in the 1970s and 1980s. Those who care about the environment and the countryside are no longer just vegetarians and cranks. Indeed even vegetarians are no longer cranks.

So, there are grounds for cautious optimism on the general environment front – greater awareness, greater acceptance and a (slow) shift in values and opinions.

Equally, as regards the specific parts of Cornwall that are designated as an Area of Outstanding Natural Beauty, things are looking much better than they did thirty years ago. The Cornwall AONB, with its twelve separate, unconnected sections, has always struggled somewhat for

Dave Matthews

Dave Matthews

growing awareness of the meaning of the AONB designation and its importance.

During that same period there has been a steady increase in the appreciation of landscape and the part it plays in our economy and quality of life. Nationally and locally people have woken up to the fact that the destruction or degradation of landscape has a negative effect, not least in economic terms, while its protection and enhancement nearly always has a positive one. And whilst I, and many of my more idealistic friends, would love to see our landscape, environment and countryside valued *for its own sake*, if the only way to conserve it is to talk in terms of pounds and pence then so be it.

After all, climate change (often mistakenly termed global warming) only started to be properly discussed with the publication of the Stern Report in 2006 when effects on the world's economy and GDP were highlighted. Note, not the effect on human health or well-being nor on the earth's other species and flora but the *economy*. Money still talks loudest.

The short term

It seems to me that the future for the Cornish landscape can be looked at in three ways: short, medium and long term. In the short term we face two major changes: increased demand for housing and infrastructure and an increase in renewable energy provision.

Increased demand for housing, both 'affordable' and luxury or second home alike, shows no sign of abating. The population of the UK as a whole may be stabilizing but that of Cornwall is still increasing as more people, of all ages, but especially the retired, move here for quality of life reasons. The lack of new council housing from the early 1980s to the present has meant that there is a queue for housing in nearly every town, despite the good work of not-for-profit housing associations. And in the villages, prices are mostly so high that very few local youngsters can even think about getting on the housing ladder. House prices in some parts of Cornwall rival those of the Home Counties, even though wages are nowhere near the same level.

So there is pressure for affordable housing. This does not have to be a problem for the AONB and other scenic

recognition. But other parts of the country so designated, even when they are a homogenous unit such as the Cotswolds, Quantocks or the Forest of Bowland, suffer too. The words 'Area of Outstanding Natural Beauty' are not easily recognizable or remembered. The acronym, AONB, is very often wrongly written or spoken as ANOB! 'It's not a knob, it's much more beautiful,' one of my colleagues is wont to say. If only, we sigh often, we could have the simplicity of a National Park as our designation.

Another concern is that the words are often used (particularly by estate agents and developers) with a lower case: *area of outstanding natural beauty* suggests a pretty bit of country or coast – but with no formal value or legal protection. Yet the CRoW Act of 2000, giving our designated landscapes the specific remit to conserve and enhance natural beauty, began a slow yet significant change. So for the last twelve years there has been a

Peter Maxted

parts of the Cornish landscape. It is possible, given the right political will, using the right local materials, understanding the importance of scale and carefully taking the landscape into account at every turn, to build new homes that fit in with and enhance the landscape, especially in our towns and villages. Not easy, but possible.

The increase in relatively affluent immigration provides a different challenge. More people want to live in the AONB and other scenic landscape areas because these, of course, have the peace, the views and the natural beauty that attract settlers in the first place. Many incomers enhance the landscape they have come to appreciate – as ghastly seventies breezeblock constructions are replaced with sensitively sited buildings of local stone, or, on an ancient farm, scrub is cleared, hedges rebuilt, even footpaths re-opened. But others do not. It is their land, they believe, to do with what they will; if that involves building a four-storey Hollywood ranch house (especially if it has the 'eco' prefix) or cutting down trees to improve the view, then surely that's their right?

Appropriate planning regulations and good planners can help to keep the best, avoid the worst and improve the rest. Planners may not be universally popular but, in my view, they have largely done a very good job in Cornwall over the last decade. However, this may change, depending on how the planning system is 'improved' at

national level. Recent moves towards making a bonfire of planning laws and making all planning in thrall to 'development' is not, I would suggest, a good way forward. And it's not just me and a few woolly-minded environmentalists who think this either. The National Trust, the CPRE, the RSPB and the *Daily Telegraph* have been in the forefront of a campaign to make sure the planning baby is not thrown out with the bathwater.

Almost as contentious as housing and infrastructure development is the topic of renewable energy. To meet (fairly modest) targets for producing 15% of all energy consumed in transport, heat and power generation from renewable sources by 2020, there will have to be an increase in the two proven methods: on-shore wind and solar. Without such an increase, there would have to be a massive and successful effort to implement energy efficiency and demand reduction measures – and there isn't much sign of that happening. Other and better methods may come, but it looks as if the short term fix required will mean more turbines and more panels.

For years, AONBs, like National Parks, have been strongly in favour of small scale renewables. Larger developments, or a number of smaller ones that add up to a large one, within or near to sensitive landscapes are usually opposed. If the qualities of the landscape and the ability of people to experience and enjoy it are likely to be negatively affected then Natural England, supported by AONB Partnerships, will object. In my view it comes back (again) to sensible planning and political will.

Nick Maxted

▲ New affordable housing near falmouth

Dave Matthews

▲ Wind turbines – a contentious issue

Apart from housing and infrastructure and renewable energy, there are many other short-term pressures on all of our landscape, not just the AONB: increasing tourism, changes to farming practices and water needs and, perhaps above all, cumulative effects – small scale changes and seemingly innocuous developments, which, when taken together, slowly erode the landscape's distinctive qualities.

The problems are not just on land. Our maritime areas will become increasingly busy with shipping, leisure activities, fisheries, energy production and port development putting pressure on what's left of the beauty and tranquillity of our coast and seascapes.

But, on the whole, in the short term change will probably be gradual and in forty years' time we may be able to repeat the words of the NAAONB: 'Over four decades have passed since the designation of the first AONBs. During these years, few major urban or industrial developments have scarred any of these areas. This is a clear vindication of what is, essentially, a policy of trust, which has left the nation's landscape treasures in capable local hands.'

The medium term

In the medium term, say half a century or so, I think we really do have problems.

Whatever the catalyst may have been to make the environment a central part of national and local policy, there has been, over the last decade, a gradual acceptance of the bigger picture. That's not to say that there seems any sense of urgency to do much about it, Kyotos and Copenhagens come and go with little action. World population continues to rise, developing countries continue to industrialize and climate change, the great medium term threat to our prosperity, and perhaps very existence, rears its head.

Climate change is not 'global warming'. The scientific evidence that the earth's temperature is increasing is pretty much irrefutable but this does not mean that everyone, everywhere will experience a rise in temperature. What is does mean is that the atmosphere and the oceans are warming, ice is being lost from glaciers and ice caps north and south, sea levels are rising and the biological world is changing. No amount of banning the final episode of David Attenborough's *Frozen Planet* from American TV will change the facts.

The Climate Commission's 2011 report, *The Critical Decade*, states: 'We know beyond reasonable doubt that the world is warming and that human emissions of greenhouse gases are the primary causes.' And before the sceptics start unpicking this not very controversial statement, allow me to quote American scientist Naomi Oreskes: 'History shows us clearly that science does not provide certainty. It does not provide proof. It only provides the consensus of experts, based on the organised accumulation and scrutiny of evidence.'

But if the naysayers are largely falling silent, at least in Europe, what about the 'ignorers'? This is a much more difficult problem. At the top level, in the realm of national or local policy-making, the problem is fear. The changes to policy and direction to even begin to tackle climate change are simply too big for them to

Peter Maxted

▲ Rising sea levels are already occurring

contemplate. They involve worldwide acceptance of the problem and then a willingness to deal with it. They need agreement, consensus and the willingness to confront people with the truth. Take a look at any politician, anywhere. How many do you think could even manage to make a start?

But don't blame them too much; they are people too. Here is Oreskes again arguing that fear is the major driver of those ignoring climate change : 'Fear that our current way of life is unsustainable. Fear that addressing the issue will limit economic growth. Fear that if we accept government interventions in the market place…it will lead to a loss of personal freedom. Or maybe just plain old fear of change.'

It was suggested recently that we have about seven to eight years to put mechanisms in place that will actually begin to slow down and then reverse climate change. Not very long. After that, it is possible, indeed probable on the latest scientific modelling, that we shall reach a tipping point after which climate change will continue and increase *regardless* of human activity. Melting ice caps that reduce the mirroring effect on the sun, melting tundra increasing methane – these are the kind of issues that will increase the rate of climate change. We won't notice them much at first. But our grandchildren will reap the whirlwind.

Further ahead

In the long term it doesn't really matter very much – the landscape will change dramatically in one way or another – whatever we do in the short run. We are overdue an ice age. Recent research from Cambridge University, which examined variations in the Earth's orbit and global climate patterns calculated that the next ice age should begin within 1,500 years. However, the impact of (largely manmade) carbon dioxide emissions on the environment means that the ice will not be able to take hold. It is just possible that whilst upsetting the 'natural' balance, mankind may have created a new one, delaying the next ice age for a considerable time. Whether the alternative, of a significant rise in temperature with its consequent devastation, will occur, is exercising finer minds than mine.

Cornwall has been under deep ocean on a number of occasions. It has been part of a mountain range and a chain of volcanoes. It has been an arid desert and been-covered in tropical forest, icy tundra, temperate forest and, only recently, has been largely industrialized. That's pretty much every possibility covered. I think that, today, we probably have one of the most attractive landscapes ever. I'm sure my farmer friend would agree.

So here we are, after umpteen pages on the natural beauty of Cornwall. But words, of course, can and should only whet your appetite for the real thing. You have to see it for yourself. Shakespeare, as usual, has it in a nutshell:

Beauty itself doth of itself persuade
The eyes of men without an orator.

Off you go then.

Dave Matthews

Dave Matthews

Index